"Roy Bhaskar's too brief life was a gift to humanity. [...]
ontological grounding for all those intuitions that m[...]
to justify, but are constantly being told by the reign... ....
can't: that the world, and other people, are real, that freedom is inherent in the
nature of the cosmos, that genuine human flourishing can never be at the expense
of others. Bhaskar lived to provide the intellectual heavy artillery for simple common decency and good sense. Much of his work was written in exceedingly difficult language. This book, however, makes it accessible to those who have the most
to gain from it: anyone trying to make the world a better place."

David Graeber, anthropologist; sometime revolutionary;
Professor at London School of Economics, UK

"Roy Bhaskar writes: 'If there is a single big idea in critical realism it is the idea of
ontology.' One big idea, perhaps, but Bhaskar developed it in three very different and
equally innovative ways. From early depth ontology, through rethinking dialectical
negativity, to the metaphysics of metaReality, Bhaskar pushed his thought – and
himself. Guided always by the lodestar of emancipation, this final work demonstrates the unity in the three phases of his thought. Always willing to go against the
mainstream, it is a fitting final tribute to a great philosopher."

Alan Norrie, Professor, University of Warwick, UK

ENLIGHTENED COMMON SENSE

Since the 1970s critical realism has grown to address a range of subjects, including economics, philosophy, science, and religion. It has become a complex and mature philosophy.

Enlightened Common Sense: The Philosophy of Critical Realism looks back over this development in one concise and accessible volume. The late Roy Bhaskar was critical realism's philosophical originator and chief exponent. He draws on a lifetime's experience to give a definitive, systematic account of this increasingly influential, international and multidisciplinary approach.

Critical realism's key element has always been its vindication and deepening of our understanding of ontology. Arguing that realist ontology is inexorable in knowledge and action, Bhaskar sees this as the key to a new enlightened common sense.

From the definition of critical realism and its applicability in the social sciences, to explanation of dialectical critical realism and the philosophy of metaReality, this is the essential introduction for students of critical realism.

Roy Bhaskar (1944–2014) was the originator of the philosophy of critical realism and the author of many acclaimed and influential works, including: *A Realist Theory of Science*; *The Possibility of Naturalism*; *Scientific Realism and Human Emancipation*; *Dialectic: The Pulse of Freedom*; *Plato Etc.*; *Reflections on MetaReality*; *From Science to Emancipation*; and (with Mervyn Hartwig) *The Formation of Critical Realism*. He was an author of: *Critical Realism: Essential Readings*; *Interdisciplinarity and Climate Change*; *Ecophilosophy in a World of Crisis*; and was the founding chair of the Centre for Critical Realism. He was also a World Scholar and Director of the International Centre of Critical Realism at the University of London Institute of Education.

Mervyn Hartwig is the founding editor of *Journal of Critical Realism* and editor and principal author of *Dictionary of Critical Realism*.

Ontological Explorations

ENLIGHTENED COMMON SENSE

The philosophy of critical realism

Roy Bhaskar

Edited with a preface by Mervyn Hartwig

Routledge
Taylor & Francis Group

LONDON AND NEW YORK

First published 2016
by Routledge
2 Park Square, Milton Park, Abingdon, Oxon OX14 4RN

and by Routledge
711 Third Avenue, New York, NY 10017

Routledge is an imprint of the Taylor & Francis Group, an informa business

British Library Cataloguing in Publication Data
A catalogue record for this book is available from the British Library

Library of Congress Cataloging-in-Publication Data
Names: Bhaskar, Roy, 1944–2014, author. | Hartwig, Mervyn, editor.
Title: Enlightened common sense: the philosophy of critical
realism/Roy Bhaskar; edited with a preface by Mervyn Hartwig.
Description: New York: Routledge, 2016. | Series: Ontological
explorations
Identifiers: LCCN 2016002746| ISBN 9780415583787 (hardback) |
ISBN 9780415583794 (pbk.) | ISBN 9781315542942 (e-book)
Subjects: LCSH: Critical realism. | Common sense.
Classification: LCC B835 .B346 2016 | DDC 149/.2–dc23
LC record available at http://lccn.loc.gov/2016002746

ISBN: 978-0-415-58378-7 (hbk)
ISBN: 978-0-415-58379-4 (pbk)
ISBN: 978-1-315-54294-2 (ebk)

Typeset in Bembo
by Sunrise Setting Ltd, Brixham, UK

CONTENTS

FIGURES

TABLES

ABBREVIATIONS

Editor's note. Abbreviations explained immediately below the titles of figures and tables or confined to one location in the text have not been included. Those for the various phases of development of the philosophy of critical realism (TR, CN, EC, DCR, TDCR and PMR) are used, as a rule, only in the tables.

1M	first moment (non-identity) of the system of critical realist categories
2E	second edge (process)
3L	third level (totality)
4D	fourth dimension (transformative praxis)
5A	fifth aspect (reflexivity)
6R	sixth realm ((re-)enchantment)
7A/Z	seventh zone (non-duality)
MELDARA/Z	acronym for the system of critical realist categories considered as a whole
CDA	critical discourse analysis
CN	critical naturalism
CP	*ceteris paribus* (other things being equal)
CR	critical realism
DCR	dialectical critical realism
DREI(C)	description, retroduction, elimination, identification, (correction)
EC	explanatory critique
LF	the linguistic fallacy
LS	laminated system
M/M	the morphogenetic/morphostatic approach
PMR	the philosophy of metaReality
RRREI(C)	resolution, redescription, retrodiction, elimination, identification, (correction)
RRRIREI(C)	resolution, redescription, retrodiction, inference to best explanation, retrodiction, elimination, identification, (correction)
TDCR	transcendental dialectical critical realism
TINA	there is no alternative
TMSA	transformational model of social activity
TR	transcendental realism

EDITOR'S PREFACE

Thoas
Do you believe
that the crude Scythian,
the barbarian, will hear the voice
of truth and humanity that Atreus,
the Greek, did not?

Iphigenia
Everyone,
born under every sky,
in whose breast
life's source flows pure
and unhindered hears it

(Goethe)[1]

This is Roy Bhaskar's last solo-authored book.[2] The 'Final Table of Contents' of his manuscript is dated 30 December 2013.[3] In January 2014 he was diagnosed with heart failure and on 19 November 2014 he died.

Bhaskar will long be remembered I think for three great achievements, all of which are evident in this book. First, his work arguably provides the most adequate solution yet arrived at to the nexus of problems that constitute post-Kantian philosophy. This is the working hypothesis of a brilliant young American philosopher now domiciled in the UK, Dustin McWherter.[4] If borne out it will rank Bhaskar above the likes of Nietzsche, Heidegger and Derrida. Second, it articulates a powerful metatheory for orienting or underlabouring for emancipatory science, that is, science capable of making discoveries that can assist in promoting human emancipation. Finally, it develops the most thoroughgoing and devastating metacritique ever penned of capitalist modernity and its intellectual underpinnings (and indeed of master–slave-type social forms in all their guises) and offers a metatheoretical roadmap out of it to a global eudaimonian constellation of societies in which the free flourishing of each human being is a condition of the free flourishing of all. The overall message of Bhaskar's work, as of this book, is that people can rationally change the world decisively for the better.

Enlightened Common Sense: The Philosophy of Critical Realism brilliantly fills an egregious void in the critical realist corpus: the absence of an introductory account in a single volume of Bhaskar's philosophy as a whole. Andrew Collier's *Critical Realism: An Introduction to Roy Bhaskar's Philosophy* (1994) is superb, but because of the time of its writing could say little about dialectical critical realism and nothing as such about the philosophy of metaReality. *Enlightened Common Sense* provides an accessible, lucid and coherent account of Bhaskar's system overall, achieving a high level of simplicity and clarity without sacrificing profundity. It will finally lay to rest at least one of the libels Bhaskar had to endure, that he was an abominable writer who cared not a jot for his readers. As will be evident to any impartial reader, before one can attain the high level of clarity and perspicacity achieved here an immense amount of difficult and complex argumentation and analysis has to be engaged in at the highest level. The most difficult and 'impenetrable' Bhaskarian text is by no means as difficult or impenetrable as its Heideggerian or Kantian counterpart – and all Bhaskar's main works are indispensable to the lucid distillation presented here. This is not to suggest that readers who are relatively new to critical realism and/or philosophy will find the book plain sailing. It operates at the highest level of abstraction on matters that are intrinsically difficult, adroitly following Albert Einstein's wise advice that 'things should be made as simple as possible, but not any simpler'.

I would like to underline a related point that Bhaskar makes in Chapter 1.2. Although dialectical critical realism goes beyond basic critical realism and the philosophy of metaReality goes beyond dialectical critical realism, they arguably both presuppose and are broadly presupposed by basic critical realism, such that the three form a single system. What I want to emphasise is that this carries no implication that deploying critical realist metatheory to orient one's research or practice entails accepting 'the whole package'. On the contrary, since the later phases presuppose the earlier, work making use of any of the phases in either their specificity or their constellational unity is equally valuable and important from the perspective of the system as a whole. Whatever critical realist work scholars do, it matters! Of course, emancipatory philosophy and science, while indispensable for making a transition to eudaimonia, are not the only, or even the main thing. If we are ever to get much further with that project, philosophical and scientific work will need to be articulated creatively with proliferating social and political movements, as this book emphasises. Our greatest resource for building the good society is people everywhere and their inexhaustible capacities for freedom and creativity, love and hope – for hearing and living by 'the voice of truth and humanity', as Goethe understood so profoundly.

The manuscript Bhaskar left (an invaluable gift to humanity, in my estimation) is 70,000 words long. The book before you is some 92,000 words. It is evident from the manuscript that, working to a deadline and over very long hours, Bhaskar's energies were flagging during the writing of the last section of Chapter 6 and the whole of Chapters 7 and 8. (The concluding Chapter 9, which is appropriately shorter, is in relatively good shape; Bhaskar evidently gave it a certain priority.) Leigh Price, who most generously typed and checked most of the manuscript on an unpaid basis (much of it was dictated to her over the telephone!) confirms that parts of the later chapters were written under intense pressure in a few days before she flew to Zimbabwe at short notice after receiving news that her mother was terminally ill. Although the overall structure of the argument is clear to a reader who is familiar with Bhaskar's work, the writing becomes elliptical and definitions sparse. When at the suggestion of Bhaskar's literary executor, Hilary Wainwright (who had invited me to join her in that role), I sent the manuscript to Alan Jarvis of Routledge with a recommendation to publish it, Alan got back to us in a few days with a commitment to do so, providing that it was edited. Courtesy of Alan, Routledge quickly entered into an arrangement with me to accomplish this.

Meanwhile a team of people willing and very able to assist in bringing the manuscript to publication had already formed via the Centre for Critical Realism: Maggie Archer offered to 'copyedit' all of it – which she proceeded to do with remarkable alacrity – and Hilary and Leigh offered to read it with an eye to improving its accessibility. When Maggie had worked her way through to the more gnomic sections of the manuscript, she urged me to 'help Roy' by fleshing them out. This I resolved to do, in consultation with the team. Our procedure in broad outline was as follows. I produced an overall editor version and then incorporated Maggie's edits and made changes in the light of her comments as seemed appropriate. I then circulated the result with changes tracked to the team and also to Alan Norrie, who had meanwhile kindly offered to give advice on Chapters 6, 8 and 9, and invited further suggested changes and comments. Then I reviewed these and either made changes as seemed appropriate or, where I disagreed on matters of evident importance took them back to the team for discussion, until consensus was reached.[5]

In fleshing out the manuscript I have tried to write as if I were Bhaskar. I have not hesitated to draw directly on his writings (and also on my own expositions of them), usually without using quotation marks (but indicating sources in Bhaskar's corpus); and I have not confined my changes to the chapters indicated above, though my elaborations are concentrated there. In the interest of readability the only occasions on which I differentiate my additions (as *Editor's notes*) from Bhaskar's original are the few times when I make comments on material that has been published since his death (but that he knew was in the offing). Scholars who wish to know which passages and notes in the book are to be found in the original manuscript and which I have added will readily be able to discover this by consulting the original in the Bhaskar archives (which will be housed at the UCL Institute of Education, London) or by applying for an e-copy to me or any other member of the team that brought this book to press. Well over a third of my additions in terms of number of words take the form of the bibliography, which is entirely new, and additional notes and references. My main innovation in the text, leaving aside elaboration, is the introduction of a selection of the many (more than 200) illuminating figures and tables (especially the former)[6] that Bhaskar incorporated in his books down to and including *Plato Etc.* (1994). The drawing of the figures, Bhaskar once told me, came mostly *after* the writing as part of the dialectics of recapitulation to double check the analysis and embed it within his innermost being. It is hoped that they will serve that purpose for the reader too, but after illuminating the analysis.

I am most grateful to members of the editorial team for their excellent work, especially to Maggie, who encouraged me to do what needed to be done and whose experienced eye picked up many things of importance that I missed on a first edit or that served as valuable prompts for me to clarify or elaborate. The usual disclaimers apply. As Bhaskar was fond of pointing out, the 'paradox of the preface', like many of the other so called paradoxes and problems of Western philosophy, is readily resolved on critical realist terrain: in an open, developing world I can be sure that weaknesses and mistakes in my elaborations will come to light, but I can't know now with any confidence which or where. I have done my best to be true to Roy's thought.

Mervyn Hartwig
January 2016

Notes

1   J. W. von Goethe, *Iphigenia in Tauris* (1787), lines 1936–42. *Thoas*: Du glaubst, es höre/ der rohe Skythe, der Barbar, die Stimme / der Wahrheit und der Menschlichkeit, die Atreus, /der Grieche, nicht vernahm? *Iphigenie*: Es hört sie jeder, / geboren unter jedem Himmel, dem/des Lebens Quelle durch den Busen rein/und ungehindert fließt.
2   There may of course be a *Nachlass* of unpublished manuscripts, addresses, and so on.
3   The manuscript is entitled *Critical Realism in a Nutshell: An Introduction to the Philosophy of Critical Realism*, reflecting the brief Bhaskar had been given by the Templeton-funded project 'Human Flourishing and Critical Realism in the Social Sciences', which provided the financial support necessary for its writing. The decision to change this was a collective one taken by the editorial team (see below) on the grounds that the book is summative rather than a basic summary of Bhaskar's philosophy; that is, it adds to and enhances, while recapitulating it.
4   See Dustin McWherter, 'Roy Bhaskar and post-Kantian philosophy', in Ruth Porter Groff, Lena Gunnarsson, Dustin McWherter, Paul Marshall, Lee Martin, Leigh Price, Matthew L. N. Wilkinson and Nick Wilson, 'In memoriam Roy Bhaskar', *Journal of Critical Realism* 14:2 (2015), 119–36, 124–7.
5   The title *Enlightened Common Sense* was chosen by Bhaskar's literary executors. There was some concern within the editorial team that readers might interpret 'enlightened' primarily (1) in a spiritual or religious sense; or (2) in the sense of the eighteenth century European Enlightenment. This is far from our intention. The concept 'enlightened common sense' was first deployed (in print) by Bhaskar in 1989 in a context that explicitly envisages a new, post-capitalist enlightenment. See Roy Bhaskar, *Reclaiming Reality: A Critical Introduction to Contemporary Philosophy* (London: Routledge, 1989/2011),

1. The concept calls attention to 'the transcendental necessity of transcendental realism' (see Chapter 2.8), that is, the inexorability of transcendental or critical realist ontology, and to the importance of critique to demystify or enlighten common-sense understandings – themes that are at the core of Bhaskar's philosophy in all its phases.

6   The 20 figures included are all by Bhaskar, whereas only two of the 10 tables are (1.1 and 2.1, though two more – 3.1 and 3.2 – were strongly implicit in the original text and were compiled by me mainly on that basis). The original manuscript called for the inclusion of two tables from my own writings (6.1 and 8.1); I have taken the liberty to include four more (6.2, 6.3, 7.1 and 7.2), as I am aware that Bhaskar thought them very useful. They display in a spatial spread the correspondences that Bhaskar carried around in his consciousness and deployed to ordinate his presentational, systematic and critical dialectics. Figures and tables are not included in the total word counts given above.

ACKNOWLEDGEMENTS

The writing of this book was funded by the John Templeton Foundation and would not have been possible without the loving assistance of Roy Bhaskar's partner and carer, Rebecca Long, the support of Hilary Wainwright and the provision of accessible accommodation by the Wainwright family. Its published version is dedicated to Rebecca.

Also indispensable was the selfless voluntary work of Leigh Price, who typed and checked the greater part of the manuscript that Roy left us. Rebecca took over these responsibilities after Leigh flew to Zimbabwe.

I am very grateful to Alan Jarvis of Routledge, who acted so decisively to bring this book to publication, and to the critical realists who gave me much valuable advice in the editing process: Hilary Wainwright, Leigh Price, Alan Norrie and (above all) Maggie Archer.

On behalf of Roy and the publisher, I also wish to thank Guardian News and Media Limited for permission to reproduce the following copyright material:

> Will Hutton, 'In language and action, there's a new brutalism in Westminster'. *The Observer* (London), 29 June 2013.

1

ON THE PRESUPPOSITIONS AND ORIGINS OF THE PHILOSOPHY OF CRITICAL REALISM

I begin by introducing some distinctive features of the critical realist approach to philosophy (section 1.1). These are: (i) its intent to philosophically *underlabour* for science and practices oriented to human well-being; (ii) its *seriousness*, that is, commitment to the unity of theory and practice; (iii) its method of *immanent critique*; (iv) its realism about philosophy, namely, its conception of its goal as the elucidation of the normally unreflected *presuppositions of social practices* of various kinds and its commitment to *transcendental argument* (understood as a species of retroduction); (v) its aim of enhanced *reflexivity* and/or *transformed practice;* (vi) its endorsement of the *hermetic principle*, that it should be applicable to and verifiable by everyone and in the context of everyday life; and (vii) its *criticality* and commitment to *dispositional realism*.

After this introductory section, I describe the origins of the philosophy of critical realism and explain how the organisation of the book is related to its subsequent development (section 1.2). In this section I also differentiate the philosophy of critical realism, which is relatively new, from its practice, which is not, and distinguish it from some of its namesakes. I then briefly look at some of the consequences of the ontological turn in the philosophy of science for sociology and social theory, anticipating to some extent the argument in Chapter 3.3 (section 1.3). Finally, I survey, topically and thematically, the argument to come in the book (section 1.4).

1.1 Distinctive features of the critical realist approach to philosophy

(i) Underlabouring

Philosophical underlabouring is most characteristically what critical realist philosophy does. The metaphor of underlabouring comes from the eighteenth-century British empiricist philosopher, John Locke, who said:

> The commonwealth of learning is not at this time without master-builders, whose mighty designs in advancing the sciences, will leave lasting monuments to the admiration of posterity: but everyone must not hope to be a Boyle or a Sydenham; and in an age that produces such masters as the great Huygenius and the incomparable Mr Newton, with some others of that strain, it is ambition enough to be employed as an under-labourer in clearing the ground a little, and removing some of the rubbish that lies in the way to knowledge.[1]

Critical realism aspires to clear the ground a little, removing, in the first place, the philosophical rubbish that lies in the way of scientific knowledge, especially but not only in the domain of the social sciences; and in this way to underlabour for science and (partly in virtue of this, it argues) more generally for practices oriented to human well-being and flourishing. These philosophies have been inherited largely unthinkingly from the past. At one time they may have played a progressive role, but they have long since ceased to do so. Indeed, we can say with Albert Einstein that 'the world we have created today as a result of our thinking thus far has problems which cannot be solved by thinking the way we thought when we created them'.

(ii) Seriousness

Seriousness is a term of art deriving from the great German idealist philosopher, G. W. F. Hegel. It involves the idea of the unity of theory and practice, of being able to walk one's talk, of not saying one thing and doing something completely different. I shall be arguing that much modern, including contemporary, Western philosophy is palpably unserious. For instance, when one of John Locke's successors, David Hume tells us that there is no better reason to leave the building by the ground-floor door than by the second-floor window, he cannot be being serious.[2] For if he really believed what he claimed to believe, then surely he should have left such buildings by their second-floor windows on some 50 per cent of all occasions!

In a similar way, when Hume avers that he has no better reason to prefer the scratching of his finger to that of the destruction of the whole world,[3] then again he is not being serious, because if he were to choose the destruction of the world, then since his finger is clearly part of the world he would lose that too! What Hume is tacitly doing here is extruding himself (and philosophy) from the rest of the world, which of course includes himself and philosophy (and the sciences and other human ways of knowing). It is, as we shall see, in such 'hypostasis', detotalisation or disconnect that the seeds of academic unseriousness very often lie.

What critical realism would like to do, then, is produce a serious philosophy that we can act on, and one moreover that is relevant to the pressing challenges we face and that ideally at least can illuminate a way forward (telling us something new).

(iii) Immanent critique

Immanent critique is an essential part of the method of critical realist philosophy. It specifies that criticism of an idea or a system should be internal, that is, involve something intrinsic to what (or the person who) is being criticised. It typically identifies a theory/practice inconsistency, showing that the position being disputed involves a claim or analysis that would undermine the point, values or substance of the position; so that it undermines or 'deconstructs' itself. A moment's reflection shows indeed that this is the only way an argument can ever ultimately be won. Merely to assert what one believes will get nowhere unless it impinges in some way on what one's opponent believes.

Thus, if someone says 'everyone should eat more meat' and I disagree, what I have to do to begin to be rationally persuasive is to find something within their belief or value system or customary practices that would be undermined by eating more meat.

The most devastating form of immanent critique is Achilles' Heel critique. This identifies a weakness or blind spot at a point in a theory deemed by its proponents to be its strongest.

(iv) Philosophy as explicating presuppositions

For critical realism, philosophy does not speak about a world apart from the world of science and everyday life. There is not a separate world for philosophy and another world for everything else: there is only one world,[4] and philosophy speaks about it too. What differentiates the discourse of philosophy is that it talks about the most abstract or general features of that world, which are not normally discussed in, but are tacitly presupposed by our practices.

These abstract features are expressed by philosophical categories such as causality, substance, and so on. For critical realism, such categories refer to real but very general features of the world. Thus for it the world contains not only specific causal laws[5] but causality as such. (This is a position that can be called *categorial realism* (see Chapter 6.4).) And it is the characteristic task of critical realist philosophy to explicate these higher-order or abstract features, which are for the most part taken for granted in, or unreflectively but tacitly presupposed by our practices. What philosophy typically does, then, is to explicate the normally undisclosed or otherwise not topicalised assumptions embodied in our activities or underpinning our practices, which are for the most part 'given', but as 'tacit' and very often 'confused'.

If philosophy is mainly about elucidating the normally unreflected presuppositions of our practices, then we can begin to see the importance of a key feature of critical realist philosophy, namely its commitment to a form of argument initiated by Immanuel Kant: *transcendental argument*. A transcendental argument asks what must be the case for some feature of our experience to be possible, or more generally what must the world be like for some social practice (as conceptualised in our experience) to be possible. As such it is clearly a species of a genus that plays a large part in science, which I call *retroductive argument*. A retroductive argument asks what would, if it were real, bring about, produce, cause or explain a phenomenon; and retroduction is the imaginative activity in science by which the scientist thinks up causes or, as we shall say, generative mechanisms which, if they were real, would explain the phenomenon in question.

(v) Enhanced reflexivity and/or transformed practice

Pre-existing philosophy has seriously misdescribed the presuppositions of most of our everyday and scientific practices. So it involves theory/practice disjuncture or incoherence and performative contradiction, characteristically constituting what I call a TINA compromise formation, in which basically a truth in practice is combined or held in tension with a falsity in theory. (TINA stands for 'there is no alternative'; see further Chapter 6.4.)

The aim of critical realist philosophy can now be clarified. When a practice is more or less adequate, as we can perhaps grant it is most of the time in the natural sciences, but nevertheless theory (that is, understanding of its presuppositions or, we could also say, *metatheory*) falls woefully short, the aim is to provide a better or more adequate account or theory of the practice. However, where the practice is itself flawed, as patently must be the case with at least some of the large array of contested and conflicting social scientific practices, the ultimate goal of critical realist philosophy becomes the transformation of practice in the appropriate way (albeit mediated, of course, by the better understanding and self-understanding of the agents directly involved). That is to say, the most general goal of critical realist philosophy is enhanced reflexivity or transformed practice (or both).

(vi) The principle of hermeticism

Hermes is the Greek name for an ancient Egyptian sage[6] who argued that we should accept nothing on authority, but test every proposition for ourselves in our everyday practices. This is very much in keeping with the radical spirit of critical realism. I would enjoin the reader, as we go along in this book, to refer constantly to their experience (whether lay or research), to attempt to apply to it the arguments, theories and concepts put forward, and to see whether they cohere or fit with it.

For since there is only one world, albeit there are very variant descriptions of it, the theories and principles of critical realist philosophy should also apply to our everyday lives. If they do not, then something is seriously wrong. This means that our theories and explanations should be tested in everyday life as well as in specialist research contexts.

(vii) Criticality and dispositional realism

Since the time of Socrates philosophers have rightly deplored the 'unexamined life'; but, for the examination to be worthy of the name, another life and another world must be possible, which presupposes that change must be possible, and that possibility must be real. This is the position I call *dispositional realism*, namely that possibilities, as well as the actualities that are instances of them, must be real. But it also presupposes that agency is real, and that I can transform it, that is, that a transformed transformative praxis is possible and that reflection (including philosophical critique) can play a part in ushering in a better life and a better world.

If this is so, an underlabouring philosophy such as critical realism, seriously committed to the project of universal human flourishing, can aspire to be more than a nuisance, a Nietzschean gadfly on the neck of the powers that be; it can become a spark, a liberation, lifting the weight of the (Lockean) rubbish that mires us. This is philosophy as enlightened common sense[7] and as midwife, an agent of emancipatory change.

1.2 On the origins, development and *differentiae* of the philosophy of critical realism and the organisation of the book

I now describe how I came to critical realism. I did an undergraduate degree at Oxford University in philosophy, politics and economics (PPE) and enjoyed each of the subjects more or less equally. But it struck me that economics dealt with questions that were perhaps more immediately important, concerned as I was with issues such as poverty in the 'third world', so I decided to plump for further work in economics. Now the question that concerned me most was how relevant the economic theory that had been developed in the advanced capitalist countries of the West was to the needs and situations of the newly developing, so called 'under-developed' countries. My intuition was that current economic theory was not very relevant, since, though subject to many of the same structures, these were neverthe-less very different and rapidly changing societies.

So I enrolled for graduate studies and commenced work on a thesis on *The Relevance of Economic Theory for Developing Countries*. However, it gradually dawned on me that I had chosen an impossible topic, since the dominant metatheories did not allow for a comparison between a body of theory and the world. I was of course shocked to find that reference to reality was taboo, so I reverted to philosophy, and in particular the philosophy of science and social science, to find out why this was so. Alas, I did not fare much better here in sifting through the textbooks of orthodoxy. There was much on confirmation and falsification, explanation and prediction and other epistemic activities but nothing about the nature of the world to which they were presumably attempting to refer, and no explanation as to this silence. So I delved deeper and, returning to the philosophies of Hume and Kant, the source of the trouble at last became clear: it lay in their injunction *not to do ontology* or the philosophical study of being. And so I embarked on the project of my first book, on the terrain of the philosophy of science – *A Realist Theory of Science* – which had the two-fold aim of at once revindicating ontology and estab-lishing a new non-Humean ontology characterised by structure, difference and the possibility of change.

The origins of critical realism and the duplex argument for (a new) ontology

The context of philosophy of science in the 1970s was one in which Humean empiricism provided the baseline for most contemporary discussion. In particular, the Humean theory of causal laws, the idea that a constant conjunction of atomistic events was either necessary and sufficient (the empiricist variant) or at least necessary (the neo-Kantian variant) for the attribution of a law, underpinned the standard (Popper–Hempel) deductive-nomological or covering-law model of explanation and almost all the other theories of orthodox philosophy of science.[8]

This theory went alongside a metatheory, championed by Hume and especially Kant, that ontology was impossible, a mistake; that it was sufficient for philosophy, in the words of the early Wittgenstein, only to 'treat of the network, and not what the network describes'.[9] This metatheory is what I call the *epistemic fallacy*, that ontology can be completely defined in terms of, or reduced to epistemology.[10] This supposition is clearly wrong because the Humean theory of causal laws implies that the world is uniform, flat and repetitive, undifferentiated, unstructured and unchanging, and it is evident that this is not the case. However, it is one thing to 'know' this and quite another to establish it in the discourse of philosophy. This set the double task of the work that initiated critical realism, namely, to establish that ontology was possible and necessary; and to establish the outlines of a new, non-Humean ontology.

That both aims were necessary was very clear to me from my earlier reflections on economics. For the prohibition on ontology, in the guise of the possibility of reference to reality independently of the descriptions of a particular body of theory, had by no means banished ontology, but merely covered and disguised the generation of an *implicit* Humean *ontology*, which presupposed that the world was without structure or depth, difference and context, let alone the possibility of emergence, change and development.

Employing the method of immanent critique coupled with transcendental argument meant that I had to find a feature of social practice that my opponents thought was important; so I picked on experimental activity (which everyone agreed was vital to science). The question I asked was what must the world be like for experimentation to be possible; and my analysis showed that it must be independently real, structured and differentiated. So I had provided at once an argument for ontology and an argument for a new (non-Humean) ontology.

This duplex argument generated a pair of double distinctions that are fundamental to critical realism.

First, the distinctions between (i) *philosophical* and *scientific ontology* and (ii) the *transitive* and the *intransitive dimensions* of science, together with the critique of the epistemic fallacy, or the reduction of ontology to epistemology. The understanding of science as at once a (transitive) social process in which knowledge about an independently existing and acting (intransitive) world is produced situates the mutual compatibility and entailment of *ontological realism*, *epistemological relativism* and *judgemental rationalism*, which I call the *holy trinity*[11] of critical realism. At the same time the limits of what I call our *natural attitude*, in which we do not distinguish ontology and epistemology, but merely talk (in an undifferentiated way) about the *known world*, a standpoint that Hume and Kant merely reflected, are clearly visible. This attitude breaks down when there are competing claims about the same world (such as in periods of scientific revolution or contestation, as in the contemporary social sciences). For in this case we have explicitly to differentiate the independently existing (intransitive) world from our (transitive) socially pro-duced and fallible claims to knowledge of it.

Second, there are the substantive ontological distinctions between (i) *open* and *closed systems* and (ii) *structures* and *events* or what I call the *domain of the real* and the *domain of the actual*, together with a corresponding critique of the implicit actualist ontology of *empirical realism*. Thus we have the theorem of the irreducibility of structures, mechanisms and the like to patterns of events (or of the domain of the real to that of the actual) and of patterns of events to our experiences (or of the domain of the actual to the *domain of the empirical*) (see Table 1.1).

The immediate implications of this ontological turn in the philosophy of sci-ence can now be registered. The transcendental argument from experimental activity, together with other arguments from the context of applied and practical science, establishes the inexorability and irreducibility of philosophical ontology and the necessarily stratified and differentiated character of this ontology. Moreover, it now becomes important to see science as a creative activity, essentially moving from descriptions of events and other phenomena to their causal explanation in terms of the structures and mechanisms that produce them. Furthermore, the his-tory of science reveals a multi-tiered stratification in nature, which accordingly defines a continually reiterated dialectic of discovery and development in science. Following on from this, there is the *DREI(C) model of theoretical explanation*, in which science moves continually from the description of phenomena to the retro-duction of possible explanatory causal mechanisms for them, the elimination of competing explanations, through to the identification of the generative mechanism at work (followed by the correction of previous results) (see Chapter 2.4). Science then proceeds to describe this newly identified level of reality and a further round of discovery and development follows.

On this new view of science, it is a dynamic social activity continually opening up deeper and more recondite levels of reality to the curious investigator; while on the new ontology *stratification* emerges as a key property. Three forms of stratifica-tion are immediately identifiable. There is the simple stratification implied by the distinction between structures (generative mechanisms and so forth) and the pat-terns of events (or the domains of the real and the actual); the multi-tiered stratifi-cation revealed by the history of science; and that special form of stratification shown by *emergence* (about which more in a moment).

TABLE 1.1 Domains of the real, actual and empirical[12]

	Domain of Real	Domain of Actual	Domain of Empirical
Mechanisms	✓		
Events	✓	✓	
Experiences	✓	✓	✓

Generalising and developing the core argument

The question of transapplicability

The original argument of critical realism raises the question as to whether this characteristic retroductive pattern of activity, involving the movement from descriptions of events to that of the explanatory structures producing them, can take place in other sciences, domains and practices. More specifically, it raises the question of the transapplicability of the results of the philosophy of the experimental natural sciences to the social sciences[13] or (for example) the biological sciences;[14] or to new domains of the social sciences, for example, of language (which is explored in Chapter 5.2, when we discuss the programme of critical discourse analysis) and the contexts of the variety of human practices (from architecture to archaeology).

However, it is important to note that the method of immanent critique prohibits any simple-minded or unmediated transfer of results from one context to another. There must always be an independent analysis of the new domain before the possibility of any transapplication can be considered. Thus, when I turned to investigate the compatibility of the social (and more generally human) sciences with the new transcendental realist ontology, I had first to latch onto something there that would be of comparable immanent weight to experimental activity in the natural sciences. I found this in the endemic *dualism* (and dualisms) of contemporary philosophy of social science. There was an overarching dualism between positivistic naturalism and anti-naturalist hermeneutics, and a plethora of regional or topical dualisms or antinomies, including structure/agency, individual/collective (or whole), meaning/behaviour (or law) and conceptuality/materiality, which I call the *macrodualisms*; and the *microdualisms* of reason/cause, mind/body, fact/value and theory/practice upon which the macrodualisms depend. The critical realist response to these dualisms is explored in Chapter 3 (especially).

Other ways of developing the original argument

The original argument can also be developed in a variety of other ways. Thus there is its concrete and *applied* development, which involves the move, not from events to mechanisms, but into the nature of the particular concrete event, phenomenon or situation itself. Then there is its *critical*, including *metacritical* development, which involves exploring the conditions of possibility of false or otherwise inadequate accounts and the practices they inform. Finally there is the possibility of the *theoretical deepening of the ontology* to incorporate categories other than structure and difference, such as change and process, or internal as well as external relations, and so on. It is this further deepening of the ontology of critical realism, which will be addressed in detail in Chapters 6 and 7, that I am concerned with now.

It is not difficult to see that this deepening is in fact implied by the nature of the foundational arguments. Clearly, activities such as experimentation presuppose social life, and this in turn implies that we, as materially embodied social beings, are emergent conceptualising parts of nature, capable of acting back on the material out of which we are formed. Here a distinction is mandatory between our possession, *synchronically*, of emergent powers and the *diachronic* (both ontogenetic and phylogenetic) processes of their formation. So the explicit ontology of transcendental realist philosophy of science in fact implies both *society* (and hence critical naturalism) and *emergence*, and therefore both *change*, including the possibility of progressive or *negentropic change* or development, and (differentiated) *unity*; change and unity are key themes in the deepening of ontology within dialectical critical realism and the philosophy of metaReality, respectively. In other words, the dialectical and metaReal developments of ontology are, like critical realism (including, as a condition of its efficacy, explanatory critique) implicit in the programme of transcendental realism, and not, as is sometimes suggested, gratuitous excrudescences of it.

If ontology is the initiating big idea of critical realism, the subsequent development of critical realism is most perspicaciously presented as founded on successive further deepenings of ontology, around each wave of which we can organise characteristic categorial/conceptual, epistemological, ethical and methodological tropes.

Delineating the terrain of the book

In fact, it has now become customary to divide critical realism into three phases and to sub-divide these phases further still. These divisions will inform the organisation of the book. Thus critical realism (CR) is divided into *basic* (or original or first-wave) *critical realism*, which is sometimes also just called 'critical realism', *dialectical critical realism* and the *philosophy of metaReality*; and basic critical realism is itself subdivided into *transcendental realism* or critical realist philosophy of science, *critical naturalism* or critical realist philosophy of social science, and the *theory of explanatory critique*, which forms part of critical realist ethics. *Transcendental dialectical critical realism* is regarded as a form of dialectical critical realism transitional to the philosophy of metaReality. The reader will have noticed that I use the term 'critical realism' in two distinct ways, which refer to (1) original critical realism; and (2) my system of philosophy overall; the context determines which meaning is intended. Also worth mentioning is the associated *seven-level schema for the development of ontology*[15] that embraces these three phases. Here we progress from

understanding being as *non-identity*, as structured, and differentiated; to
understanding being as *process*, as involving absence, negativity and change; to
understanding being together or as a whole or *totality*, as involving internal relations, holistic causality and concrete universality = singularity; to
understanding being as incorporating *transformative praxis* in four-planar social being; to
understanding being as *reflexive* and inward (and 'spiritual' in a certain sense of that term); to

understanding being as *re-enchanted*, as intrinsically valuable and meaningful; to understanding being as *non-dual*, as involving the primacy of underlying identity over difference and unity over split.

Besides these divisions, I like to talk of *applied critical realism*, which is the subject of Chapter 4.

The primary focus of this book is on basic critical realism, and within that on the work of the social sciences, both theoretical and applied. Nevertheless, as behoves a book with the subtitle *The Philosophy of Critical Realism*, I will discuss the other spheres of critical realism too. This is in any case necessary, as I have just indicated, for its coherent articulation. Thus Chapters 2, 3 and 5 deal with the fundamentals of basic critical realism in the philosophy of science, social science and ethics, that is, transcendental realism, critical naturalism and explanatory critique, respectively; but Chapter 5 also looks further at the critical realist approach to language and in particular at the CR-inspired and -influenced research tradition in this field known as critical discourse analysis, which is related back to the programme of explanatory critique. Chapter 4 looks at applied critical realism, and Chapters 6 and 7 at dialectical critical realism and the philosophy of metaReality, respectively, while Chapter 8 deals with the critique of the philosophical discourse of modernity (first formally broached in the philosophy of metaReality, but in process from transcendental realism onwards) and its roots in the Western philosophical tradition critiqued in dialectical critical realism. Chapters 4 and 9 (and to an extent 6 and 7), like the presentation of applied critical realism in Chapter 4, extend the presentation of critical naturalism initiated in Chapter 3; so at least half the book is explicitly on the terrain of the social sciences – and all of it is pertinent to articulating a metatheory capable of underlabouring for them.

Differentiating the philosophy of critical realism

I differentiate fairly sharply the philosophy of critical realism, which *A Realist Theory of Science* may be said to have initiated,[16] from the practice of critical realism which has characterised (normally unselfconsciously) much great science, and probably at least most natural science. I also distinguish it from various other philosophies that have been accorded the same name.

The term 'critical realism' arose from the running together of the 'critical' in critical naturalism and the 'realism' in transcendental realism. I decided at the time that it would be overly stuffy to reject it. For Kant had after all used 'critical' as a synonym for 'transcendental' and critical realism is also critical in so far as it is oriented to the transformation of inadequate beliefs, practices and indeed (in explanatory critique) structures; while its credentials as a realism were obvious.

However, when I accepted the label I was unaware of the variety of other philosophies that had chosen or been given this designation.[17] The most prominent of these include the philosophy of science of Roy Wood Sellars and his co-thinkers of the 1920s (so called 'American critical realism'), and the 'theological critical realism' of the school of British philosopher-theologians that included Ian Barbour, John Polkinghorne and Arthur Peacocke. But 'critical realism' has also been used to characterise such diverse philosophies as the aesthetics of György Lukács, the Thomism of Jacques Maritain and the positivism of Moritz Schlick. Although there are areas of overlap with American and theological critical realism (and of course Thomism too) none of these have an ontology of intransitive and transfactually active structures and generative mechanisms, though Alistair McGrath has begun to import one from my philosophical critical realism into theological critical realism.[18]

A further qualification is necessary. Although most critical realists would accept most of transcendental realism and critical naturalism, there is not the same unanimity about dialectical critical realism and the philosophy of metaReality (or even, within basic critical realism, about explanatory critique), some aspects of which have indeed been hotly disputed. However, while many critical realists have chosen not to explore or (in their research) use the dialectical and metaReal developments, there is by now widespread appreciation of at least their potential value and interest. Moreover, it should be borne in mind that, according to critical realism, it is in the last instance the nature of the object that determines how it should be studied (together with the current state of the research process). Thus it is incumbent on every researcher to determine, in the light of this maxim, which parts of the expanding toolkit of critical realism they wish, in any given instance, to utilise.

Finally, it may be worth differentiating critical realism from its ignorant and possibly wilful misinterpretation as a species of neo-positivism committed to the idea of incorrigible foundations of knowledge. Nothing could be further from the truth. This interpretation completely ignores the transitive dimension, committing in effect the *ontic fallacy* by overlooking the fact that knowledge is an irreducibly social and changing product and that our access to reality is always mediated by the research process, and overlooking too the continuing critique within critical realism of all forms of foundationalism and any claim to incorrigibility, and the fact that the development of (at least theoretical) critical realism is best viewed as a process of continuing self-critique (or metacritique). The ontic fallacy, namely that the world determines our knowledge, is the hidden social meaning of the epistemic fallacy. Whereas the latter reduces the world to our knowledge, the ontic fallacy reduces the resulting knowledge to the world: it ontologises, hence naturalises or *eternalises* our knowledge and makes the social status quo seem permanent and ineluctable. Because they play complementary roles in generating the idea of incorrigible foundations of knowledge, I sometimes refer to these two fallacies as one: the *epistemic-ontic fallacy*. Its deeper ramifications will be explored in Chapter 8 in particular.

1.3 Consequences of the vindication of ontology for social theory

The critical realist philosophy of social science is established by the immanent critique and resolution of the dualisms of the contemporary philosophy of social science and social theory. The result is a *critical naturalism*, which steers a *via media* between positivistic hyper-naturalism and hermeneutical anti-naturalism and which could indeed be as well styled a 'critical hermeneutics' as a 'critical naturalism', a *via media* that is also equally a transcendence of both duals.

Resolution of the antinomy between *structure and agency* is achieved by the *transformational model of social activity* (TMSA), on which society, and social forms generally, are conceived of as pre-existing, but reproduced or transformed by human agency.[19] This transformational model appears prima facie similar to Anthony Giddens's theory of structuration, published in the same year (1979).[20] However, Margaret Archer pointed out (in *Realist Social Theory*[21] and elsewhere) that time and tense are intrinsic to the TMSA, but not to or in structuration theory. Thus on the TMSA, structure always pre-exists any round of human agency and the heavy weight of the presence of the past precludes voluntarism. The TMSA can be further deepened by situating it in the context of *four-planar social being*.[22] On this conception, every social event occurs along each of the following dimensions: material transactions with nature; social interactions between people; social structure proper; and the stratification of the embodied personality.

The antinomy between *individualism and collectivism* is resolved by an understanding of the subject matter of social science as paradigmatically, not behaviour, but the enduring relations that govern, condition and circumscribe behaviour (and their transformation). This relational model of the subject matter of social science is in turn developed through a conception of its subject matter as occurring on any of the following seven *levels of scale*: a *sub-individual* level, typified by the unconscious or the play of motives; an *individual* level, typically invoked by novelists and existentialists, such as Jean-Paul Sartre; a *micro-level* of small-scale social interactions, typically studied by ethnomethodologists and the followers of Harold Garfinkel and Erving Goffman; a *meso-level*, which is the field of classical sociological analysis, as practiced for example by Karl Marx, Emile Durkheim and Max Weber; a *macro-level* which looks at the properties of whole societies, such as contemporary Norway; a *mega-level* which looks at whole geo-historical swathes and trajectories, such as the development of medieval Christianity; and a level which takes as its subject matter the global or *planetary* or *cosmic* whole.

In relation to the antinomy between *meaning and law*, critical realism accepts the hermeneutical thesis of the conceptuality of social life. But it argues that social life, though concept-dependent, is not exhausted by its conceptuality. Thus it has a material as well as a conceptual dimension. War is not just a question of employing certain concepts in the correct way; it is the bloody fighting as well. Homelessness is not only a conceptual question, it is also not having a roof over one's head. Although hermeneutics defines the starting point of social science, conceptualisations are corrigible and subject to critique – a theme that is taken up in the critical realist theory of explanatory critique.

The above three paragraphs indicate briefly how critical realism resolves the main macrodualisms of the philosophy of social science; I defer setting out the resolution of the microdualisms to Chapter 3.

On this critical naturalist conception, there are important differences between the social and natural sciences. The most significant *epistemological differences* turn on the unperceivability of social phenomena (which must therefore be detected by their effects); the absence of naturally occurring closed systems and the impossibility of experimentally establishing them; and the importance of context in social life. The most significant *ontological differences* turn on the activity-dependence, concept-dependence and characteristically greater space–time specificity[23] of social structures and forms; together with the internality of social science to its subject matter, which defines a *relational difference*. However, it is just in virtue of these differences, critical realism contends, that social science is possible. The social and natural sciences can both be sciences in the same sense, but not in the same way.

We can now identify the chief defects in pre-existing metatheories of social science. Contra *empiricism*, empirical regularities can be neither necessary nor sufficient for a causal law. Contra *neo-Kantianism*, structure is not only imposed on the empirical manifold by the human mind or the social community, but is a feature of being itself. Contra *hermeneutics*, although conceptuality is important and hermeneutics defines the starting point of social science, social forms are not exhausted by the conceptuality on which they depend, and conceptualisations are corrigible and subject to critique. *Strong social constructivism* can be seen to involve either a neo-Kantianism in the transitive dimension or a form of hermeneutics in the intransitive dimension. But from the fact that we have to define, say an illness, linguistically, in order to study it, it does not follow that it is constituted by our definition or that it would not exist apart from it. Similarly, although social agents' understanding of social reality may be an intrinsic part of the reality, (a) the reality has an irreducible material dimension to it as well and (b) our understandings of it may be false or otherwise inadequate.

As for *critical theory*, it is affected by the weaknesses of the neo-Kantianism that informs it. Thus, the absence of explicit ontology means that (as in Jürgen Habermas's theory of knowledge-constitutive interests) what are in reality ontological mediations are rendered as epistemological divisions. For critical realism, the causality of reasons means that what is described in the meta-language of hermeneutics is intrinsically part of the very same reality as that described by physical-action discourse. Indeed, human action typically takes the form of the manifestation of intentionality in the physical world.

Furthermore, critical theory, like most pre-existing metatheories of social science, fails to see that factual discourse may and, indeed must, license values (as I argue in Chapter 5.1). To criticise a belief is *ipso facto* to criticise actions informed by that belief, and if we can also explain the belief in question, that is *ceteris paribus* to criticise whatever it is that explains the belief as well.[24] It follows from this that values are not so much a presupposition or condition as an implication or consequence of explanatorily powerful social theory.[25]

1.4 Preview of the argument to come

Chapter 2 is situated on the terrain of the philosophy of science and sets out to give a simple exposition of transcendental realism. After describing tensions in recent and contemporary philosophy of science, the chapter rehearses the double argument that initiates critical realism: for the *revindication of ontology*, or the *explicit* study of being, as distinct from and irreducible to epistemology, or the study of knowledge; and for the *development of a new ontology*, in which structure, differentiation and change move to the fore, as against the flat and undifferentiated *implicit* ontology of empiricism and orthodox accounts of science. The transcendental analysis of experimental activity is shown to establish the existence of a level of reality independent of human activity and thus to demonstrate both that an ontology is possible and that it is independently existing, structured and differentiated.

The distinction between *transitive* and *intransitive dimensions* is now introduced and explained, the critique of the *epistemic fallacy* is developed and its basis in the *natural attitude* is shown. The *holy trinity* of critical realism, involving the compatibility of ontological realism, epistemological relativism and judgemental rationalism, is now unfurled. The distinctions between *open* and *closed systems* and the *domains of the real, the actual* and *the empirical* are outlined and the basis of the critique of the Humean theory of causal laws, and the doctrines of orthodox philosophy of science that depend upon it are seen to involve *actualism* (the reduction of the real to the actual) and the collapse of all domains of reality into one in *empirical realism*.

Three senses of the *stratification* of reality are distinguished and the three criteria for *emergence* discussed. The transcendental realist vision of *science as a social process* moving essentially from description of patterns of events to identification of the structures that explain them is outlined; and a logic or *dialectic of scientific discovery*, involving description, retroduction, elimination, identification and correction, is displayed. In this way Chapter 2 articulates the basic ontology and epistemology of the critical realist account of science. Some implications of this are explored and the weaknesses of empiricist, neo-Kantian and superidealist philosophies of science are demonstrated, and the resolution of the aporias they create (such as the problem of induction) is sketched. (An aporia is an interminably irresolvable indeterminacy or puzzle.)

Chapter 3 considers the transapplicability of this account of science to the social world. As I have already noted, the method of immanent critique rules out reliance on a simple transplant. Instead, a pincer movement is deployed. First the *possibility of naturalism* is developed through immanent critique of the dualisms or dichotomies and antinomies of social theory and the human sciences. These dualisms are most prominently those between structure and agency, holism and individualism and meaning and law (the macrodualisms), which in turn rest upon the dualisms between mind and body, reasons and causes, facts and values and theory and practice (the microdualisms). Then we can display the emergence from the natural order of human beings as persons, and of a social world similarly emergent from human being. Concepts of *intentional causality*, on which reasons can be causes, and of *mind as a synchronic emergent power of body* are developed, and *social structure* is seen to be the condition and outcome (normally unintended) of human agency.

As already indicated, resolution of the antinomy of structure and agency is shown to lie in the TMSA (of which the morphogenetic approach is a development).

This is then developed and generalised in the concept of *four-planar social being*, on which all social activity, and all social being, is seen to occur simultaneously[26] on each of the planes of material transactions with nature, social interactions between people, social structure *sui generis* and the stratification of the embodied personality.

The dichotomy between individualism and holism is resolved first in a relational conception of social reality, and second in the development of a hierarchy of orders of scale involving up to seven levels of agency and structure, from the sub-individual to the planetary and cosmic. Finally, the oppositions between meaning and law, and anti-naturalist hermeneutics and hyper-naturalist positivism are resolved in a view of social life as dependent upon, but not exhausted by, conceptuality; and of the social as both material and conceptual. On this view, hermeneutics is the starting point of social science, but conceptualisations are both corrigible and in principle subject to causal explanation in a research process in which qualitative and quantitative considerations can both find a place.

Chapter 3 moves on to consider the *differences between the social and natural sciences*. Epistemological, ontological and relational differences emerge. The most important epistemological differences lie in the impossibility of establishing experimentally closed systems, which entails that there is a necessary asymmetry between explanation and prediction; and the relative unperceivability of social structures. The most important ontological differences are the activity- and concept-dependence of social structures, which make possible a quasi-transcendental mode of argumentation in conceptually fundamental social science. The most important relational difference is the fact that social science is part of its own subject matter, which presages the transition from facts to values discussed in Chapter 5. The implications of the context-dependence of the operation of social mechanisms and the character of social science as involving a double hermeneutics are then traced. Finally, the consequences of the complexity and greater space–time dependence of social phenomena are explored. This chapter also extends the critique of empiricism and neo-Kantianism (and superidealist theories of science), established in Chapter 2, to hermeneutic, social constructivist (and poststructuralist) philosophies of social science.

In Chapter 4 our attention turns to *the logic of the concrete*. Social phenomena (like most natural) phenomena only ever occur in open systems, characterised by complexity and emergence. The explanation of concrete open-system phenomena (events, situations) is shown to involve the resolution, redescription, retrodiction,[27] elimination, identification and correction of claims about their component parts. This characteristic multiplicity of causes, mechanisms and theories does not, however, in itself license the transition to multidisciplinarity. For that we need also the emergence of levels, such that some of the mechanisms in an applied or concrete explanation are ontologically distinct and irreducible to the more basic ones. This gives us multidisciplinarity. But that is not yet interdisciplinarity. For interdisciplinarity one needs non-additive relations between the distinct levels, or the emergence of outcomes. Emergence of the mechanisms themselves yields intradisciplinarity. Turning from ontology to epistemology, the concepts of transdisciplinarity and cross-disciplinary understanding are introduced. Cross-disciplinary understanding is essential for the effective epistemic integration that must inform a united or integrated policy intervention or response to the open-systemic phenomenon, which could be climate change, an increase in demand for a commodity or a car crash.

The important concept of a *laminated system* is then introduced. Four kinds of laminated system are discussed: those constituted by (i) different (emergent) ontological levels, as in the original introduction of the concept for a case of disability;[28] (ii) different dimensions of social life, such as the four planes of social being; (iii) different levels of scale, such as the seven-tier model introduced in Chapter 3; and (iv) different (emergent) spatio-temporalities, such as in the Opening of Parliament or a New Delhi street scene.[29] The idea of a 'lamination' is designed to underwrite the irreducibility of, and necessity for, the various levels used in an applied or concrete interdisciplinary investigation. The deleterious consequences of reductionism, and the actualism that underpins it, is now exemplified in various domains. The *holy trinity of interdisciplinary research* and inter-professional cooperation quickly follows: this involves metatheoretical unity, methodological specificity and substantive theoretical pluralism and tolerance. The applied critical realist research process itself is conceived of as *doubly specific*: both to its place in the research cycle of the science concerned and also to the nature of the subject matter under investigation. This chapter ends by describing the ways in which critical realism can empower and facilitate a typical research project and showing how this in turn can avail itself of the resources provided by critical realism in its enquiry.

Chapter 5 outlines how the criticality of discourse establishes a basic argument for the evaluative implications of all factual discourse. This is further developed in the critical realist *theory of explanatory critique*, on which one can pass from negative valuations of beliefs, to negative evaluations of actions informed by them, and thence to negative evaluations of their causes and to positive valuations of action rationally directed at their removal. This model of cognitive explanatory critique can both be generalised to embrace non-cognitive and non-communicative ills and be embedded within a depth-emancipatory praxis. At its heart lies an ontology of human being in which our desires, needs and unfulfilled potential depend on the understanding and actions of others, that is, in which freedom and solidarity are interdependent – an ontology to be further developed in the course of this book.

The various senses of objectivity are now distinguished and the ways in which the intrinsic criticality of the social sciences is, and is not, consistent with objectivity are explored. The consequences of the reflexivity of social life are then traced. The important idea of *concrete utopianism* is now introduced and explained. The manner in which it forms an indispensable component in all ethical thinking is detailed and the ways in which it provides a moment that can be progressively radicalised within the structures of a deepened and enriched democracy and community social life are developed. The nature of ideology and ideology-critique are examined; and the characteristic pattern of critical realist critique as moving progressively through immanent critique, omissive critique and explanatory critique is demonstrated. Finally, a justification for the elision of transcendental realism and critical naturalism in 'critical realism' is offered, along with further reflection on the character of philosophical discourse and the role and nature of critical realism.

Chapter 5 then continues by considering in greater depth *the phenomenon of language*. The most characteristic form the epistemic fallacy takes today is that of the *linguistic fallacy*, involving the denegation[30] of both being and the materiality of social life. The basis of semiotics in the *semiotic triangle* (signifier, signified and referent) and the relationship between it and hermeneutics is explored. The importance of the *referent* and of the activity of *referential detachment* is emphasised. Poststructuralism follows Saussure in eliding the referent, while Anglo-Saxon linguistics typically elides the signified.

This chapter then explores the nature of language as an essential condition of social life, as both causally conditioned and causally efficacious, and as a diagnostic clue to extra-linguistic features of social reality, such as power relations and the distribution of resources, all of which furnish a basis for *critical discourse analysis* as an indispensable tool of social scientific analysis. Critical discourse analysis is related to the practice of explanatory critique, and two examples of evaluatively significant explanatory critique are discussed in some detail. This leads on to a discussion of the ways in which CDA enhances the criticality and reflexivity of social life.

Chapters 6–8 could in principle be skipped in a first reading of the book. They develop themes from dialectical critical realism and the philosophy of metaReality, as distinct from the basic critical realism that is outlined in the earlier part of the book. However, it is important to incorporate presentations of these bodies of theory in so far as they are (as we have seen) already implied by basic critical realism and in so far as they bear on the arguments and subject matter of Chapter 9. Moreover, dialectical critical realism and the philosophy of metaReality are part of critical realism and *Enlightened Common Sense: The Philosophy of Critical Realism* must, for completeness, say something about them.

Chapters 6 and 7 are concerned with the development of critical realism through the theoretical deepening of its ontology. This can be seen to involve *seven levels* or stadia[31] *of development*, each remedying absences in its predecessor level in a process of self-transcendence. The first (known as 1M or 'first moment') establishes being as such, as *non-identical* (differentiated) and as stratified; this is the level of basic critical realism. The second level (2E or 'second edge') involves the idea of being as *process*; the third (3L or 'third level') that of being together or as a *whole*; and the fourth (4D or 'fourth dimension') that of being as incorporating *transformative praxis* or agency. These form the basis for the so called MELD system of dialectical critical realism. The fifth level (5A or 'fifth aspect') involves the ideas of being as incorporating *reflexivity* and inwardness, the sixth (6R or 'sixth realm') that of being as *re-enchanted* (that is, as intrinsically valuable and meaningful in its own right) and the seventh (7Z/A or 'seventh zone or awakening') involves the idea of being as *non-dual* or as incorporating the primacy of underlying identity over difference and unity over split. These last three levels are taken up and theorised in the philosophy of metaReality. All seven levels comprise the so called MELDARZ or MELDARA[32] system of critical realism considered as a whole.

Chapter 6 begins with the analysis of *absence* and the critique of the *ontological monovalence* characteristic of the Western philosophical tradition since the time of Parmenides (*c*. 515–460 BCE). Ontological monovalence is the view that being is purely positive. It is shown that absence or the negative is not only necessary for being, but that change, properly understood, presupposes absence. Moreover, the key category of absence yields the clue to the vexed problem of dialectic. For this may be seen to depend on the rectification of real absences (omissions, incompleteness) in a move to greater completeness, inclusiveness and coherence. Absence is also necessary for a full understanding of intentional agency. For agency is the absenting of absence or lack. This generates an *axiology of freedom* conceived of as depending upon the absence of constraints and unwanted and unneeded sources of determination generally. Absence is further shown to be the root concept of a group of categories necessary for the understanding of change, including most importantly the idea of *contradiction*, which is argued to be ontological and not just epistemological. Also theorised under this stadion of dialectical critical realism are space, time, tense, process, *rhythmic* (or tensed, spatialising causal process), and the *presence of the past*.

We then track back to note some further implications of the first categorial level, involving the ideas of being as such, and as non-identity or difference and as structured. These include deepening our understanding of emergence, tracing the consequences of the inexorability and all-inclusiveness of ontology and investigating the nature of *dispositional*, *categorial* and *moral realism*. The theory of reference and referential detachment is further developed and a four-componential analysis of truth, which situates the possibility of *alethic* and *ontological truth*, is given. The nature of *TINA formations* and the characteristic logic of emancipatory discourse, as involving both transformation and shedding, are displayed.

The third level of categories, clustering around the idea of internal relations between elements, takes us into conceptions of *holistic causality*, the *concrete universal*, *constellationality*, *reflexivity*, *alienation* and *totality* generally, and a characteristic combination of *moral realism* and *ethical naturalism*. The fourth level of categories, revolving around the idea of being as incorporating transformative praxis, is situated within the structures of four-planar social being; and the dialectic of freedom, involving a *tendential rational geo-historical directionality* towards the eudaimonistic or good society, is presented. A developing set of understandings of *freedom*, and of its interdependence with *solidarity*, takes us from simple agentive freedom, through concepts of negative and positive freedom, via emancipation and autonomy, to notions of well-being and flourishing, and thence to the idea of universal human flourishing.

Chapter 7 begins with a brief discussion of the fifth level of reflexivity and interiority (and of the transition to the philosophy of metaReality through *transcendental dialectical critical realism*). It then discusses the sixth level of *re-enchantment*, and introduces the *philosophy of metaReality*. The main theme of metaReality is the *primacy of identity over difference* and *unity over split*. After a brief informal introduction and a discussion of the fate of Hegel's 'life-and-death struggle', the senses of identify and unity in the philosophy of metaReality are shown to be very different from our normal atomistic and abstract concepts. This is followed by a presentation of the basic justification for metaReality. Three senses in which identity is essential to social life are then differentiated, namely as *basis* (ground state – the state without which no other states could exist), *mode of constitution* or reproduction and transformation (non-duality) and as *deep interiority* (fine structure). Four types of non-duality are distinguished: the transcendental self, transcendental identification in consciousness, transcendental agency and transcendental holism (or teamwork). And three mechanisms of identification, namely, *reciprocity*, *transcendental identification* and *co-presence* are delineated.

A tripartite analysis of the *self*, as consisting in (absolute) ground state, (relative) embodied personality, and an illusory ego is given, and the axiology of freedom developed in dialectical critical realism is further extended. A discussion of the *axiological asymmetry* between the heteronomous features of social life and their non-dual grounds leads into an investigation of a normally unremarked *spiritual substructure of social life*, in which principles of reciprocity, solidarity and trust hold sway, reason is non-instrumental and unconditional love and spontaneous creativity abound. It is argued that this level underpins the other more visible ones, such as those of all commercial transactions and all relations of oppression or exploitation (characterised as relations of $power_2$ or power-over to differentiate it from the sense of $power_1$ or transformative capacity). Finally, rationales for the axioms of *universal solidarity* and *axial rationality* are provided and it is shown how they can be used both in the resolution of conflicts in social life and in collective decision-making.

Chapter 8 outlines the development of the philosophical discourse of modernity through five phases: the *classical discourse of modernity*, *high modernism*, the *theory of modernisation*, *postmodernism* and *bourgeois triumphalism*. The onset of each of these phases is marked by a revolutionary moment: 1640–60/1789; 1848/1917; 1945–49; 1968; and 1989.[33] The fundamental feature of the classical discourse of modernity is defined by an atomistic individualism and abstract universality, but it is already present in the Cartesian *cogito*[34] which opposes thought to body (and emotion, and consciousness generally); 'I' to other human beings and society; humanity to the natural world and other species; and the present to past and future. It leads inexorably to the situation of a Hobbesian world, in which atomised individuals are set apart from each other and, in Humean fashion, related to each other and similarly punctiform objects only by attachment or aversion, desire and/or fear. In stark contrast to this is the *Ubuntu* of some southern African peoples. This means 'I am because you are' (or 'we are', in some variants).

This chapter then shows how the problematic[35] of atomistic possessive individualism and reified abstract universality has given rise to the characteristic theories of science and social science we have been critiquing. It then explores its fundamental basis in three profound category mistakes: the *epistemic fallacy*; *ontological monovalence*; and *primal* squeeze, which entrains an actualist collapse on what I call the *Platonic/Aristotelian fault-line* characteristic of destratifying ontologies. The basis for a comprehensive explanatory critique of the Western philosophical tradition is thus established.

In Chapter 9 further features of the ontology necessary for the social sciences are developed. In Chapter 3 we conceptually distinguished the person and the agent. We now further distinguish the *person* qua embodied personality from the *self*. Following the analyses in Chapters 6 and 7 we can further develop the *dialectic of freedom and solidarity* to sketch some contours of the good society characterised by an orientation to universal flourishing in four-planar social being. The chapter goes on to consider what needs to be done to move towards universal flourishing in the context of the present multiple global crises (ecological, economic and moral) or *crisis system*, raising concerns about capability and legitimacy alike.

This leads into a recapitulation of the *dialectic of desire to freedom*, which is the ethical high point of dialectical critical realism, and its radicalisation in the philosophy of metaReality in the idea of the eudaimonistic society as dependent upon and oriented towards the project of *universal flourishing and self-realisation*.

The chapter looks critically at some contemporary currents in social and philosophical theory, specifically the new speculative realists in continental philosophy and the analytical causal powers or dispositional realists in analytical philosophy of science. In volumes planned I will examine actor network theory, rational economic actor theory, genetic reductionism and the proponents of 'evidence-based' empiricism in social theory and, in the more philosophical field consider the contemporary legacy of Nietzsche and Heidegger, contemporary critical theory, the new Neo-Aristotelians, the new Neo-Platonists and the new right-wing post-structuralist Hegelians.

The main themes of the book are then summarised and the advantages of critical realism briefly sketched. These include its ontological inclusiveness, epistemological coherence and comprehensiveness and methodological fertility; the susceptibility of alternative theories to devastating immanent and Achilles' Heel critique; their proneness to and dependence upon TINA formations, implicitly relying on a tacit and under-theorised critical realism; and the need for explicit *ex ante* methodological commitment to critical realism in an epistemic situation riven by the claims of competing metatheories. Following this we describe the *critical realist embrace*, sketching a mechanism by which irrealists can become aware of their implicit critical realism and learn to enjoy it!

After rebutting some common misconceptions about critical realism, the book then turns critically and self-reflexively to the respects in which critical realism remains weak and considers the ways in which it needs to develop today to underlabour for the challenges humanity and its sciences face.

Notes

1 John Locke, *An Essay Concerning Human Understanding* (Oxford: Oxford University Press, 1690/1975), 'Epistle to the Reader'.
2 See David Hume, *Dialogues Concerning Natural Religion* (Oxford: Oxford University Press, 1779/2008). The best argument against practical scepticism – that realism is

axiologically necessary – comes from the pen of Hume himself, but Hume did not accept this in theory. See Roy Bhaskar, *Scientific Realism and Human Emancipation* (London: Routledge, 1986/2009), 32–3.

3 David Hume, *A Treatise of Human Nature, Vol. II* (London: J. M. Dent, 1740/1934), Book II, Section III, 128.

4 And if our universe is part of a multiverse, that is one world too.

5 I use the terms 'law' and 'causal law' to refer both to statements of law in the transitive (epistemological) dimension and to what such statements designate in the intransitive (ontological) dimension. See Roy Bhaskar, *A Realist Theory of Science* (London: Routledge, 1975/2008), Chapter 2, Postscript to the Second Edition [1978], 251. The context determines the usage intended. Concerning the transitive and intransitive dimensions, see section 1.2.

6 The purported author of the founding corpus of the religious and philosophical tradition of hermeticism was Hermes Trismegistus, which may be a syncretic representation of Hermes, the Greek god of interpretive communication (hence 'hermeneutics') and Thoth, the Egyptian god of wisdom.

7 cf. Roy Bhaskar, *Reclaiming Reality: A Critical Introduction to Contemporary Philosophy* (London: Routledge, 1989/2011), 1.

8 Bhaskar, *A Realist Theory of Science*, Chapter 2, Appendix, 'Orthodox philosophies of science and the implications of open systems', 127–42.

9 Ludwig Wittgenstein, *Tractatus Logico-Philosophicus*, trans. Frank Ramsey and C. K. Ogden (London: Kegan Paul, 1921/1922), 6.35.

10 Bhaskar, *A Realist Theory of Science*, 37.

11 'Holy' puns on 'holes' (real absences). See Roy Bhaskar, *Dialectic: The Pulse of Freedom* (London: Routledge, 1993/2008), 42n.

12 Bhaskar, *A Realist Theory of Science*, Table 0.1, 13.

13 Roy Bhaskar, *The Possibility of Naturalism: A Philosophical Critique of the Contemporary Human Sciences* (London: Routledge, 1979/2015).

14 Bhaskar, *Scientific Realism and Human Emancipation*.

15 This is known as the 1M-7Z/A or MELDARZ/A chain of presuppositions, which I expound in Chapter 6.1 and subsequently.

16 According to a common view, my supervisor at Oxford, Rom Harré was co-initiator of transcendental or scientific realism. Although Harré's philosophy of science of the early 1970s was perhaps the most advanced antecedent of transcendental realism, I do not regard Harré as its co-originator, for reasons indicated in Chapter 2.7. See also Roy Bhaskar with Mervyn Hartwig, *The Formation of Critical Realism: A Personal Perspective* (London: Routledge, 2010), 31, 35–7, 47–9, 70, 216 n4.

17 Brad Shipway, *A Critical Realist Perspective of Education* (London: Routledge 2011), Chapter 1 and Mervyn Hartwig, 'Critical realism' in M. Hartwig, ed., *Dictionary of Critical Realism* (London: Routledge, 2007), 97–8.

18 Alistair McGrath, *A Scientific Theology: Volume 1, Nature; Volume 2, Reality; Volume 3, Theory* (London and New York: T&T Clark 2001, 2002, 2003 respectively); see esp. Vol. 2. See also the work of Andrew Wright.

19 Bhaskar, *The Possibility of Naturalism*, Chapter 2.

20 Anthony Giddens, *Central Problems of Social Theory* (London: MacMillan, 1979).

21 Margaret S. Archer, *Realist Social Theory: The Morphogenetic Approach* (Cambridge: Cambridge University Press, 1995).

22 See Bhaskar, *Scientific Realism and Human Emancipation*, 130 and *Dialectic*, 160.

23 Hence agent-dependency and variability.

24 Bhaskar, *Scientific Realism and Human Emancipation*, Chapter 2.5–2.7.

25 See also Craig Reeves, *The Idea of Critique* (London: Routledge, in press).

26 Roy Bhaskar, *The Philosophy of MetaReality: Creativity, Love and Freedom* (London: Routledge, 2002/2012), lxvi, 269–70, 301.

27 Retrodiction or postdiction is 'inference from effects to causes or from later to earlier states of systems via retroduced explanatory structures, for example, when a doctor infers

from a symptom in a patient that one of the generative mechanisms involved is a flu virus'. Stathis Psillos, 'Inference', in *Dictionary of Critical Realism*, ed. M. Hartwig (London: Routledge, 2007), 256–7, 257.

28 Roy Bhaskar and Berth Danermark, 'Metatheory, interdisciplinarity and disability research: a critical realist perspective', *Scandinavian Journal of Disability Research* 8:4 (2006), 278–97.

29 Bhaskar, *Dialectic*, 55.

30 I use this term in the specific dialectical sense of 'denial in theory, affirmation in practice' (Roy Bhaskar, *Plato Etc.: The Problems of Philosophy and their Resolution* (London: Routledge 1994/2010), 242). Denegation is the inverse of unseriousness, or 'affirmation in theory, denial in practice'. Both are a form of theory/practice contradiction or inconsistency.

31 *Stadion* (plural *stadia*) is classical Greek for (i) a unit of length and (ii) a course for a foot-race, usually with tiers of seats for spectators. I use it synonymously with *moment* (from Hegel), *a stage* (in a process), *level*, *phase*, and so on.

32 *Editor's note*. The deployment of such schemas is not of course peculiar to Bhaskar. The four truth procedures of Alain Badiou's philosophy, for example – science, art, love and politics – correspond to the moments of MELD, but in an anthropic register. For explanation and justification of the names given to the different levels, see the sources indicated in Chapter 6, Note 2, below.

33 See Roy Bhaskar, *Reflections on MetaReality: Transcendence, Emancipation and Everyday Life* (London: Routledge, 2002/2012), Chapter 4.

34 *Editor's note*. Contra Doug Porpora, one does not have to accept the Cartesian *cogito* in order to sustain a notion of human beings as coherent selves. See Douglas V. Porpora, *Reconstructing Sociology: A Critical Realist Approach* (Cambridge: Cambridge University Press, 2016), 23. There is a great deal in this excellent book that I find myself in agreement with. For Bhaskar's critique of the Cartesian *cogito*, see also Chapters 7.6 and 8.1, below.

35 A 'problematic' (n.) in my usage is the structured field constituted by philosophies, philosophical traditions, theories, and so on within which alone meaningful questions can be asked or problems posed. It typically screens out or occludes some questions and problems. It overlaps with 'paradigm', but specifically calls attention to screening. A 'problem-field' or 'theory problem-field solution set' is a specifically ideological problematic or TINA compromise formation that is systematically misleading and occlusive (see esp. Chapter 6.4). I sometimes use the terms interchangeably.

2

TRANSCENDENTAL REALISM AND THE PHILOSOPHY OF SCIENCE

2.1 The double argument: for ontology, and for a new ontology

When we talk about the world in the normal way we do not make a distinction that will be crucial to critical realism and in particular its philosophy of science. Thus if I ask you how far London is from New York and you tell me that it is about 3,500 miles, and I then ask you whether that is a statement about your knowledge or about the world, you might, understandably, be taken aback. For your statement would not have been so much about one *or* the other, but about *both*: about the *known world*. Indeed in the normal course of things, in what I call the *natural attitude*,[1] we do not disambiguate or differentiate knowledge from being, what we know from what there is. Accordingly, it is perhaps not easy to see the need to distinguish them. But they are not in fact the same. On the contrary, there is always in principle a distinction between knowledge and what it is knowledge of or about. Moreover, whenever there is a doubt about our knowledge, or there are competing claims to knowledge, we will need to make a distinction between knowledge and being; and accordingly between *epistemology*, or the philosophical study of knowledge, and *ontology*, or the philosophical study of being.

When I began work on the text that introduced philosophical critical realism (or, perhaps better, the philosophy of critical realism), *A Realist Theory of Science*, ontology was pretty much taboo. Indeed, there was an assumption, which I call the *epistemic fallacy*, that statements about being could always be analysed in terms of or reduced to statements about knowledge;[2] that it was sufficient for philosophy only to 'treat of the network, and not what the network describes'.[3] A problem with this mistaken assumption is that there is no way that a claim to knowledge of the world can fail to embody assumptions about the nature of the known world; so that the epistemic fallacy will merely mask or cover the generation of an *implicit ontology*. Thus, if one holds to the Humean theory of causal laws, whereby laws merely report constant conjunctions of atomistic events or states of affairs, then this pre-supposes that the world is unstructured, undifferentiated and unchanging, that is, flat, uniform and repetitive. For only a world so constituted is consistent with the availability of Humean causal laws.

The implicit ontology of most mainstream (non-critical realist) epistemology continues to be dominated by this shibboleth, that is, the idea that causal laws and the other objects of scientific knowledge either just are, or at the very least depend upon empirical regularities. This assumption underpins the familiar deductive-nomological or Popper–Hempel theory of explanation, that to explain an event is to deduce it from universal covering laws conceived of as invariant empirical regu-larities. But it also underpins a kindred theory of prediction (and of its symmetry with explanation), and theories of confirmation, falsification, theory production and the development of science, and so on.[4]

However, the deductive-nomological theory is clearly wrong. One only gets a unique result under experimentally or otherwise closed conditions. Outside such a context there is no invariant regularity; but inside it, the significance of the regularity lies entirely in the fact that it represents access to something (such as the operation of a natural structure or mechanism), at a different ontological level, something that continues to prevail outside that context. In experimental activity we do not produce a causal law, but rather the empirical grounds for such a law. That is to say, we pro-duce the conditions under which it can be realised in actuality and empirically tested.

What the Humean theory of causal laws does is to collapse three levels of reality, which I call the *domains* of the *real*, the *actual* and the *empirical* (see Figure 1.1), into one; and to assume that all systems are closed (that is, to collapse *open* to *closed* sys-tems). The collapse of the real to the actual is what I call *actualism*;[5] it presupposes the collapse of open to closed systems and, when coupled with the additional col-lapse of the actual to the empirical, results in *empirical realism*.[6] Both actualism and empirical realism are forms of *subject–object identity theory*.[7]

We are now almost in a position where we can display the basic architecture of critical realist philosophy of science or transcendental realism. However, before we can do so, we need to consider the way in which critical realism approaches the traditional terrain of the theory of (scientific) knowledge. It does so by introducing a distinction between two aspects or dimensions of science, both of which are necessary and irreducible.

Thus critical realism reworks the traditional distinction between epistemology and ontology in terms of a distinction between two dimensions necessary for our understanding of science. The first dimension depends upon the sense, or refers to the way in which science is a social process, dependent on anterior social products. This aspect of science is called the *transitive dimension*. The second dimension depends upon the sense, or refers to the way in which, though a social process, science studies objects that exist and act independently of it. This aspect of science is called the *intransitive dimension*. (This concept is further refined in Chapter 3.2.)

This gives us the basic structure of the transcendental realist account of science. The aim is to revindicate ontology against the strictures of Hume and Kant, encapsulating the epistemic fallacy; and at the same time to establish a new non-Humean ontology, committed to the reality of structure, difference and change against actualism, as encapsulated in the Humean theory of causal laws and the covering-law model of explanation.[8]

To achieve this anti-Kantian end, transcendental realism uses Kantian means, employing in particular *transcendental arguments*. Transcendental arguments ask what the world must be like for such-and-such a human activity to be possible. Commitment to the strategy of immanent critique means that the particular human activity analysed, forming the minor premise of such arguments, must be that selected by our adversary. One thing that mainstream accounts of science all agree on is the importance of experience, especially under experimental conditions in science. The argument from experimental activity that I have already advanced indicates that its significance lies in its capacity to afford us access to objects of knowledge such as causal laws that exist and act independently of our activity. So, we have at once:

(i)   an argument for ontology, distinct from epistemology; and
(ii) an argument for causal laws distinct from patterns of events, and correspondingly for a new non-Humean ontology.

Transcendental realism employs other transcendental or kindred arguments from science, for example, from applied activity (with the instrumentalists and pragmatists especially in mind), from scientific change and from the possibility of incommensurability; but it also, as we shall see, employs transcendental-type arguments from much more humdrum, everyday activities, such as the use of language or our interaction with other material objects in our world of material objects. For the moment, however, let us look at some of the more immediate implications of (i) and (ii).

2.2 Implications of the argument for ontology

Pursuing the implications of (i), we have the themes of the critique of the epistemic fallacy and of the necessity and irreducibility of ontology; of the need to understand science as a social process studying a world that exists and acts (wholly or at least in part) independently of it, that is, in terms of intransitive and transitive dimensions; and of the mutual entailment and compatibility of ontological realism and epistemological relativism. We can allow without strain that our knowledge is socially produced and changeable, but that it is of (or about) things and structures that are existentially quite independent of us and our knowledge, and relatively or absolutely independent causally.

This point is further developed in the holy trinity of critical realism, which (as we have seen) consists in commitment to ontological realism, epistemological relativism and judgemental rationalism. The combination of epistemological relativism and judgemental rationalism allows us to assert that, although our knowledge is fallible and without sure foundations and is always knowledge under particular socially and linguistically mediated descriptions, nevertheless there can be rational grounds for preferring one to another competing description (belief or theory). In this way critical realism is able to sustain the realist intuitions of positivistic modernisms without succumbing to their foundationalism; while acknowledging, along with post-modernist constructivism, the social relativity of all our beliefs without resorting to their judgemental irrationalism.

Since the end of the nineteenth century the epistemic fallacy has often taken the form of the *linguistic fallacy*. This is the idea that statements about being can be reduced to or analysed in terms of language.[9] Generally the epistemic fallacy represents a profound anthropocentricity in modern and contemporary philosophical thought;[10] indeed, one can think of it as an instance of a more general fallacy, the *anthropic fallacy*, in which the conditions and interests of being (and beings) are reduced to or analysed exclusively in terms of those of human being(s). As we will see in Chapter 6, the anthropic fallacy, together with the reciprocating *ontic fallacy*, constitutes a characteristic form of *anthroporealism* or *subject–object identity theory*, which necessitates a complementary *transcendent realism*.

The epistemic fallacy, in whatever form it is conducted, collapses the intransitive to the transitive dimension. In this way it can be seen to subvert the rationale of science. For science, at least understood in realist terms, is an *ontological investigation*. Indeed, we can now appreciate that realist science involves the *suspension of the natural attitude*, that is, our normal, but conflationary way of thinking in terms of the *known world*. (This is also, at least if Thomas Kuhn is right, our way of thinking in what he calls 'normal science'.)[11]

What then are we to say about the a priori ontology produced by transcendental argument? In particular, how do we differentiate such a *philosophical ontology* from the substantive *scientific ontology* produced as a result of, or in the context of irreducibly empirical a posteriori scientific (ontological) investigations? A philosophical ontology, formed by transcendental argument from a specific epistemological premise such as experimental activity, will tell us only about the general form of the world (what the world must be like for that activity to be possible), for example, that it must be intransitive, and structured and differentiated. Its detailed content, the particular ways in which it is structured and differentiated, must be furnished by the substantive investigations of a posteriori, irreducibly empirical science.

Another way to look at this is to see transcendental philosophy as supplying only the most abstract, highest order or categorial descriptions, with empirically-informed substantive science supplying their detailed content. Of course, if we are to understand philosophy as speaking about the same world as science – the one world, not a hypostasis or dual – we must make some distinction such as this.

A Kantian, or someone who wishes to tie ontology always to some epistemology, might object that our transcendental argument does always involve a specific epistemology and that you cannot talk about things in themselves apart from our ways of knowing them. But if you can't talk about the world apart from our ways of knowing it or our grounds for certain cognitive claims, you will never be able to talk about anything. For if you can't make a claim about the world without bringing in its supportive context, then you are never going to have any local, sectoral, separate or particular knowledge. For if you can't establish a conclusion about anything apart from our way of proving or establishing it, then ultimately the only knowledge you can have will involve the whole, indeed possibly everything, and indeed the process of everything. If we are going to have knowledge of particular things or of any discrete subject matter, we must be able to (and regularly do) *detach* the (ontological) conclusion of some epistemic investigation from the epistemic investigation itself.

A similar fallacy is often committed in the sociology of science when the argument is put forward that one cannot talk about a natural ontology, because scientists are always working in a social context without which the ontology might, at least arguably, have been different. This is of course to confuse what a claim is about, its *referent*, with all the conditions without which it might have been different. And without the *detachment of conclusions*, you are not going to have any science, argument or investigation (which depends on the *referential detachment* of the outcome of the investigation).[12]

There is of course a fine balance to be struck about exactly when, and how far, ontological detachment from epistemological premises and conditions should be taken. Thus Kant's strictures against ontology can be understood partly as a warning that ontological reflection should never become too severed from epistemological considerations, as well as continuing the polemic of Bacon and Descartes against scholastic metaphysics and for the new experimentally based sciences of physics and chemistry. But I take it that we can in principle distinguish the transcendental and critical underlabouring philosophical ontology of critical realism from the dogmatic metaphysical and largely a priori ontology of classical rationalism.

In sum, it follows that critical realism

(i) respects a difference between philosophy and science, form and content, with detailed content being supplied by empirically-grounded science; and
(ii) regards ontological detachment as only relatively autonomous from epistemological considerations, and sees philosophy in the last instance as needing to be consistent with the findings of science.

2.3 Implications of the argument for a new ontology

Here the big category mistake is actualism, namely the reduction of the domain of the real to (or its exhaustive definition in terms of) the domain of the actual. This is expressed most starkly in the Humean theory of causal laws; and for this, and for actualism generally, the presupposition of closed systems is (as we have seen) necessary.

The Humean theory of causal laws and the covering-law model of explanation imply an ontology that is flat, undifferentiated and repetitive. In contrast to this, the critical realist ontology is structured, differentiated and (in virtue of the transitive/intransitive distinction) susceptible to change. There are two cardinal or core distinctions here:

(i) the *real/actual* distinction, an index of the (vertical) *stratification* of the world; and
(ii) the *open/closed systems* distinction, an index of the (horizontal) *differentiation* of reality.

It is important to appreciate that the distinction between the domains of the real and the actual involves a commitment, not just to the *independent existence* of generative mechanisms apart from events, or of powers (and dispositions generally) apart from their manifestation or actualisation, but also to their *transfactual exercise* apart from particular patterns or sequences of events or the contingent actualisation of the disposition concerned. That is to say, what is involved in the real/actual distinction is a *three-tiered* (powers, exercise, manifestation or actualisation) *dynamic and transfactual form of dispositional realism* – not just a two-tiered (powers, exercise = actualisation) form of it.[13] This differentiates transcendental realism from other dispositional realisms currently in vogue (see Chapter 9.1).

Whereas the whole significance of open systems derives from the fact that one can no longer explain what happens in terms of a single type (or level) of mechanism, actualism tends pretty quickly to generate reductionist and mono-disciplinary approaches, and these tend very often to physicalism or in a physicalist direction, that is, to see the biological, psychological and social features of the world as nothing but (patterns in) the physical features of the world.[14] *Necessarily, in open systems, more than one type (or level of) mechanism is involved.* (We will be exploring some of the consequences of this in Chapter 4.)

As I have already indicated, actualism, especially in the forms of the Humean theory of causal laws and the deductive-nomological model of explanation, constitutes the core of deductivism and mainstream philosophy of science. But, considered epistemologically (rather than implicit-ontologically), it also generates *inductive scepticism*. For if all we have to go on for a law or any other universal statement are its instances, then clearly we can never verify it, since no matter how many positive instances turn up it is always conceivable that a negative one will be uncovered.

The ontology of empirical realism, which collapses three levels of reality into one, immediately generates the *problem of induction*. For if the evidence for a law of nature is restricted to its instances, we can never be certain that a counter-instance will not turn up (as Europeans discovered when they found black swans in South America and Australia). There are numerous variants of the classical problem of induction. There is the problem that if all emeralds examined up to midnight tonight have been green, what is to justify the supposition that after midnight tonight they will continue to be green rather than blue? This is because the evidence for 'all emeralds are green' is equally evidence for 'all emeralds are green until midnight tonight and thereafter blue', that is, 'all emeralds are grue'. This is Nelson Goodman's 'new riddle of induction'.[15] Then there is the problem of how you can distinguish a necessary from an accidental sequence of events: if there is a perfect correlation between the importation of bananas into Sweden and the UK birth rate, why is that not a necessary connection? There is also the problem of subjunctive conditionals: what justifies my supposition that if I walked out the front door into the rain, I would get wet? Then there is Hempel's paradox: there is no reason why the sighting of a black raven should confirm the proposition that all ravens are black better than the sighting of a red herring or a white shoe, which are logically equivalent contrapositives, non-black things that are not ravens.[16]

These problems are all unresolvable on empirical realist or actualist grounds. What is the critical realist resolution of them? There is a real reason, located in their molecular structure, why emeralds differentially reflect green light. However, this reason is located at a *deeper* level of structure than that described by their manifest colour of green. Given this reason, emeralds must be green; that is to say, anything that did not possess the structure would not be an emerald, and anything that does possess the structure must appear, or tend to appear green. Moreover, the absurdity of the empirical realist or actualist response to the problem of induction, namely seeking out yet further positive instances, like Don Quixote, in the impossible project of corroborating it, is shown by the fact that scientists in practice, once there is evidence that two properties may be connected, do not waste time totting up further confirming instances but move immediately to the process of discovering the connection in question, following a logic I describe in the next section.

The problem of induction has any number of open-systemic homeomorphs or duals[17] and can be generalised as the *problem of transdiction* or of the *transdictive complex*.[18] It is rationally resolved by remedying the absence that accounts for it, namely of the missing concept of *ontological stratification*. This is its theoretical or formal resolution. Its practical resolution comes from seeing that real scientists, once they have grounds for suspecting a real connection, do not endlessly seek out confirming instances of the association, but move always to seek to explain *why*, in an account of the mechanism in terms of which, when we have x, we must also have (or tend to have) y. (This is at the Lockean and Leibnizian levels of *natural necessity* in the DREI(C) model of scientific discovery and development to be discussed below.)

The Popperian 'falsificationist' response to the problem of induction, without the concept of ontological stratification (an immanent surrogate of which was given by the Lakatosian 'hard core' or basic assumptions of a theory), is equally eristic.[19] First, because few law-like statements, if interpreted empirically, are unfalsified (given the prevalence of open systems). In general a statement can be empirical or universal but not both. Second, because the refuting instance must be repeatable and in general universalisable. This again raises the original problem of induction and the non-existing warrant for the supposition of the uniformity of nature.[20] And third, because the actual response to a putatively falsifying instance is invariably modification of the statement or theory rather than its outright rejection (as Imre Lakatos, from within the Popperian camp, well appreciated).

Since the time of Hume, and especially Kant, many have indeed felt that there must be something wrong with deductivist criteria for a causal law, explanation, and so on, namely, that a constant conjunction of events cannot be *sufficient* for an explanation. However, critical realism, while underlining the lack of sufficiency of Humean criteria, denies even the *necessity* of such criteria (see Table 2.1). For we can certainly have a law of nature, that is to say the operation of a generative mechanism, in open systems where there is no regularity. This is just as well because, upon inspection, it is extremely difficult to find informative,

TABLE 2.1 Status of constant conjunctions of events[21]

	Necessary	Sufficient for Law
Classical empiricism	✓	✓
Transcendental idealism	✓	✗
Transcendental realism	✗	✗

non-trivial, non-falsified law-like statements or explanations conforming to deductivist criteria in open systems, either in the natural or the social domains. Moreover, in practice deductivism generates epistemically disastrous reductionist and interactionist regresses.

2.4 Tracing the consequences of transcendental realism

A new vision of science

On transcendental realism the world is seen to be stratified and differentiated, and corresponding to this we have a striking new vision of science as exploratory, essentially concerned with explaining why, searching for the currently unknown causes of known phenomena; always on the move from manifest phenomena to the mechanisms that generate them. In short, science comes to be seen as something wonderful again. It tells us about a world that we did not previously know and about the currently unknown causes of known phenomena; that is, why (and also how) things work in the world that we do know. It is an exciting, creative process of discovery that expands our knowledge and experience rather than producing (inevitably, in open systems, increasingly complicated) redescriptions of our everyday knowledge and ordinary experience.

The DREI(C) model of scientific discovery and development

A simple model of scientific discovery and development follows from this ontology and account of science as consisting essentially in the movement from events to the structures that generate them (see Figure 2.1).

What I call the DREI(C) schema defines a characteristic *logic of scientific discovery*. The first step, D, consists in the description of some pattern of events or phenomena. The next step involves retroduction, R. This consists in the imagining of possible mechanisms, which, if they were real, would account for the phenomenon or pattern in question. Since, clearly there will often in practice be a large, and perhaps infinite, number of mechanisms which may be imagined, the next stage in this process will be the elimination, E, of those which do not apply in this case. There then follows a most exciting stage consisting in the identification, I, of the causally efficacious generative mechanism or structure at work. The final stage, (C), stands for the iterative correction of earlier findings in the light of this identification.

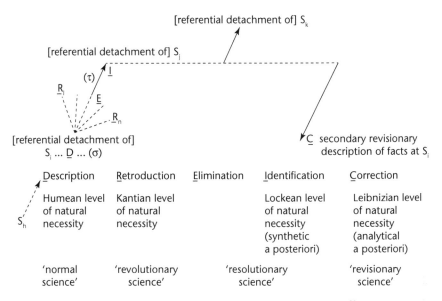

FIGURE 2.1 The DREI(C) model of theoretical scientific explanation[22]

Note: S = structure (real reason); (σ) = period of anomaly; (τ) = period of revolution.

When a science has moved through this cycle to the identification of the structure or generative mechanism causing the phenomenon or pattern in question, it does not proceed to endlessly confirm – or to disconfirm – its descriptions (as in the aporetic scenarios of 'the problem of induction' problem-field), but moves immediately on to a new round of discovery, beginning retroductively with the imagining of plausible mechanisms which, if they were real, would account for the phenomena of the newly identified level of reality.

This model also allows us to reconcile competing accounts of *natural necessity*. On it, science moves successively through *Humean, Kantian, Lockean* and *Leibnizian levels of natural necessity*. At D, we have simple Humean necessity, a correlation, but no causal connection, between the events described. At R, we have a Kantian level in which the necessity is a product of the scientific imagination. At I, we have a Lockean level where the generative mechanism or structure responsible can be empirically identified. This is then followed by a Leibnizian level at C where the (initially empirically identified) mechanism or structure is now taken as defining the kind of thing in question. At this level, having discovered that the possession of a free electron is what accounts for the fact that metals conduct electricity, the possession of a free electron comes to be regarded as defining what it is to be a metal, so that anything that did not conduct electricity would not be metal at all.

Three senses of stratification

The stratification of reality is a striking feature of the transcendental realist account. For convenience, we can distinguish three senses of stratification. There is, first, the stratification involved in any scientific explanation that is involved in positing a structural or generative cause of some phenomena. This first sense of stratification turns, then, on the distinction between *structures* and *events* or between the domains of the real and the actual. The second sense involves the iterative reapplication of this distinction, and the third involves a special case of the second.

The second sense consists in the kind of *multi-tiered stratification* of reality revealed in the development of science. The overt properties of material objects such as tables and chairs and molecules are explained by recourse to a deeper level of reality that is described by the theory of atomic number and valency. This, in turn, is explained by the theory of electrons and atomic structure, itself explained at a still deeper level of reality in terms of quantum fields, string theory or some other competing theory of sub-atomic structure.[23]

A third sense of stratification is defined by the special case of this multi-tiered stratification that consists in *emergence*.

Emergence

We are talking here of course about *ontological*, not merely *epistemic* emergence. In order to get a good handle on ontological emergence, it is important to distinguish synchronic from diachronic emergence, and focus on the former; that is, to look at the relationship between the emergent or higher-order and the lower-order levels of reality once the emergent level has been constituted. There are three criteria for emergence, considered ontologically and synchronically:

(i)   The unilateral dependence of the higher-order or emergent level on the lower level. Thus mind is unilaterally dependent on body, in the sense that we do not (as far as we know) have mind without body, but the converse is not the case.

(ii) The taxonomic and causal irreducibility of higher-order properties or powers to lower-order ones in the domain of the higher order. That is to say, we cannot explain features and phenomena at the higher-order level using the concepts of the lower-order level alone.

(iii) The causal irreducibility of higher-order powers in the domain of the lower order. This is top-down causation.[24]

The third criteria is especially noteworthy. Once a higher-order level has been constituted, there is no alternative but to take into account its causal efficacy at the lower level. This is of course the kind of causality that is involved in anthropic (human activity-induced) climate change in our own times, but it is also involved generically in all intentional action, and its effects in agriculture and industry have proved momentous in the development of civilisation and social life.

There is a fourth condition which can be added to these three, that is the sense in which the lower contains the higher order as a possibility implicit or enfolded within it.[25] This is the sense in which, ontogenetically, the child's knowledge of mathematics may be regarded as implicit or enfolded in its first utterances, or the sense in which, phylogenetically, the possibility of human language is enfolded within the genes of the higher primates.

2.5 A note on the disjuncture between the domains of the real and the actual

We are concerned here with two familiar types of situation for the investigator:

(i) where there is the continuing efficacy of a mechanism, but no regularity; and
(ii) where there are regularities, but no connecting mechanism.

In situations of type (i), we have two familiar kinds of cases in which a connecting mechanism may be overlooked:

(ia) *case studies*, where the mechanism is active in the particular case (and can indeed also be generalised to other cases of this particular type), but where there are no regularities – for example, the stimulus and/or releasing conditions for a mechanism are satisfied in this particular kind of local context, but are not generally met outside it; and

(ib) *counteracting mechanisms* (ongoing mechanisms and transfactually efficacious tendencies), where the stimulus and releasing conditions for the operation of the generative mechanism or exercise of the tendency are generally satisfied over a region of space–time – for example, those involved in anthropic climate change (such as the burning of fossil fuels) – but are not actualised or empirically manifest as regularities due to a flux (often variable) of counteracting mechanisms and circumstances.

In situations of type (ii), we again have two familiar kinds of cases, but here an assumed connection is wrongly projected, rather than a real one overlooked:

(iia) *illicit generalisation* or inference of a law-like or connecting mechanism where the posited mechanism either does not exist at all or is at any rate not instantiated;

(iib) *use of empirical regularities to justify counterfactuals*, subjunctive conditionals, and so on, either where there is no mechanism or where it is not actualised.

But there are other frequently occurring types of situation, including

(iii) a form of *misplaced concreteness* where there are regularities and a connection, but where the connection is the result of other deeper or mediating mechanisms; and

(iv) *contra-positive counteracting mechanisms* where the absence of a correlation (regularity) is wrongly taken as grounds for the absence of a connection – for there is a mechanism present, but its operation (and therefore the connection) is masked, overridden or undermined by the operation of other mechanisms and conditions.

2.6 Deepening the argument for transcendental realism

The argument for transcendental realism can be developed by an examination of scientific activities other than experimentation and the phases or logic of scientific discovery, as we have seen in section 2.4. But it can also be deepened by arguments from ordinary life, which is what I will be concerned with here.

We live in an incompletely described world of agents[26] and our praxis everywhere presupposes the independent existence and activity of transfactually efficacious mechanisms.[27] Thus, reflect upon the conditions of intelligibility of the most quotidian activity, like making a pot of coffee. We presuppose the independent existence of both the pot and the coffee, that the nature of water, coffee, pots and cups will not change, that if a cup breaks there is a reason for it and that sugar will continue to dissolve in the coffee. Everywhere we assume the independent existence (that is, the *existential intransitivity*) and the enduring properties or causal powers (that is, the *transfactual efficacy*) of things. These are presupposed by our material practices.

Moreover, language use presupposes the activity of *referential detachment*, that is, the non-anthropic detachment of both the referent and oneself from the act of picking out the referent. I am working with the assumption here that the intelligibility of language use and the possibility of meaning presupposes at a minimum the *semiotic triangle* (see Figure 2.2), constituted by the signifier (for example, word), signified (concept or meaning) and referent (thing or object);[28] but it is important to appreciate that this argument for the necessity of referential detachment entails not only the independent existence but also the transfactual activity (and hence the causal properties of kinds) of things.

Consideration of the intelligibility, or indeed the possibility of both material practices and language use presupposes that the world in which they occur is not a closed system constituted by invariant empirical regularities, but that it is

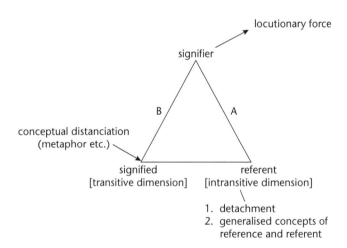

FIGURE 2.2 The semiotic triangle[29]

nevertheless (multiply) determined (caused) at a deeper level of reality by existentially intransitive and transfactually efficacious things; in other words, the world of everyday life, as much as that of the objects of scientific activity, presupposes the ontology of transcendental realism. Indeed, this can be argued to be a necessary condition for our *sense of self*, as we increasingly learn to pick out, describe and manipulate objects that are objectively other than, and so must be subjectively detached from ourselves. More about this in section 2.8.

2.7 The aporias of actualism

Undergirding actualism is the assumption of *regularity determinism*. This is the thesis that for every event y there is an event x or set of events $x_1...x_n$, such that x or $x_1...x_n$ are regularly conjoined under some set of descriptions; that is, that there are Humean causal laws such that for every event the simple formula 'whenever this, then that' applies. Regularity determinism must be differentiated from *ubiquity determinism*, which asserts merely that every event has real causes or that there are explanations for differences – which is acceptable and arguably presupposed by science.[30]

Regularity determinism of course assumes closed systems. Elsewhere, I have set out the very restrictive conditions for closed systems.[31] These are: for the systems, either isolation or the constancy of extrinsic conditions; for the individuals within them, either atomicity or the constancy of intrinsic conditions; and for the principle of organisation (or composition) of the system, either additivity or the constancy of any non-additive principle. Failure to satisfy these conditions generates in practice notorious 'interactionist' and 'reductionist' regresses.[32] The requirements of atomicity and additivity strongly insinuate what I have called *the classical paradigm of action*, and more generally the classical corpuscularian/mechanical worldview, which can be summarised as follows:[33]

(i) the externality of causation;
(ii) the absence of internal structure and complexity;
(iii) the absence of pre-formation, and of material continuity;
(iv) the passivity of matter and the immediacy of effects;
(v) the atomicity of fundamental entities; and
(vi) the subjectivity of transformation and of apparent variety in nature (that is, metaphysically, qualitative diversity and change are Lockean 'secondary qualities' and 'nominal essences', not 'primary qualities' and 'real essences').

Reductionism strongly encourages *physicalism*, a prevalent perspective among physicists and many other natural scientists, on which emergence is denied and qualitative change and variety is regarded as illusory, so making intentional agency impossible (in physicalism's own terms). This is, from the standpoint of critical realism, a self-referential paradox[34] and renders espousal of reductionism nugatory: for it cannot, in its own terms, have any real effects on the natural world, and hence any effect on other people's thoughts and opinions. Ontologically, regularity determinism of this

Laplacean sort was widely held to follow from the celestial closure achieved by Newtonian mechanics; and in its wake, epistemologically, a view of science as proceeding *algorithmically* became widespread. The role of human agency in experimentally establishing closed systems and in imaginatively retroducing scientific theories was ignored. Sooner or later a reaction to this tacit view of human beings as mechanistically determined was bound to be forthcoming, and when it arrived in the shape of romanticism the human world was typically held to be totally distinct and separate from the world of nature studied by (natural) science. The implied view of agency still did not see human beings as endowed with transformative powers capable of engaging in and affecting the course of the natural world.

Epistemologically, of course, the Humean theory of causal laws generated the insuperable *problem of induction* (in its own terms), and indeed the whole problem-field of what I call the *transdictive complex*.[35] The problem can be resolved only if one allows for a *non-algorithmic* response to an apparent regularity, involving the introduction of *new* concepts that can neither be induced nor deduced from existing data. From a critical realist standpoint, these new concepts refer to a newly discovered (but not created) mechanism located at a deeper or fuller level of reality, the understanding of which explains *why* the world is the way the problem of induction and the covering-law model assumes that it is (or is not).

Induction and deduction form the 'upward' and 'downward' limbs or curves of the *arch of knowledge tradition*, the founding principles of which were laid down by Aristotle; the keystone of the arch is supposedly comprised of general laws or principles.[36] But an induction is only valid if there *is* a generative mechanism connecting the instances concerned and one has established a closed system. And deducibility is only possible if one has *knowledge* of that generative mechanism as well; that is, not *that* they are, but the reason *why* the events in question are connected – that is to say, if and when one has moved, through a process of abductive redescription or retrodiction, elimination and identification to a new, deeper or fuller account of reality. The limbs of the arch of knowledge tradition could never have met in a keystone of general laws – the keystone was in reality lacking. To supply the keystone, the sceptic in theory (cf. the upward limb) had to be a dogmatist in practice (cf. the downward limb).[37] But once we have knowledge of natural necessity we have no need of induction; and what one can deduce from such knowledge is a *tendency of a natural kind* of thing, which is by no means an inductive generalisation of any number of instances or empirical regularities. The whole arch of knowledge tradition presupposes actualism.[38] We will discuss it further in Chapters 8 and 9.

2.8 The immanent context and transcendental necessity of transcendental realism

Transcendental realism was formed by a combination and deepening of two contemporary currents in the philosophy of science of the early and mid-1970s. The first was an anti-monist current represented by the work of Karl Popper, Thomas Kuhn, Imre Lakatos and Paul Feyerabend. This yielded the necessity for a distinction between the transitive and the intransitive dimensions as essential for the coherent description of scientific change.[39] Without this distinction the anti-monist current quickly fell into a more or less self-acknowledged incoherence. Take, for example, a well-known passage in Kuhn's *The Structure of Scientific Revolutions* where he says that he is convinced that we must learn to make sense of sentences like 'though the world does not change with a change of paradigm, the scientist afterward works in a different world'.[40] Unfortunately Kuhn does *not* make sense of such sentences. However, once we recognise the necessity for both the intransitive and transitive dimensions and their irreducibility to each other, we can transcribe the puzzling sentence without strain as 'though the [intransitive, ontological, natural] world does not change with a change of paradigm, the scientist afterward works in a different [transitive, epistemic, theoretical] world'.

The second, anti-deductivist current, associated with the work of Norwood Hanson, Stephen Toulmin, Mary Hesse and Rom Harré, showed that scientific knowledge was stratified. However, lacking the concept of ontology, it had great difficulty in sustaining real depth in the world, so that the stratification involved in science always appeared somewhat arbitrary and lacking rational justification. This is indeed the aporia of this tradition's 'theory of models', which recognises that science needs something more than empirical regularities or constant conjunctions of events but locates this extra or 'surplus element' in the scientific mind or community rather than the world. Such a neo-Kantianism or transcendental idealism is an advance on empiricism but, without ontological stratification, it is still subject to the aporias of the problem of induction. Moreover, it faces a difficulty in justifying the particular surplus element posited for knowledge. This problem is there in the Kantian original: what grounds are there for assuming that the categories will be valid or applicable to all domains of reality and whatever the development of our worldviews or belief systems? Anyway how can we talk of the synthesising powers of the categories of the understanding unless they are assumed to be real?

The philosophy of science of Rom Harré in the early 1970s[41] represents perhaps the most advanced antecedent to transcendental realism, but lacks three ingredients essential to it. First, there is no notion of the lack of necessity to complement the neo-Kantian critique of the insufficiency of a constant conjunction of events or invariant empirical regularity for a law or scientific explanation; nor, following on from this, is there the notion of the transfactual exercise as well as existence of the causal powers of things. Second, it lacks explicit thematisation of ontology, and of ontology as distinct from epistemology. Third, it lacks a metatheory or principled methods of philosophical argument – neither transcendental argumentation nor immanent critique are theorised or systematically employed. In other words, Harré lacks critiques of ontological actualism, of the epistemic fallacy and of non-transcendental philosophy.

The transcendental necessity of transcendental realism

Transcendental realism involves a *categorial realism*, that is, the supposition that *the principles of philosophy, if true, are true to the world* (see further Chapter 6.4). So causality, for instance, is not just something designed to make sense of the world but rather an intrinsic feature of the world itself. As such the principles elaborated by transcendental realism will constitute *axiological necessities* for science, that is, principles that must be met in its practice.[42] Now, no physicist or chemist could possibly work without a tacit distinction between experimentally constructed closed systems and the open systems to which the knowledge garnered in the laboratory is supposed to apply. As such, this distinction, though not licensed by mainstream philosophy of science, will inform their practice. Thus to apply scientific knowledge, the physicist or engineer will have to presuppose *in practice* its transfactual efficacy. This defines a sense in which *transcendental realism is an essential part of the practice of any working scientist*, a sense that imparts to their practice a key aspect of what I call a TINA compromise form, where TINA stands for 'there is no alternative' (see Chapter 6.4).

A TINA compromise form, which holds truth in practice in tension with falsity in theory, will of course readily lend itself to immanent critique. But consideration of the axiological necessity of the distinction between epistemology and ontology allows us to see that in practice every philosophy of science and every continuing scientific practice must be, contain or involve a realism, and indeed a transcendental realism of some sort. Transcendental realism is axiologically necessary also in the more general sense that it is a necessary condition of the ability of intentional agents to navigate their way in the world, a *ubiquitous practical presupposition* that underpins all currency of mind, in whichever particular practices minted.[43] Hence all human societies always already possess a proto-scientific account of the world and any serious science or philosophy is always necessarily trying to transform this account into a more adequate account, that is, to demystify and enlighten common sense.[44] The relevant questions will then be how far this realism is developed (whether so as to include causal laws or universals, for example) and in what form it is manifest (empirical, conceptual, and so on). This of course gives the immanent critic of some position adopted in practice a way in which explicitly to critique it. But by the same token it becomes important for us not just to identify lazily as a realist, but to specify exactly what kind of realism the position being advanced is committed to – for example, in our case transcendental or critical realism as distinct from empirical realism and other forms of *anthroporealism* (conceptual, intuitional, voluntarist, and so on).[45]

The contemporary resurgence of realism

Recently there has been a resurgence of interest in ontology and, paralleling it, in realism, in metaphysics and philosophy of science in the analytical tradition and in the camp of the so called speculative realists in the tradition of 'continental philosophy'.[46] At the same time within analytical philosophy of science there has been a move away from Humean and actualist thought to locating the basis of a causal claim in the existence of the causal powers of a structure or thing.[47] However, it should be noted that the dispositional realism of these traditions has mainly been of the two-tiered, static variety, not three-tiered and dynamic (see section 2.3, above); that is, it has sustained the existence of powers irrespective of their exercise, but not their transfactual exercise irrespective of the closure or otherwise of the systems in which they occur, that is, of the actualisation of the tendency concerned. Moreover, the realism of the speculative realists has mainly concerned the existence of things, not the operation of their causal powers; it is a realism about things rather than (also) about causality and hence the activity of things.

2.9 The further development of ontology within critical realism

If critical realism begins with an argument for ontology and an argument for a new ontology (as distinct from the old implicit ontology of empirical realism), it is important to see that its interest in ontology does not end there. This is because important corollaries of the argument for ontology are (i) the *inexorability* and (ii) the *all-inclusiveness of ontology*. There is no way that one can talk about knowledge or language or activity in the world without presupposing some account of the world. So ontology will inevitably be extended and developed in the further development of critical realism. But ontology is not only inexorable, it is also all-inclusive. For a moment's reflection shows that ontology must also contain epistemology, that is, the world must include our beliefs about the world (a relationship that dialectical critical realism will specifically theorise using the idea of *constellational containment* or overreaching – see Chapter 6.5). Moreover, ontology will not only include beliefs, but specifically *false beliefs* and illusions, and indeed errors of all kinds. For anything that has a causal effect must be admitted to be real.

Although every development within critical realism will involve an *extension and development of ontology*, the way is also open for the specific systematic theoretical *development of the philosophical categories* or concepts elaborated within critical realism. In dialectical critical realism and the philosophy of metaReality, the critical realist understanding of being as such and as non-identity, structure and difference is developed in two ways. First, by elaborating categorial levels thematising being as process, as internally related, as incorporating transformative agency, inwardness, re-enchantment and non-duality (the 1M-7Z/A or MELDARZ/A hierarchy of presuppositions, which I expound in Chapter 6.1 and thereafter). Second, by introducing a deeper reflection on categories of the non-identity form, of the difference and the structure kind, that is, specifically at the first level, 1M. Here the simple elaboration of non-identity, difference and structure and with it the abstract possibility of change in transcendental realism is built on enormously to include *dispositional realism*, that is, realism about possibilities and powers; and *categorial realism*, that is, realism about the referents of philosophy; realism about truth, and in particular an *alethic realism*; and about *reference, compromise formation* and error, and the *logic of emancipatory discourse*.

2.10 Critique of irrealist alternatives and anthropocentricity

By irrealism I mean any philosophy that is not a transcendental realism.[48] This section is a prolegomenon to the critique of irrealism I develop throughout the book but especially in Chapters 6 and 8.

Classical empiricism

Philosophical problems of the problem-of-induction genre may be further gener-alised as the problem of *transduction* (inference from closed to open systems) and the problems of the *transdictive complex* (transdiction is inference from the observed to the unobserved).[49] Such problems are insoluble on empiricist assumptions, and admitted to be insoluble. This means that strictly speaking there is no way that clas-sical empiricism can reach even the first rung of knowledge, the Humean level of natural necessity. However, if the existence of an empirical generalisation is assumed, there is no way its survival can be secured in open systems, where events are gener-ated by a conjunctive multiplicity of mechanisms and where any particular tendency is bound, on occasion, to be defeated. These two lines of argument are totally dam-aging to classical empiricism.

Neo-Kantianism

This accepts the ontology of classical empiricism (turning on the Humean theory of causal laws) but adds to it a surplus element deriving from the nature of the scientific mind or community. However, even if the surplus element is regarded as providing some inductive warrant over and above instances, its nature and specific content require justification. Epistemological stratification may enhance our understanding of the scientific enterprise but leaves us no better off ontologically or epistemologi-cally, at least in terms of judgemental rationality. For that, one requires ontological stratification and the dialectic or logic of discovery outlined in section 2.4.

Superidealism

By superidealism I mean the view that when our theories change, the world they investigate changes with them.[50] The superidealism, for example, of Kuhn or Feyerabend, together with the strong social constructivism in much sociology of science and knowledge (and indeed in the social sciences generally) are all based on the collapse of the intransitive dimension, that is, of the independently existing and transfactually efficacious referents of scientific discourse. As such they cannot coher-ently account for critique of, or change in our knowledge, which presuppose for their coherence relatively unchanging objects. They therefore succumb to a judge-mental relativism. In contrast, the epistemic relativism of critical realism, embedded within ontological realism, is consistent with the possibility of judgemental ration-alism in what I call the holy trinity of critical realism.

Non-anthropocentricity

Kant's so called Copernican revolution can now be seen to be in effect an anti-Copernican revolution, anthropocentrically placing humanity at the centre of the known world (see further Chapter 8.3). To correct this we need the concept of the

FIGURE 2.3 Our meta-reflexively totalising situation[51]

Note: O = objectivity; S = subjectivity; W = world; L = language.

unity of subjectivity and objectivity in the known world as situated within an over-arching objectivity. This can also be theorised in terms of the concept of a *meta-reflexively totalising situation* (see Figure 2.3).[52] We know of course that our world came into existence long before human beings and that it or the cosmos, which is after all being, will survive our species, human beings. We know that the laws of nature, to which for example a golf ball is subject, exist and operate quite independently of our activities, just as we cannot alter the speed of light or the specific gravity of alcohol. The standpoint of critical realism, which here depends upon ontological detachment, is the only standpoint consistent with *enlightened* common sense.

However, it is also a standpoint that can see science, and in particular natural science as a (qualified) success story, telling us far more about the natural world than we could have known without it. This is in contrast to the aporetic and trivialising caricatures of science in the mainstream and other irrealist traditions.

Critical realism is indeed a new philosophy but, as I argued in section 2.8, it is not a new practice; genuine science, whether great or ordinary, revolutionary or normal, has always been critical realist.

Notes

1 Roy Bhaskar, 'Theorising ontology', in *Contributions to Social Ontology*, eds Clive Lawson, John Latsis and Nuno Martins (London: Routledge, 2007), 192–202, 193–4. cf. *The Possibility of Naturalism*, 151 (my concept of the natural attitude is adapted from Alfred Schutz's phenomenology, but without Schutz's irrealist commitments).

2 See Bhaskar, *A Realist Theory of Science*, 36.

3 Wittgenstein, *Tractatus*, 6.35.

4 See Bhaskar, *A Realist Theory of Science*, Appendix to Chapter 2, 127–42.

5 See Bhaskar, *A Realist Theory of Science*, 64.

6 See Bhaskar, *A Realist Theory of Science*, 56.

7 Bhaskar, *Plato Etc.*, 31.

8 For an excellent recent account of my rehabilitation of ontology in transcendental realism, see Dustin McWherter, *The Problem of Critical Ontology: Bhaskar* Contra *Kant* (London: Palgrave Macmillan, 2013).

9 cf. Bhaskar, *The Possibility of Naturalism*, 155–6.

10 MinGyu Seo, 'Bhaskar's philosophy as anti-anthropism: a comparative study of Eastern and Western thought', *Journal of Critical Realism*, 7:1 (2008), 5–28, 10–12.

11 Thomas Kuhn, *The Structure of Scientific Revolutions* (Chicago: University of Chicago Press, 1962/1970).

12 See Roy Bhaskar, 'Theorising ontology', in *Contributions to Social Ontology*, eds Clive Lawson, John Latsis and Nuno Martins (London: Routledge, 2007), 192–202, 193–4.

13 See for example, Roy Bhaskar, 'On the ontological status of ideas', *Journal for the Theory of Social Behaviour* 27: 2/3 (1997) 139–47, 140.

14 Daniel Stoljar, 'Physicalism', *The Stanford Encyclopedia of Philosophy* (Spring 2015 Edition), Edward N. Zalta (ed.), retrieved on 24 February 2016 from http://plato.stanford.edu/archives/spr2015/entries/physicalism/.

15 Nelson Goodman, *Fact, Fiction, and Forecast* (Harvard: Harvard University Press, 1955).

16 See Carl G. Hempel, *Aspects of Scientific Explanation and Other Philosophical Essays* (The Free Press: New York, 1965), Chapter 1.

17 See Bhaskar, *A Realist Theory of Science,* Chapter 3.5–3.6 and *Dialectic*, Chapter 4.2.

18 See Bhaskar, *Plato Etc.*, 29–31.

19 Bhaskar, *A Realist Theory of Science*, 86–7, 160–63.

20 See Bhaskar, *A Realist Theory of Science*, 217–8.

21 Bhaskar, *A Realist Theory of Science*, Table 3.1, 164.

22 Bhaskar, *Plato Etc.*, 25, Figure 2.2.

23 See Bhaskar, *A Realist Theory of Science*, 169.

24 See Bhaskar, *Scientific Realism and Human Emancipation*, 113.

25 See Roy Bhaskar, 'Critical realism in resonance with Nordic ecophilosophy', in *Ecophilosophy in a World of Crisis*, eds Roy Bhaskar, Karl Georg Høyer and Petter Næss (London: Routledge 2012), 9–24, 12.

26 See Bhaskar, *A Realist Theory of Science*, 105.

27 See Bhaskar, *Dialectic*, 230.

28 See Bhaskar, *Dialectic*, 223 and *Plato Etc.*, 52.

29 Bhaskar, *Plato Etc.*, 52, Figure 3.4.

30 Bhaskar, *A Realist Theory of Science*, 69–70.

31 See Bhaskar, *A Realist Theory of Science*, 76.

32 See Bhaskar, *A Realist Theory of Science*, 77.

33 Bhaskar, *A Realist Theory of Science*, 78 f.

34 The denial of emergence etc. presupposes that intentional agency is real, that is, not – as is affirmed by physicalism – illusory.

35 See Bhaskar, *Plato Etc.*, 29.

36 See David Oldroyd, *The Arch of Knowledge: An Introductory Study of the History of the Philosophy and Methodology of Science* (London: Methuen, 1986).

37 Bhaskar, *Plato Etc.*, 41.

38 Bhaskar, *Plato Etc.*, 17–23, 35–6, 41.

39 Roy Bhaskar, 'Feyerabend and Bachelard: two philosophies of science', *New Left Review*, 94 (1975), 31–55; reprinted in my *Reclaiming Reality: A Critical Introduction to Contemporary Philosophy* (London: Routledge, 1989/2011), Chapter 3, 26–48.

40 Kuhn, *The Structure of Scientific Revolutions*, 121.

41 Rom Harré, *The Principles of Scientific Thinking* (London: Macmillan, 1972).

42 For the concept of axiological necessity see Bhaskar, *Dialectic*, esp. 118–19.

43 Bhaskar, *Scientific Realism and Human Emancipation*, 246; see also 32–3.

44 Bhaskar, *The Possibility of Naturalism*, 48 f.

45 Bhaskar, *Scientific Realism and Human Emancipation*, 7–10.

46 Alison Assiter, 'Speculative and critical realism', *Journal of Critical Realism* 12:3 (2013), 283–300.

47 Ruth Groff, 'Introduction to the special issue on causal powers', *Journal of Critical Realism* 8.3 (2009): 267–76 and *Ontology Revisited: Metaphysics in Social and Political Philosophy* (London: Routledge 2013).

48 Bhaskar, *Scientific Realism and Human Emancipation*, 9.

49 See Bhaskar, *Plato Etc.*, 30–1.

50 See Bhaskar, *Scientific Realism and Human Emancipation*, 70–92.

51 Bhaskar, *Plato Etc.,* 15, Figure 1.4.

52 See Roy Bhaskar, *Dialectic*, 150, 272. The unity of subject and object may also be conceptualised in terms of the idea of the 'expressive-referential duality' of truth in the dialectic of truth (see ibid., 217 f. and Chapter 6.4, below).

3

CRITICAL NATURALISM AND THE PHILOSOPHY OF SOCIAL SCIENCE

3.1 Methodological preliminaries

The argument of Chapter 2 can be developed, extended and/or generalised in various ways. In particular, we can ask to what extent the basic move within science – from events, or more generally phenomena, to the generative mechanisms, explanatory structures or (generically[1]) causes that explain them – can be made in fields other than the experimental natural sciences. We can ask whether this move occurs, or can occur in say the social field (the task I set myself in my second book, *The Possibility of Naturalism*, revisited in this chapter), or the biological realm (which I began to explore in my third book, *Scientific Realism and Human Emancipation*) or to whole domains such as language (explored in the present book in Chapter 5). Alternatively, we can, as indicated in Chapter 2, seek to develop theoretically and extend the newly established philosophical science of ontology (as is done in dialectical critical realism and the philosophy of metaReality). Or we can pursue the metacritical question of the conditions under which the accounts of science critiqued in Chapter 2 are possible.[2] Or we can take a concrete turn, concerning ourselves not so much with the move from events to structures but with the constitution, structure or formation of the event itself and how it should be explained. (This will be discussed in the next chapter under the rubric of applied critical realism.) Then of course we may decide to adopt a more specific focus, corresponding to which are the large number of sectoral critiques, reconstructions, analyses and engagements pursued by critical realists in specific subject domains or on particular topics of enquiry; for instance in an area or field such as education or on a particular topic within it, say, the nature of assessment practices in secondary schools in the UK today.

In this chapter we are concerned with the applicability of the general account of science outlined in Chapter 2 to the field of the social, and to an extent the psychological sciences, that is, the human sciences. However, as we have already seen, our commitment to the method of immanent critique prohibits the simple transapplication of results from the philosophy of the experimental natural sciences to another field. That would beg the question of the extent to which their subject matters are indeed comparable. Rather, an independent analysis of the subject matter of the social sciences is required.

A prominent feature of the philosophy of social science, social theory and indeed the practice of the social sciences today, as in the 1970s when I first considered this question, is the *prevalence of dualisms*. It will thus be convenient to take the dualisms of social science as our immanent starting point. These may be conventionally divided into the *macrodualisms* and the *microdualisms*. They are displayed in Table 3.1, together with their critical naturalist resolution. The main macrodualisms are those of structure and agency; society and the individual; and the dualism between those who would explain human affairs by reference to our conceptuality or some feature (such as language or subjectivity) associated with it, and those who would explain it by reference to our behaviour or at any rate to properties associated with our being materially embodied objects or things. The main microdualisms are those between mind and body; reasons and causes; fact and value; and, to an extent, theory and practice.[3]

The macrodualisms rest squarely on the microdualisms, but the microdualisms derive much of their plausibility from the macrodualisms. The macrodualisms converge on perhaps the *overarching dualism* of the field as whole, that between naturalism, the dominant form of which has been positivism, and anti-naturalism, the dominant form of which has been hermeneutics. This overarching dualism is between the *naturalists*, who hold that social (or more generally human) affairs can be studied in the same kind of way as nature is studied in the natural sciences, and the *anti-naturalists*, who believe that human affairs must be studied in a radically different way.

TABLE 3.1 Dualisms in irrealist social thought and their resolution in critical naturalism

Dualism	*Critical naturalist resolution*
Overarching macrodualism	
naturalism/anti-naturalism (positivism/ hermeneutics)	qualified critical naturalism
Other macrodualisms	
society/individual (collectivism [or holism]/individualism)	relationism, emergentism
structure/agency (reification/voluntarism)	transformational model of social activity
materiality/conceptuality	conception of materially embodied and conceptualising agentive human and social being
Microdualisms	
body/mind (macroscopically: nature/ society)	synchronic emergent powers materialist theory of mind
causes/reasons	reasons can be causes
facts/values and theory/practice	explanatory critique, ethical naturalism

Critical realism adopts a *via media* between naturalism and anti-naturalism, but of course it does so on the basis of a radically different account of (natural) science and a radically different ontology or account of the world presupposed by it. I call this middle way *critical naturalism*, but it could also be called, fairly enough, *critical hermeneutics*. The critical naturalist response to these macro and microdualisms will be to

(i) critique the account of the terms typically opposed,

(ii) enabling us to transcend their opposition,

(iii) thus resolving the dualism, and moreover

(iv) in such a way that justice can be done to both terms of the erstwhile dualism, but now on radically transformed grounds.

3.2 Transcendental realism, the philosophy of the social sciences and the problem of naturalism

The problem of naturalism, namely, of the scientificity of social and psychological studies, has been linked inextricably in the domain of the human sciences to the debate over the adequacy of the Humean theory of causal laws, the Popper–Hempel model of explanation and indeed the whole structure of the deductivist account of science. But as we have already seen, there must be serious reservations (to say the least) about the adequacy of deductivism in the domain of the natural sciences. Indeed, it will be recalled, the deductivist theory of scientific structure had already come under fire before critical realism (from, among others, Michael Scriven,[4] Mary Hesse and Rom Harré) for the *lack of sufficiency* of Humean criteria for causality and law, of Hempelian criteria for explanation and of the associated Nagelian criteria[5] for the reduction of one science to another more basic one. Transcendental realism generalised this critique to incorporate in addition the *lack of necessity* of such criteria (see Table 2.1). Thus positivism is seen to be unable to sustain either the necessity or the universality – and in particular the transfactuality (in open and closed systems alike) – of laws. And the way is cleared for an ontology that

(i) is irreducible to epistemology;

(ii) does not identify the domains of the real, the actual and the empirical with one another; and

(iii) is both stratified, allowing emergence, and differentiated.

That is to say, transcendental realism establishes the necessity for three kinds of ontological distinction, distance and depth that may be summarised by the concepts of *intransitivity*, *transfactuality* and *stratification*.

The lynchpin of deductivism is of course the Popper–Hempel theory of explanation, according to which explanation proceeds by deductive subsumption under universal laws (interpreted as empirical regularities). Its critics pointed out, however, that deductive subsumption typically does not explain but merely generalises the problem (for instance, from 'why does $x\,f$?' to 'why do all x's f?'). What is required for a genuine explanation is, as William Whewell had argued against John Stuart Mill in the 1850s and Norman Campbell against Mill's latter-day successors in the 1910s,[6] the introduction of *new concepts* not already contained in the explanandum, such as models picturing plausible generative mechanisms and the like. But critical realism breaks with Campbell's neo-Kantianism by allowing that, under some conditions, these concepts or models could describe newly identified deeper, subtler or otherwise more recondite levels of reality. Theoretical entities and processes, initially imaginatively posited as plausible explanations of observed phenomena, could come to be established as real through the construction of sense-extending equipment or of instruments capable of detecting the effects of the phenomena. In the latter case we invoke a *causal* criterion for attributing reality; to be is now fundamentally to (be able to) do, and no longer to be perceived. All this strongly suggests a *vertical* or *theoretical realism*. As we saw in Chapter 2.4, science could now be seen as a continuous or reiterated process of movement from manifest phenomena through creative modelling and experimentation or other empirical controls, to the identification of their generative causes (at a deeper and qualitatively different level of reality), which now become the new phenomena to be explained. The stratification of nature thus imposes a certain dynamic logic upon scientific discovery in which progressively deeper knowledge of natural necessity is uncovered a posteriori, that is, as a result of an irreducibly empirical process.

However, transcendental realism argues that a *horizontal* or *transfactual realism* is additionally necessary to sustain the *universality* (within their range) of the workings of generative mechanisms or laws. Thus, as we have seen, it is a condition of the intelligibility of experimentation that the laws that science identifies under experimental or analogously closed conditions continue to hold extra-experimentally; but they do so transfactually, not as empirical regularities. This provides the rationale or ground for practical and applied explanatory, exploratory and diagnostic scientific work too. Indeed, the whole point of an experiment is to identify a law that is universal (within its range) that, by virtue of the very need for an experiment, is not actually, and even less empirically, manifest and so not actually or empirically universal. It follows from the combination of vertical and horizontal realisms that the laws and the workings of nature generally have to be analysed *dispositionally* as the powers, or more precisely *tendencies*[7] of underlying generative mechanisms. These mechanisms may, on the one hand, be possessed unexercised, exercised unactualised, and actualised undetected or unperceived by human beings; and, on the other, be discovered in an ongoing irreducibly empirical open-ended process of scientific development.

A transcendental argument from the conditions of possibility of experimentation in science thus establishes at once the irreducibility of ontology (the theory of being) to epistemology and a novel non-empiricist but non-rationalist, non-actualist stratified and differentiated ontology; that is, an ontology characterised by the existence of structures as well as events (stratification) and open systems as well as closed ones (differentiation).

As we saw in Chapter 2, there are thus three new kinds of ontological distance or depth in transcendental realism, which I now explicate more fully.

(i) Intransitivity

The Western philosophical tradition has mistakenly and anthropocentrically reduced the question of *what is* to the question of *what we can know*. This is the *epistemic fallacy*, epitomised by concepts like *the empirical world*. Science is a social product, but the mechanisms it identifies operate prior to, and independently of their discovery; this is *existential intransitivity*.[8] I distinguish existential intransitivity from the *causal interdependence* that obtains in the social sphere (including its material infrastructure) to varying degrees. Existential intransitivity obtains as much in the social as the natural world, constituting a unifying principle for critical naturalism: everything within space–time is existentially intransitive or determined and determinate the moment it comes to be, for nothing can now alter that and why it has occurred; there is thus always an ontological distinction between beliefs and concepts and what they are about, even where what they are about is itself a belief or concept. Existential intransitivity is distinct from *causal intransitivity*. The latter is of two kinds: *absolute*, which pertains to things that cannot be changed by humans – for example, the speed of light; and *relative*, which pertains to things that can be changed by humans with varying degrees of difficulty – for example, the thawing tundra or a social structure – though only of course in the future-in-the present, not in regard of the past. While existentially intransitive, most social phenomena, unlike the fundamental laws of nature, are only relatively intransitive causally. But the most important distinction is between the intransitive and transitive dimensions as such, ontology and epistemology. Failure to distinguish them results among other things in the reification of the fallible social products of science. Of course, being contains, but it is not reducible to knowledge, experience or any other human attribute or product. The domain of the real is distinct from, and greater than the domain of the empirical.

(ii) Transfactuality

The laws of nature operate independently of the closure or otherwise of the systems in which they occur. And the domain of the real is distinct from, and greater than, the domain of the actual (and hence the empirical too). Failure to appreciate this results in the fallacy of *actualism*, which collapses and homogenises reality. Once the ubiquity of open systems and the necessity for experimentation or analogous procedures are appreciated, then laws must be analysed as transfactual, as universal (within their range) but neither actual nor empirical. Constant conjunctions are produced, not found. Generative mechanisms and laws operate independently of both the conditions for their identification (closed systems) and their empirical identification alike. Theoretical explanations, for their part, explain laws in terms of the structures that account for them; while they are applied transfactually in the practical explanation of the phenomena they co-produce in open systems.

(iii) Stratification

There is stratification both in nature and, reflecting it, in science, and both (a) within a single science or subject matter and (b) within a related series of them.

(a) Recognition of the stratification of nature and the DREI(C) logic of scientific development, in which natural necessity comes to be discovered empirically, that is, identified a posteriori, allows the resolution of a whole host of philosophical problems, most strikingly the notorious problem of induction. The unanalysed or tacit condition of possibility of this problem, indeed problem-field, may now be seen to be actualism, itself presupposing the ubiquity of closed systems. Thus if there is a real reason, located in its molecular or atomic constitution, why water boils rather than freezes when it is heated, then it *must* do so.

(b) The real multiplicity of natural mechanisms grounds a real plurality of sciences that study them. Even though one kind of mechanism may be explained or grounded in terms of another, it cannot necessarily be reduced to or explained away in terms of it. In particular, such grounding is consistent with its emergence. Given ontological emergence, the course of nature is now different from what it would have been if the more basic stratum alone operated. Hence – to invoke a causal criterion for reality – the higher-order structure is real and worthy of scientific investigation in its own right.

This takes us nicely to the domain of the social sciences, where what William Outhwaite has called the 'law-explanation orthodoxy'[9] was never even remotely plausible.

As we have noted, for most of its recognised history the philosophy of the human sciences has been dominated by dichotomies and dualisms, which critical realism seeks to transcend (see Table 3.1). Once again, the main ones are:

(i) The overriding dichotomy or split has been between a *hyper-naturalistic positivism* and an *anti-naturalistic hermeneutics*, which is resolved in the generation of a *qualified critical naturalism*.

(ii) Then there is the split between *individualism* and *collectivism* (or holism), which critical naturalism resolves by seeing society *relationally* and as *emergent*.

(iii) The connected split, upon which the debate about *structure* and *agency* was superimposed, is between the *voluntarism* associated with the Weberian tradition and the *reification* associated with the Durkheimian one.[10] This critical naturalism transcends in its *transformational model of social activity*.

(iv) Then there is the split between meaning and law, language and behaviour or *conceptuality* and *materiality*, which critical naturalism transcends in its conception of *materially embodied and conceptualising agentive human and social being*.

(v) Then, fuelling the positivism/hermeneutics debate has been the dichotomy between *reasons* and *causes*, which critical naturalism resolves by showing how, once Humean causality is rejected, reasons can be causes *sui generis* on a critical realist conception of causality.

(vi) Underpinning many of these dichotomies is the dualism between *mind* and *body* (or, more macroscopically, between society and nature), which critical naturalism seeks to overcome by seeing mind as an emergent power of matter in its *synchronic emergent powers materialism*.

(vii) Finally there is the dichotomy between *facts* and *values*, most sharply expressed in 'Hume's Law' to the effect that there is no legitimate way of inferring values from facts, which critical naturalism refutes in its theory of *explanatory critique*. Discussion of this is postponed until Chapter 5.1.

The Possibility of Naturalism (Bhaskar 1979) was oriented primarily to the first of these questions, which was whether or not society and human phenomena generally could be studied in the same way as nature, that is, 'scientifically'. It was oriented against two main positions, dualistically opposed:

(1) A more or less unqualified naturalism that asserted that they could be so studied. This normally took the form of *positivism*, dominant in the philosophy and practice of the social sciences. Its immediate philosophical antecedents lay in the work of Hume, Mill, Mach and the Vienna Circle, providing the spine of the orthodox conception of science, which it transplanted to the social world.

(2) An anti-naturalism, based on a distinctive conception of the subject matter of the social realm, that is, as pre-interpreted, conceptualised or linguistic in character: *hermeneutics*, the official opposition to positivism. The philosophical ancestry of hermeneutics derived from Dilthey, Simmel, Rickert and Weber, who fused Hegelian and Kantian dichotomies to produce a contrast between the phenomenal world of nature and the intelligible world of human freedom, so as to ground dichotomies between causal explanation and interpretive understanding, the nomothetic and idiographic, the repeatable and unique, the realms of physics and of history.

Whereas positivism found expression in the Durkheimian sociological tradition and in behaviourism, structuralism and functionalism, hermeneutics did so in aspects of the Weberian tradition and in phenomenological, ethnomethodological and interpretive studies. Within the second camp it is important to discriminate between those who sought to synthesise or combine positivist and hermeneutical principles, such as Weber and Habermas, and those, such as Hans Gadamer or Peter Winch, who denied positivism any purchase in the human sphere.

Both positivist and hermeneutical views – that is, the standard baseline naturalist and anti-naturalist positions – share an essentially positivist account of natural science. If this is, as I have contended, *false*, then the possibility arises of a third position:

(3) A qualified, *critical* and non-reductionist *naturalism*, based upon a transcendental realist account of science and, as such, necessarily respecting (indeed grounded

in) the specificity and emergent properties of the social realm. Moreover, if the positivist account of natural science is false, then positivists in the domain of the social sciences have to make out a special case as to why positivism should be uniquely and (most implausibly) applicable to the human realm. And hermeneuticists, for their part, have to reassess their contrasts. Thus both of Winch's two main arguments in his very influential *The Idea of a Social Science* (1958)[11] are parasitic on positivist ontology. The first argument is that, whereas the natural sciences are concerned with constant conjunctions of events, the social sciences are concerned with intelligible connections in their subject matter.[12] But constant conjunctions of events are neither necessary nor sufficient either for natural or for social scientific understanding; and both alike are concerned with the discovery of intelligible connections in their subject matter. The second argument is that social things have no existence, other than a purely physical existence, that is, as social things, apart from the concepts that agents possess of them. But the conceptual and the empirical do not jointly exhaust the real. In natural science, leaving aside thought, to be is not just to be perceived; it is also more generally to have a causal effect, whether or not it is detected or perceived by human beings. Critical realism can allow that conceptuality is distinctively social, without supposing that it is exhaustive of social life.

Let me elaborate on this. The social world is characterised by the complete absence of laws and explanations conforming to the positivist canon. In response to this, positivists plead that the social world is much more complex than the natural world (interactionism) or that the laws that govern it can only be identified at some more basic, for example, neurophysiological level (reductionism). But positivists are wrong to expect the social sciences to find constant conjunctions in the human world, for they are scarce enough in the natural realm; while hermeneuticists are wrong to conclude from the absence of such conjunctions that the human sciences must be radically different from the natural sciences. Closed systems cannot be established artificially in the human world. But this does not mean that one cannot identify generative mechanisms at work in specific contexts or construct theoretical generalisations for them; or that there are no criteria for theory choice or development, or that there are no empirical controls on theory. Rather, it follows from the absence of closed systems that criteria for choice and development of theory will be explanatory, not predictive, and that empirical controls will turn on the extent to which events indicate or reveal the presence of structures.[13] Moreover, the fact that social life is pre-interpreted provides a ready-made starting point for the social sciences. That said, there are no grounds for treating these data (such interpretations) as exhaustive of the subject matter of social science, or as incorrigible, or for that matter as non-causal, that is, as neither causally produced nor causally efficacious. Thus, rejecting the Humean account of causality and acknowledging emergence allows us to see reasons as causes, but causes that may, for instance, be rationalisations or otherwise false.

The positive case for critical naturalism turns on the extent to which an independent analysis of the objects of social and psychological knowledge is consistent with the transcendental realist theory of science. It is this analysis that the resolutions of the dualisms argued for in the next two sections are designed to yield.

3.3 Transcending the macrodualisms and the critique of social theory

The three macrodualisms with which I will be immediately concerned here are, as already mentioned, those between structure and agency; society and the individual; and conceptuality and behaviour.

In the *Possibility of Naturalism*, the first two dualisms were taken together (as for instance Margaret Archer also does in her book *Realist Social Theory* (1995)), but it is normally better to differentiate the two. Given this, strong cases could be made for starting with either dualism. However, I will begin here with the structure/agency one.

Structure/agency

The perspective of critical naturalism here is that of the transformational model of social activity (TMSA) (see Figure 3.1).

The nature of the TMSA

The characteristically quasi-teleological or goal-oriented character of human action suggests an essentially Aristotelian model of agency as creative or productive (*poïetic*), such that it involves work on *pre-given materials*, at least some/one of which are/is transformed into a product or result, such as a speech act, a chair or a wedding.

Among the pre-givens are social structures. Our society always stands to us as something that we have not created (on pain of voluntarism), into which we are 'thrown' or indeed 'hurled',[14] but that would not exist without our continuing activity (on pain of reification). Social forms then (i) pre-exist human agency. Such forms are deployed by agents in their activity which (ii) they (the forms) enable or constrain, and so are, in virtue of this deployment, (iii) reproduced or more or less transformed by that activity.

Thus human beings, in their substantive activities, must not only do/make things (their first-order praxis or activity), for example, get married; they must also do or re-make the conditions of their doing/making (their second-order activity), reproducing (or more or less transforming), for example, the institution of marriage – a making that is for the most part unintended and indeed may be unconscious.

This then is the TMSA. It has close affinities with Margaret Archer's morphogenetic/morphostatic (M/M) model.[16] In fact, the M/M model can be regarded as an elaboration of the ontology of the TMSA, with three clearly successive

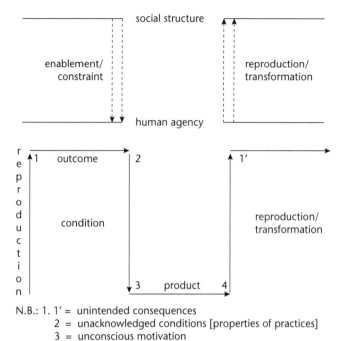

N.B.: 1. 1' = unintended consequences
  2 = unacknowledged conditions [properties of practices]
  3 = unconscious motivation
  4 = tacit skills [properties of agents]

FIGURE 3.1 The transformational model of social activity[15]

Note: The second diagram draws out some of the temporal and other implications of the first.

temporal phases, namely of structural conditioning, sociocultural interaction and structural elaboration in any round or cycle of structural transformation or reproduction.[17] However the TMSA does not depend on the assumption that change comes from interaction between elements; on it, change can occur endogenously or by 'inner action' and as a result of incompleteness or contradictions within or between elements, which are, nevertheless, activity-dependent.

Time plays a crucial role in both the TMSA and the M/M models. Structure always pre-exists the actions that transform it and always post-dates the actions by which it is transformed. However, I would prefer to identify the relationship between structure and agency as one of 'analytical duality', rather than, as in Archer's work, 'analytical dualism'.[18]

In elaborating the crucial role of time and temporal difference, it is important to note that social structure is dependent not only on the present activity (and conceptions) of human beings but on their past activity (and conceptions).[19]

The second important feature that the TMSA and the M/M model share is their highlighting of the non-identity of social structure and human agency, that they constitute *radically different kinds of thing*. This is the second reason why it is important not to conflate structure and agency.

The TMSA versus structure/agency conflation

It is convenient to differentiate three inadequate, conflationary stereotypes that serve to obliterate the autonomy and efficacy of structure or agency or the difference and connection between them. On the *upwards conflation* of the Weberian and utilitarian stereotypes, structures are in effect the immediate products of actions, and on the *downwards conflation* of the Durkheimian and social constructivist stereotypes, actions are effectively pre-determined by structures, whereas on *central conflation* actions and structures are mutually constitutive – different moments of the same process or different aspects of, or perspectives on fundamentally the same thing.[20] I will revisit these stereotypes shortly.

Here it is worth dwelling on *central conflationism* a bit. There is the illicit identification of society and persons in the model of Peter Berger and Thomas Luckmann, on which society is conceived of as an objectification or externalisation of human beings and human beings, for their part, are regarded as the internalisation or reappropriation in consciousness of society.[21] But the most influential form of central conflationism is Anthony Giddens's theory of 'structuration' on which structure exists only as the skilled accomplishment of knowledgeable actors. This encourages a picture of the social structure packing up or dissolving when we go to sleep, so that in the morning we might invent an entirely new one. The trouble with this idea, attractive though it is, is its voluntarism and neglect of the massive weight of the past. Change always involves material as well as efficient causality, chipping away at the given, work on the old, *transformation* properly so called.

Later in this chapter we will see how the ontological asymmetry and radical differences between the personal and the social, mediated by the distinction between persons and agents, is further accentuated in what can be described as the historic dominance of the social over the personal, especially in the form of the experience of the social as involving the preponderance of constraint over enablement for the vast majority of human beings, for whom mere survival, rather than specific achievements, let alone the condition of flourishing has been the goal of existence.

The further elaboration of the TMSA

The TMSA can be further elaborated in the conception of *four-planar social being* (see Figure 3.2). This is the idea that all social activity, and all social being, occurs simultaneously on the four dimensions of:

(a) material transactions with nature;
(b) social interactions between people;
(c) social structure; and
(d) the stratification of the embodied personality.[22]

More on this below.

In relation to the first big dualism, of structure and agency, we have identified three forms of conflation: model I, the upwards conflation of the Weberian and

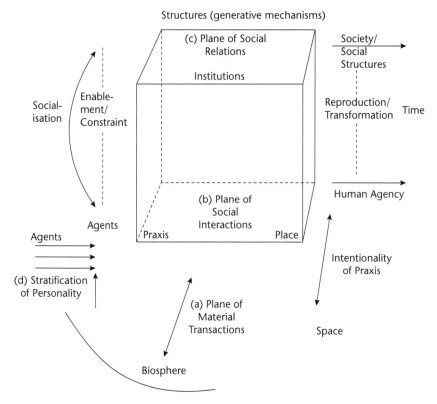

FIGURE 3.2 Four-planar social being[23]

utilitarian stereotypes, and model II, the downwards conflation of the Durkheimian and social constructivist stereotypes. Both of these are reductionist and epiphenomenalist, holding that either structure or agency is inert and a dependent variable. Model III, central conflation, is illustrated by the Berger and Luckmann model of 'illicit identification' and Giddens's theory of structuration. This variant is a-reductionist, holding that the terms are mutually constitutive. Thus we have the idea of the duality of structure, namely that structure is the simultaneous medium and outcome of action. But this ignores, of course, that whereas it is the medium of present activity, it is the outcome of past activity.

Similarly, in regarding praxis as both productive and reproductive or transformative the difference between the first-order product and the second-order reproduction of the conditions of production is elided in the theory of structuration, and the point is overlooked that the reproduction (or transformation), that is, the social elaboration is a joint product of social action/interaction and the given pre-existing structure, a vector involving two terms; in virtue of which, moreover, production and reproduction refer to distinct moments or phases of time. It is worth reiterating what Archer calls the two basic theorems of this approach:[24]

(i)   structure necessarily pre-dates the actions that transform it; and
(ii)   structure necessarily post-dates (or survives) the actions that have transformed it.

Finally, it is worth bearing in mind the following huge difference. For Giddens, '[s]tructure has no existence independent of the knowledge that agents have about what they do in their day-to-day activity',[25] whereas for critical realism society is 'an articulated ensemble of such relatively independent [existentially intransitive] and enduring structures'.[26]

However, there is an important asymmetry here: at any moment of time society is pre-given for the individuals, who never create it, but merely reproduce or transform it. The social world is always pre-structured. This means that agents are always acting in a world of structural constraints and possibilities that they did not produce. Social structure, then, is both the ever-present condition and the continually reproduced outcome of intentional human agency. People do not marry in order to reproduce the nuclear family or work in order to sustain the capitalist economy. The social world is nevertheless the unintended consequence (and inexorable result) of, as it is the necessary condition for their activity.

Society/individual

The second dualism is that between society and the individual. Historically, this dualism has taken the form of a clash between *methodological individualists* and *methodological holists* or *collectivists*. Unfortunately, the holist camp has not normally been informed by a robust concept of the social, normally identifying it with a mass of individuals, such as a crowd or audience. The argument has been over whether the behaviour of such entities can be reduced to the behaviour of the individuals who compose it. For critical naturalism, this is a very inadequate conception of the social. For the social is not primarily about either individuals or groups of individuals as such, nor their behaviour. Indeed it is not concerned in the first instance with behaviour at all. Instead, it is concerned with the more or less enduring *relations* between individuals and groups, such as (for example) between husband and wife or parents and children in the family, or between debtors and creditors, or owners, managers and workers, or politicians and their constituents.[27]

Such a *relational conception of the subject matter of social science* is well adapted to thematise relations of oppression and exploitation alongside other forms of domination or subjugation, such as exclusion. I call such relations of oppression *master–slave-type relations* or $power_2$ relations. It is important here to disambiguate two frequently confused senses of power: power in the sense of transformative capacity, which I call $power_1$, from power in the sense of domination or oppression, $power_2$. Clearly, emancipation from $power_2$ relations will in general depend on an augmentation of the transformative capacity or $power_1$ of the oppressed. Equally clearly, this will normally depend on, or indeed consist in part in knowledge of the $power_2$ relation, that is, of the explanatory structures and mechanisms that account for $power_2$, and of the conditions under which they can be transformed. The goal of emancipation from any set of master–slave-type relations is not only or primarily the liberation of those who are slaves, but the overthrow of the master–slave relation itself, that is, a transformation at plane (c), not just plane (b) of social being. These themes will be further discussed in Chapter 6.

This relational conception of social science accords well with the TMSA's conception of social structure, with the primary social structures of concern being defined relationally. The relations may often, but not always be understood as between the points of contact between structure and agency in what I called the *position-practice system*,[28] which define relations between the individuals and groups of individuals who fill the positions.

However, the relational conception is itself perhaps unduly restrictive, in so far as it would seem to prohibit the study of entities and properties in the social world that cannot be defined relationally. So I have subsequently further elaborated this in terms of a conception of social science as operating at different *levels of scale*.[29] On this conception we can define various distinct levels of agency and structure with which social explanation may be concerned, including (I have suggested illustratively) the following seven levels:

(i) the *sub-individual*, psychological level, including the Freudian unconscious and that of our ordinary attributions of motives and reasons for action;

(ii) the *individual* or biographical level, typically adopted by novelists but also argued by some (such as Sartre), not just individualists, to be the most important in the social sciences;

(iii) the *micro-level* studied for example by ethnomethodologists, concerned with such issues as turn-taking in conversation or how we avoid bumping into each other on the pavement;

(iv) the *meso-level* at which we might be concerned with the relations between functional roles, such as capitalist and worker or politician and citizen (as on the original relational model);

(v) the *macro-level*, oriented to understanding the functioning of whole sectors of society, such as the Norwegian economy;

(vi) the *mega-level*, concerned with the tracing and analysis of trajectories of whole traditions or formations, such as feudalism or contemporary Islamic fundamentalism; and

(vii) the *planetary* (or *cosmological*) level, at which we are concerned with the planet (or cosmos) as a whole, as for example in Immanuel Wallerstein's world-systems theory. This level may also be extended to cover the whole *geo-history*[30] of humanity or the planet, and so on.

Conceptuality and behaviour

Critical realism is in accord with hermeneutics on the methodological importance of the fact that social life is for the most part conceptualised, and moreover that this will normally be the starting point for any social investigation. For it must, at the very least, find out what the agents whose activity is sustaining some social institution, practice or social structure think they are doing in their activity and why they (think they) are doing it. However critical realism does not regard conceptuality as exhausting the matter. This is because we are not just conceptualising (language-using) beings, but materially embodied ones. Hence in talking about war, for example, we are not only saying that the criteria for the use of the concept of war are satisfied, but talking about the bloody fighting. Critical realism sees social activity as *concept-dependent*, but not *concept-exhausted*; that is, as dependent on, but not exhausted by its conceptuality. Thus we would not characterise a situation as one of homelessness unless we had a clear concept of, and criteria for the use of the idea (for human beings) of *home*. But homelessness is not just a condition in which the criteria for the concept are satisfied, it is importantly also having the *embodied experience* of not having a roof over one's head. Similarly, just as war involves bloody fighting and homelessness getting wet at night, so hunger involves excruciating pains. These are left out by a purely hermeneutical account. Moreover, the particular conceptualisations we have are both *corrigible* and subject to *critique*; and there may be dimensions of the social that have not been conceptualised. Again, the possibility of saying this depends on the fact that we can continue to refer to the material aspect of the social reality, while criticising its conceptualisation. Finally, because we are materially embodied as well as conceptualising beings, the human sciences must be prepared to use quantitative as well as qualitative research, that is, to measure and count our material features, as well as interpret and record our conceptual activity – to employ, in effect, 'mixed methods' research.

Critical naturalists, then, see social activity as both material and conceptual. We remain materially embodied and engaged in the natural and practical orders (see the next section) as well as the social order, even if much of our natural and practical activity is socially and linguistically mediated. Indeed, as we will see in Chapter 5.2, these two aspects of the social world (material/embodied and conceptual/discursive) are seamlessly united in a critical realist/critical discourse analysis of language, in which the linguistic is seen as at once causally conditioned by and causally efficacious on extra-linguistic reality.

The increasing prominence given to language in the twentieth century has led to at least two philosophically significant ways of overstating the importance of language, two forms of the linguistic fallacy. The first is the reduction of *all reality* to, or its analysis as language, involving the epistemic fallacy and the collapse of the intransitive dimension. This is primarily an epistemological thesis. This mistake has been committed by poststructuralist philosophers employing neo-Kantianism in a linguistic key. Then there is the reduction of *social reality* to, or its analysis as language. This is primarily an ontological thesis about the nature of specifically social reality, involving the collapse of the material side of social life, the disembodiment of social reality, including the de-materialisation of planes (a) and (d) of four-planar social being. This is the characteristic fallacy of hermeneutics. Social constructivists often commit both mistakes.

Given that language constitutes an 'inside' or 'interior' to social (unlike natural) life, it is understandable to regard hermeneutics as the starting point for social investigation. Given, further, that it is subjectivity that is constitutive of this interior, it seems natural to see social life generally as, at least in part, consisting in or constituted by subject–subject interactions and relations. Social science will then partake of the character of a subject–subject relation (although always taking place in an objective context) that is carried into the investigation of subject–subject relations; and so we have the motif of a *double hermeneutic*. *Empathy* is of course the basis for hermeneutics, and our capacity for *transcendental identification in consciousness*, which will be discussed in Chapter 7, is the basis of empathy. But it is important to remember that *semiosis* or meaning-making underpins all hermeneutics, and that all semiotics has a material basis both in the irreducibility of the referent in the semiotic triangle and of the activity of referential detachment in our linguistic (conceptualising) practices; and in the materiality and forms of embodiment of the sign.[31]

The case for critical naturalism

I have argued that the positive case for critical naturalism turns on the extent to which an independent analysis of the objects of social and psychological knowledge is consistent with the transcendental realist theory of science.

Commitment to emergence, and in particular to synchronic ontological emergence characterises the TMSA and M/M. For both, the social world is a causally and taxonomically irreducible part of the natural world, such that

(i)   persons and the personal are unilaterally existentially and emergently dependent upon the biological; and

(ii) societies and the social are unilaterally existentially and emergently dependent upon the personal.

I now wish to revisit the question of the limits of (or conditions for) naturalism, that is, of the differences between natural and social structures and the forms of their appropriate science (see Table 3.2).[32]

The emergent features of social systems that, on the invocation of a causal criterion for ascribing reality, can be regarded as (I) *ontological* (intransitive) limits on (or conditions for) naturalism, now need to be stated more carefully. The (1) activity-dependence and (2) concept-dependence of society must be parsed as the dependence of social structure on the present or past activity and conceptualisations of people. It remains true of course that the effects of social structure are only operative through human agency.[33] The (3) greater space–time specificity of social structures remains unaffected, but this is only a relative difference. A lesser, but important, ontological difference is (4) social relation-dependence: any social structure is dependent for its existence and identity on other structures of social relations.

The causal interdependency between social science and its subject matter specifies a (II) *relational* (transitive/intransitive) difference, which turns on the fact that social science is part of its own subject matter. This means that the social scientist has to be reflexive in a way that the natural scientist does not have to be. The condition that social systems are intrinsically open – the most important (III) *epistemological* difference (in the transitive dimension) – accounts for the absence in principle of crucial or decisive test situations. This necessitates reliance on exclusively explanatory (not predictive) criteria for the rational assessment of theories. (A fourth, (IV) *critical* difference will be discussed in Chapter 5.)

TABLE 3.2 Differences between natural and social structures and the forms of their appropriate science

Type	Differences	Remark
I. *Ontological* (intransitive)	social, unlike natural, structures are	
	(1) activity-dependent	social structures do not exist independently of the activities of people, present and past
	(2) concept-dependent, entailing a hermeneutical starting point for social science	the activities of people (intentional actions) are informed by beliefs
	(3) relatively space–time specific and transient (variable and changing)	there is geo-historicity in the rest of the natural order, but in the emergent social sphere it is more localised spatially and happens faster
	(4) social-relation dependent	any social structure is dependent for its existence and identity on other structures of social relations
II. *Relational* (transitive/intransitive)	social science is internal to its own subject matter in a way that natural science is not, and may causally impact it	social science is part of its own field of enquiry which, though existentially intransitive (t_1), may be causally affected by it (t_2); by contrast, the fundamental laws of nature are both existentially and causally intransitive
III. *Epistemological* (transitive)	decisive predictive tests are not available for social scientific theories	social systems are radically open, experimental closure is impossible, theories must be assessed exclusively in terms of their explanatory power
IV. *Critical*	social, unlike natural, objects include beliefs about themselves and human agency may have unacknowledged conditions, unintended consequences, tacit skills, and unconscious motivations	situates the possibility of explanatory critique of consciousness and social forms as false or inadequate, hence of the collapse of the fact/value and theory/practice dichotomies

However, subject to (and arguably just in virtue of) these differences the characteristic modalities of both theoretical and applied explanation that critical realism specifies appear to be possible to some degree in the social, just as in the natural sphere. Thus, as we saw in Chapter 2.4, theoretical explanation proceeds by *d*escription of significant features, *r*etroduction to possible causes, *e*limination of alternatives and *i*dentification of the generative mechanism or causal structure at work, which now becomes a new phenomenon to be explained and in the light of which our previous theoretical understanding is *c*orrected (DREI(C)). Applied explanation proceeds by *r*esolution of a complex event (and so on) into its components, theoretical *r*edescription of these components, *r*etrodiction to possible antecedents of the components, *e*limination of alternative causes, and *i*dentification of causally efficacious components, followed by *c*orrection of earlier results (RRREI(C)) (see further Chapter 4.1).

On the critical naturalist account, then, the social sciences can be sciences in exactly the same sense as natural ones, but in ways that are as different (and specific) as their objects. If the hermeneutical starting point of the social sciences in some pre-conceptualised social practice lends to them a closer affinity with the transcendental and dialectical methods characteristic of philosophy, any slight on a critical naturalism is banished by reflection on the fact that these forms of argument are merely species of the wider genus of retroductive argument found in all the sciences.

On this conception, then, in contrast to the hermeneutical perspective, actors' accounts are both corrigible and limited by the existence of unacknowledged conditions, unintended consequences, tacit skills and unconscious motivations; but in opposition to the positivist view, actors' accounts form an indispensable starting point for social enquiry. The TMSA entails that social life possesses a recursive and non-teleological character, as agents reproduce and transform the very structures that they utilise (and are constrained by) in their substantive activities. It also indicates, as we have seen, a relational conception of the subject matter of social science, in contrast to the methodological individualist and collectivist conceptions respectively characteristic of the utilitarian (and Weberian) and Durkheimian traditions of social thought.

Related to this is the controversy about 'ideal types'. For critical realists the grounds for abstraction lie in the real stratification (and ontological depth) of nature and society. So ideal types are not subjective classifications of an undifferentiated empirical reality but attempts to grasp (for example, in terms of real definitions[34] of forms of social life already understood in a pre- or proto-scientific way) precisely the generative mechanisms and causal structures that account in all their complex and multiple determinations for the concrete phenomena of human history.

3.4 Transcending the microdualisms: intentional causality and the formation of human agency

In this section I will mainly be concerned (i) to recapitulate my resolution in earlier works of the microdualisms involved, so as to justify the critical naturalist view that citing an agent's reasons for acting can properly be treated as causal, that is, to represent my theory of intentional causality; and (ii) to situate the study of the field opened up by the idea of intentional causality (marking the site of the psychological sciences) in relation to that of the natural sciences.

Subjectivity

If there were no subjective contributions to action in a social context, then there should be no difference in the human response to the same social circumstances. The fact that there is a difference, besides highlighting the absurdity of positing Humean causal laws or empirical regularities here, clearly indicates that there *is* a subjective component. And it is intentional agency, agency performed for a reason, that marks the site of the contribution of the human agent to the social process, that is, to the reproduction or transformation of social structures (as well as quite generally to the natural and practical orders).

The emergence of the social order

How are the objects of the social (and more generally human) sciences related to the objects of the natural sciences? They may be regarded as *taxonomically* and *causally irreducible* but *dependent* and *co-variant* modes of matter:

(i) *Dependence*: the objects of the human sciences are unilaterally existentially dependent on those of the natural sciences;
(ii) *Co-variance*: fundamental changes in their natural bases will bring about fundamental changes in the objects of the human sciences;
(iii) *Taxonomic irreducibility*: the natural sciences are *at present* unable to explain the human world under non-human descriptions;
(iv) *Causal irreducibility*: reference to properties *not* designated by physical theory is necessary to explain some *physical* states, namely those resulting from intentional action.[35]

Note that this *synchronic emergent powers materialism* is consistent with a diachronic explanatory reduction, that is, a natural-historical explanation of the formation in time of emergent powers, so that it is not pre-formationist or creationist, which is to say that it is metaphysically Darwinian. It is vital to appreciate that only an emergent powers materialism is consistent with a realist interpretation of non-physical (psychological, sociological) explanations of human phenomena; and that a realist interpretation of such explanations is only justified if it can be shown that there are properties instantiated in the human world that are inexplicable in terms of different sets of conditions specified by purely natural laws. Ontologically speaking, we are confronted with a stark choice between reductionist physicalism and an emergent powers theory. Of course, explanatory realism might still be justified as an expedient pending the prospective physicalist reduction. But this interpretation of social and psychological theory as 'elliptical' suffers from the acute embarrassments that, ontologically, higher-order phenomena appear highly underdetermined under the appropriate higher-order descriptions and, epistemologically, any choice of a higher-order theory seems arbitrary.

While all human phenomena have a natural manifestation, it is clear that nature is more centrally implicated in some (for example, medical) than other (for example, literary) practices. However, even the most basic biological functions may be profoundly socially and linguistically mediated.[36] If the causal intersection of the *natural* and *social order*s defines the *practical order*, then it is clearly also the case that all human action occurs on this interface (see Figure 3.3). Hence, if one would differentiate the three orders, this must be in terms of our *differential engagement* with them, that is, in terms of the *intentionality* of the agents and practices concerned. Thus in the case of the practical order our concern is precisely with the intersection of the natural and social, for example, in technology (where the causal relation runs mainly from the social to the natural) or in social biology or geography (where it runs mainly from the natural to the social). Our engagement with the natural order would then take the form of practices concerned with our material bodies and their natural environments; while our engagements with the social order would be in terms of practices designed to produce, or oriented towards, a social effect.

Correspondingly we can differentiate three types of explanation of concrete human phenomena, namely in terms of *natural causes*, in terms of *social causes* or in terms of a combination of social and natural causes, that is, *mixed causes*.[38]

On the critical naturalist conception, social objects are the emergent powers and liabilities of natural ones subject to continual conditioning and constraint by nature. The emergence of society is shown in the causal irreducibility of social forms in the genesis of human action (or being); and the emergence of mind is shown in the causal irreducibility of beliefs in the explanation of those states of the physical world that are the outcome of intentional agency. But the known effects of natural causes are normally mediated as cultural products (for example, artefacts), so that we are dealing with mixed rather than purely natural determination.

Reasons and causes

The argument that the human sciences are concerned with the reasons for agents' behaviour and that such reasons cannot be analysed as causes is often used to

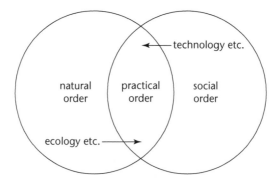

FIGURE 3.3 The natural, practical and social orders[37]

buttress the hermeneutical position. For it is said that reasons are not logically independent of the behaviour they explain; and that they operate at a different language
level (Waismann) or belong to a different language-game (Wittgenstein) from causes.
But natural events can likewise be redescribed in terms of their causes (for instance,
toast as burnt). Furthermore, unless reasons were causally efficacious in producing
one rather than another sequence of bodily movements, sounds or marks, it is difficult to see how there could be grounds for preferring one reason explanation to
another and, indeed, eventually the whole practice of giving reason explanations
must come to appear as without rationale.[39]

Mind and body

In considering the emergent powers of persons, clarity is helped by first looking at
the powers synchronically, setting aside the question of the evolutionary or historical processes of their formation. Specifically, as we have seen, the *synchronic emergent
powers materialism* advocated by critical realism is consistent with the possibility of a
diachronic explanatory reduction.[40]

The programme of any reductionist materialism (in respect of the mind–body
relation), such as central state materialism, faces enormous problems. There is, first,
the question of the analysis of psychological states. If they are regarded as real, the
reductionist must also assume that they are completely determined by neurophysiological states; in which case they would appear to be purely epiphenomenal, playing no real generative role in the life of human beings. Second, there is the problem
of causality, for the reductionist must assume that our behaviour is completely
governed by lower-order neurophysiological states. So if I get up from my desk in
order to shut the window, the reductionist must assume that my movement across
the room and the shutting of the window would have occurred just as it did, even
if I had not had the conscious intention to do so. This seems patently absurd. But
an even more acute problem is at hand.

Suppose I am having a meal with some friends and I ask one, M, to pass the
pepper. We must assume that M would have passed the pepper pot even if I had
not asked her. For my request has been completely determined by *my* neurophysiological states and her response has likewise been completely determined by *her*
neurophysiological states. But clearly there has been no interaction between our
respective neurophysiological states. We have the spectre of some universal synchronicity such as was involved in Leibniz's theory of a pre-established harmony of
monads. Discounting this far-fetched hypothesis, we would have to allow that
mind is causally efficacious on body, and body on the world; and in particular that
I am a causal agent of the acts I perform, including my request, and that M is
similarly a causal agent of her response. It can now be seen that in effect what is
involved in programmes of reductionist materialism is an abstraction from the
social context and natural environment in which embodied persons act; so what
we have in effect is the idea of the neurophysiology of a *single body* constituting a
closed system. For the programme cannot deal with the case of social interaction

or human response to a natural environment, such as is involved when I open my umbrella when it starts to rain. It is most unlikely that I would have opened my umbrella unless it had begun to rain. My friend would not have performed the action of passing the pepper pot without my request. And I would not have made the request unless I was at the dinner table, or perhaps in the supermarket.

This argument shows clearly that a world with other minds and environmental contingencies, among other things, that is, a four-planar social world, can supply us with reasons for performing one rather than another type of action; and it is clearly the reason at work that is causally responsible for the physical action performed and the ensuing result.

But the reasons we have for performing actions do not only come to us from outside. We can certainly supply ourselves with reasons for acting. But reasons can also be of a more settled, longstanding sort. Thus we have reasons in the form of longstanding beliefs and dispositions to act. Thus if I am a supporter of, say, the Labour Party, I have a reason to vote for that party in an election.[41]

I now consider the formation of action more generally.

The formation of action and of agency

Characteristically intentional human action has been seen by philosophers as dependent upon *beliefs* and *desires*, with the beliefs typically informing the desires, so that together they characteristically form a *want*, which defines the intended outcome of the action, that is, our intentionality in performing it *ceteris paribus* makes it happen. A more general account of the immediate, formative components of action would identify five kinds of component or basis involved in any action. We might enumerate these as the *cognitive* and *conative* components familiar from the traditional model, together with *affective*, *expressive* and *performative* components. Then again one might want to single out *values* and differentiate *competences, facilities* (access to resources) and *opportunities* as sub-components of the performative basis of action. In general, each component is necessary for action; and each component is learnt, formed, developed. Together these components form a matrix of the subjective sources of action, as displayed in Figure 3.4.[42]

On the TMSA, the social structure conditions actions, but this conditioning is always mediated by the actuality or possibility of *reflexive deliberation* by the agent on the course of action to be followed. This reflexive deliberation will of course be influenced by the values of the agent, and in particular by what has been called her *ultimate concerns* and commitments,[43] in relation to her capacities or capabilities and the feasibility (including chances of success) of the course of action being considered. It is always in principle possible for the agent to adopt what I have characterised as a *meta-reflexively totalising* [view of her] *situation*,[44] identifying and appraising her projects, roles and commitments in the context of her self-narrative and the totality of her life. Such reflexive deliberation may indeed, as Margaret Archer has argued, take the form of an *internal conversation*.[45] However, the actual decision taken may be the result of unconscious, as well as conscious elements, as is shown in Figure 3.5. Actions

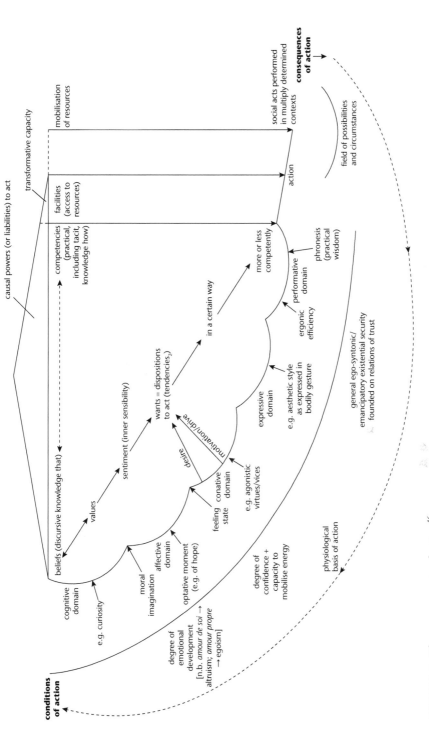

FIGURE 3.4 The components of action[46]

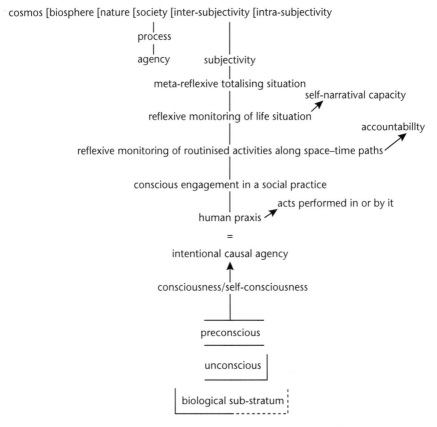

FIGURE 3.5 The stratification of agency: a moment in a person's life[47]

in principle require grounds and justification, so the *accountability* of an action will be an important consideration. Generally the agent will have to ground her agency in such a way that it is at least in principle *universalisable*, such that she would be prepared to commend her action to any other agent in exactly the same circumstances. (The importance of this will be brought out in Chapter 5 and subsequently.)

The following can be put forward as a rough formula for the formation of action:

social structural conditioning + circumstances + reflexive deliberation + values (in relation to capacities/capabilities + feasibility) = determination of the appropriate course of action

The capability approach

Much (irrealist) social science has focused on actions or behaviours, relatively atomistically, abstracting from the life projects and possibilities of the agent concerned.

An exception to this is the capability approach of Amartya Sen and Martha Nussbaum.[48] According to this approach our focus should be on:

(i) the beings and doings that agents value, which they call their *functionings*;
(ii) their opportunities or substantive freedoms to achieve them, which they call their *capabilities*; together with
(iii) the enabling or constraining personal, social and environmental *conversion factors* that account for differences between people in converting their capabilities into achievements.

Augmenting this approach with critical realism, we may regard the agent's reasons (for an action or a course of action) as a causal mechanism that triggers a particular course of action. Such a course of action may be regarded as a tendency, subject to the play of enabling and constraining conversion factors (including counter-tendencies) in the context of four-planar social being. The result will be an expanded or constrained capability on the part of the agent to achieve valued functionings. Such valued functionings will include the *development* of a set of *desired capabilities*.

One may choose a set of desired capabilities for oneself or for society overall. The development of such a set will involve a balance of negative and positive free-doms or opportunities for valued functionings, forms of solidarity that the capa-bilities entail, the universalisability of the capabilities, the degrees of empathy and co-presence encouraged and their potential contribution to the goals of well-being and flourishing for specific concretely singularised agents, with an in principle unique identity, sense of self and dharma (vocation and calling).

Agency

It is useful to distinguish *persons* and *agents*. As persons we have a continuous *sense of self* from an early age, which at a certain point matures into a conception of our *personal identity*. This will involve some balancing, sifting and sorting of our engage-ments in various practices in the three orders of reality, especially in relation to our ultimate concerns. Our personal identity will depend in part on our social position-ing, which may be established objectively in terms of our relationship to society's distribution of resources, opportunities (including capabilities or potentially desired functionings) and benefits at and from the time of birth onwards. The 'I' of self-consciousness is effectively confronted with a 'me', a 'me' defined in principle in relation to collectivities of agents who share in this respect the same life-chances. This defines what Margaret Archer has called our *primary agency*.[49] However the 'I' also has the ability to form collective projects oriented to the transformation of society's distribution of resources and opportunities. Such collective projects define a 'we', instancing our *corporate agency*. Our *social identity* will depend on the balanc-ing, sifting and sorting of our various social roles, each social role defining a social *actor* in relation to our conception of ourselves or personal identity. For it is we who as persons impart concrete singularity or coherence to our various social roles.

These distinctions between persons, agents and actors are of course merely analytical, as are the distinctions between our personal and social identities. In concrete circumstances it is, of course, only the person who acts, though we will normally have to explain what they do in terms of the various social roles they are participating in and/or transforming. Therefore in the social process it is not just social structures but agents, or more precisely kinds of agents that are reproduced or transformed, that is, there is *double morphogenesis*.[50]

3.5 Critical naturalism and personalism

The point of transcending dualisms is, among other things, to be able to establish specific connections and relations between the terms hitherto dualistically opposed. So what I want to do in this section is to explore some of the implications of the ontological asymmetry between social structures and persons stemming from the non-identity and radical differences between them already noted.

The basic orienting idea here is that critical realism and personalism, at least in the form developed by Christian Smith,[51] and in particular freed from contamination with individualism and reductionism, can not only co-exist but be happily and productively married. For what the self-conscious social animals that we call 'human beings' are and can do provides the boundary conditions for, and places absolute limits on what forms of social life are possible (though of course the nature and capacities of human beings may change). Indeed, in this way *critical realism*, at least as elaborated in and for the human sciences, *must also be or entail a personalism*.

My argument here is that in our societies, and indeed in most of human history *the social has tended to dominate the personal*, a fortiori our capacities as agents to dominate our human being and powers. The mechanisms of this domination include the necessary pre-existence and transcendental necessity of social forms, the disembedding of deeply entrenched sectors from the rest of society and human regulation, and the presence of reification and *structural sin* or fossilised master–slave-type social relations. This asymmetry and this domination has also led to a relative neglect of one particular dynamic, namely the *drive to freedom* and a conundrum that seems to me to be central to the human predicament, namely, how to harness the solidarity and reciprocity necessary to make such freedom non-eristic and conducive to generalised or *universal human flourishing*.

I will develop this argument in a series of stages.

(i) The ontological asymmetry between societies and persons

In section 3.3 I argued that there is an ontological asymmetry between the personal and the social, such that the social is existentially dependent upon the personal, just as the personal is existentially or emergently dependent upon the biological, whereas the social is not existentially, but rather only contextually and developmentally dependent on the personal. This existential dependence reflects criterion (i) of emergence, the bottom-up unilateral existential dependence of higher-order properties and strata upon lower-order ones, while the contextual and developmental dependence reflects criterion (iv), that is, the causal irreducibility, or top-down or downwards causation, of the higher upon the lower (see Chapter 2.4). This goes along with a useful contrast that can be made between the proactive ontogenetic emergence of persons and the responsive emergence of societies.

This ontological asymmetry between the personal and the social flows directly from the TMSA. The sense in which critical realism may be said to entail personalism is thus the sense in which the only efficient cause in the social world is human agency.[52] Everything that happens in the social world happens in virtue of human agency, that is, the actions of human beings. Or to put it another way, *human beings are the only moving forces in geo-history*. It is in this sense that critical realism implies personalism.

(ii) Persons and agents

This ontological asymmetry can be sharpened by the distinction between the person and the agent. This is an analytical distinction, but it reflects the real ontological distinction between a thing and its circumstances such that we explain the behaviour of the thing by reference to its nature and the conditions in which it finds itself. Thus we can imagine the same person in different social orders; and we can also analytically differentiate the natural, practical and social orders such that our engagement in the natural and practical orders provides a basis for cross-cultural comparison and a common context for the exercise of our *axial rationality*, for example, in conflict-resolution or collective decision-making.[53]

On the TMSA, society and persons have radically different kinds of properties and constitute radically different kinds of things. Thus one cannot impute intentionality to society. However, we can certainly argue that society is transcendentally necessary for any intentional agency (though not perhaps for engagement in the natural and practical orders). As already argued, another important feature of social forms is their pre-existence.

(iii) The pre-existence of society and the presence of the past

What characterises society is precisely its pre-existence in respect of any round of human agency. It is *there*, something into which we are thrown and which provides the means and media we must use in our agency. It is that which we must take into account (fallibly) in order to act, and that which, in acting, in our activity, we reproduce or transform. The difference between structure and agency can be accentuated further with the theme of the *presence of the past* in our built environments, constitutions, institutions, problem-fields, practices, languages and ideas (see Chapter 4.1, Figure 4.2).[54] Recognition of the pre-existence of social forms in respect of agency and the presence of the past form an important counterweight and corrective to voluntarism.

(iv) The disembedding of structure and the alienation of human powers

In contemporary social reality we have the radical disembedding of whole sectors and spheres of social activity from human control or direction. Thus analysis of the credit crunch of 2007–8 reveals the huge extent to which money had become dislocated from the real economy and to which the real economy had become dislocated from social control or regulation, that is, the extent to which the economy had in turn become disconnected from its social presuppositions.[55] This can also be described in the Habermasian terms of the disembedding of economic system from social life-world.

Indeed, if we take the idea of four-planar social being and conceive of every social event as occurring simultaneously on each of the four planes of (a) material transactions with nature, (b) social interactions between persons, (c) social structure proper and (d) the stratification of the embodied personality, we can trace a fundamental *alienation of human being and powers* on each of these planes, inducing (multiple) crises on each plane. ('Alienation' is the condition of being separated, split off or estranged from what is essential and intrinsic to a being's nature or identity.[56])

Thus we have (a) *ecological* crisis (b) *ethical* or moral crises, including crises of social justice raised by gross and growing inequality in the distribution of resources and opportunities, and crises of political legitimacy and democracy, alongside the familiar crises of violence, terror and war; (c) *economic* and fiscal crisis; and (d) *existential* crisis, including crises of identity and of *centricity*,[57] of addiction and apathy. These crises are not of course independent of each other, indeed they become concatenated to form in effect a *crisis system* (see Chapter 9.2).[58]

The alienation of human being and powers can be traced back at least to the *generative separation* at the dawn of capitalism and modernity[59] and, indeed, arguably to earlier Axial Age rifts,[60] but it is manifest today in potentially cataclysmic form.

Together (iii) and (iv) place limits on the priority, autonomy and causal efficacy of the personal on the social.

(v) The social as involving constraint overreaching enablement

Indeed for most people, for most of human history, the social has figured mainly as a source of constraint on, not enablement of human desires and possibilities. Not to acknowledge the constellational overreaching of enablement by constraint, the huge weight of the presence of the past, structural disembedding and structural sin (or sedimented, institutionalised master–slave-type relations of oppression) is idealistically to prioritise the personal over the social and slip back into individualism and misplaced voluntarism.

Similarly, failure to appreciate the massive role of counterfinality[61] and thwarted intentionality can encourage a corresponding neglect of the huge role played by the absenting of lack and (at a meta-level, of constraint) – that is, by the drive to satisfy desire, need and unfulfilled potential and to absent the constraints on their satisfaction – in human history.

It follows from this that not all human motivations are on a par. The first thing that must be satisfied and the prerequisite for everything else is to stay alive.

(vi) The stratification of basic motivations

Thus basic motivations or ultimate concerns are not all on a par; rather, survival is a precondition for the others, and it is on this that most of humanity has been engaged for most of its history. What well-being or flourishing is possible will depend largely on what bits of negative and positive freedom have been won and/or settled on a person in life's lottery. However, we could certainly argue that once survival is assured, the goal of a human life is or should be to flourish (see Chapter 6.7). If universal human flourishing is undoubtedly the end, then the question arises as to what is the mechanism that will take humanity there? What is the logic or dynamic that will take us to the good or eudaimonistic society?

(vii) The drive to freedom

I have argued that the desire to be free, to be self-determining, and to absent constraints on our freedom constitutes a basic mechanism, applicable both to the life of a person and to her community.[62] The drive to freedom necessitates of course commensurate *solidarity* (love and awareness of the co-presence of others as part of oneself), and entails a drive to *self-realisation* and ultimately the free flourishing *of all*. This drive connects our desire to be free with our dependence on the desires of others to be similarly free (through the logic of *dialectical universalisability*); so that our human predicament may be seen as involving our harnessing of our dependence on others in ways that enable them to fulfil their goals in universal free flourishing.

(viii) Flourishing and the purpose of a life

A person may of course choose not to flourish as best they can, but rather to work for or towards the flourishing of others, and ultimately of all. Thus a person may have as a purpose in life to heal (and to become a doctor) or to nourish (and become a cook), and this will be their specific vocation, calling or dharma, that is, a sense of what specifically they are here to do.[63] To understand a person's dharma will of course involve understanding a person in their uniqueness or their *concrete singularity* = concrete universality (see Chapters 4.3 and 6.5).[64]

(ix) The role of stratification and asymmetry

Ontological stratification and asymmetries within strata may play important roles in determining the *directionality* of process. Thus our basic agentive freedom, our capacity to do otherwise, ultimately underpins the human moral goal or object/ive of universal human flourishing (see Chapter 6.7). In the philosophy of metaReality a spiritual infrastructure is identified as underpinning the everyday world. Thus commercial transactions can be seen to presuppose trust and buying and selling to presuppose forms of reciprocity close to the Golden Rule.

Indeed, it may be argued that in the case of many social binaries or opposites the terms involved reveal a similar and profound asymmetry. Thus war presupposes some peace (some peaceful activities) for it to be possible in a way that peace does not presuppose war; arguably, hate presupposes love, and certainly the instrumental world of the workplace presupposes both the care and unconditionality of home and the tacit solidarity and right action of one's co-workers and colleagues. This is the *asymmetry of axiology and emancipation* (see Chapter 9.2).

(x) A research programme of esoteric sociology?

From the standpoint of the philosophy of metaReality the dominance of the personal by the social can now be seen more precisely as the dominance of the ordinary world (that is, the world of duality) by what I call *demi-reality*, which is constituted by generalised master–slave-type or oppressive relations and alienation at all four planes of social being. But from the exciting perspective of metaReality, our heteronomous pursuits and oppressions are actually underpinned by, and depend totally upon our ground-state capacities, such as creativity and love, and states or moments of transcendence or non-duality; capacities and states which indeed have been largely unrecognised by mainstream social science. What is opened up by this reflection is a new research programme for the social sciences, namely of *esoteric sociology*, economics, anthropology, and so on.

Good and evil are not on a par, nor logical equivalents; because evil undermines the very possibility of good (or not so good, that is, bad); and sheer evil or evil without good is not a tenable, sustainable state. Such an asymmetry can impart a weak but definite *tendential rational directionality* to human history, as I will argue in Chapter 6.

3.6 Agency and actualism

In Chapter 2 I argued that mainstream philosophy gives an inadequate account of both the world of everyday life and the world described and understood by science. A basic problem with it lies in its actualist understanding of what it means to be law-governed. Neither physics nor neurophysiology describes what happens at a dinner table (or a seminar): the flow of conversation, the precise movements of knives, forks, plates and condiments; though nothing that happens at the dinner table or in the seminar contravenes the laws of physics or neurophysiology and everything that occurs or is done (or said) remains consistent with (and indeed utilises) them – just as in a game of chess the rules constrain and define, but do not determine the play.[65]

Thus the downwards causation made possible by emergence does not involve violation of the laws governing these lower-order levels. Instead, we can think of it as the higher-order level affecting the initial and boundary conditions for the operation of lower-order laws.[66] It is highly misleading to regard the relationship between human action (that is, the exercise of our causal powers) and its neurophysiological basis or condition of possibility as standing in a one-to-one relationship between different events in a *single* (tacitly closed and unique) *causal nexus*. Human action occurs in an open system, which is neither governed nor described by actualistic, Humean causal laws or event regularities.

How does this mistake come about? We think of a single person as a single body (tacitly closed and unique) who does things. This individualism, abstracting from the social context in which we act, appears as a tacit condition of reductionism. Both are fundamental to the philosophical discourse of modernity, as I will show in Chapter 8.

In particular, human action is influenced and co-determined by social structures, mechanisms and situations, including of course the actions of other people, the natural environment, the state of the weather, and so on. Opening an umbrella when on my way to work in London is not determined by my physiology, though of course my physiology must be such that I can do it. Critical realist personalism must be committed to a non-Humean, non-actualist and non-deterministic understanding of scientific laws.

Individualism is deeply embedded in the philosophical discourse of modernity, which pivots on an *atomistic egocentricity* and an *abstract universality*. The Cartesian starting point of the discourse is profoundly mistaken. 'I think therefore I am' privileges thinking over being, epistemology over ontology (the epistemic fallacy), mind over body (emotion and spirit), the 'I' over you, we, society, and other species. Indeed, it would be better to adopt the starting point of those African peoples who begin with *Ubuntu* or 'I am because you (or perhaps we) are'.

If sociological individualism is rooted in the epistemic fallacy, reductionism is a legacy of actualism, which tends always to a monodisciplinary or a one-dimensional approach. Directly informing individualism is a particular model of (tacitly masculine gendered) human being, I have suggested, which is one of three sources or analogies of empirical realism, which together form a complementary triangle (Figure 3.6). The

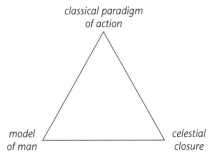

FIGURE 3.6 Three sources of empirical realism[67]

other two sources are the *classical paradigm of action* and the *celestial closure* established by Newtonian mechanics. If it is these last two that generate the abstract universalism, and thence the actualism and reductionism of mainstream approaches, it is the underlying *model of* human being (as tacitly gendered, atomistically egocentric and solipsistically possessive, *man*) that accounts for the individualism tacitly at work here.

Notes

1 That is, considered as a class or genus.
2 See for example Bhaskar, *Scientific Realism and Human Emancipation*, Chapter 3.
3 Differentiating the two sets of dualisms as 'macro' and 'micro' is not entirely satisfactory, partly because of misleading associations of size or scale, but mainly because resolution of each is necessary for the other (and each are present in the domain of the other). The macro could also be called the sociological dualisms and the micro psychological ones.
4 The attack was initiated by Michael Scriven in a path-breaking series of papers in the late 1950s and early 1960s, including 'Truisms as the grounds for historical explanation', in *Theories of History: Readings from Classical and Contemporary Sources*, ed. Patrick Gardiner (New York: Free Press, 1959), 443–75 and 'Explanations, predictions and laws', *Minnesota Studies in the Philosophy of Science* 2 (1962), 170–230.
5 See Ernest Nagel, *The Structure of Science: Problems in the Logic of Scientific Explanation* (London: Harcourt, Brace and World, 1961), Chapter 11.
6 See William Whewell, *Of Induction, With Especial Reference to Mr. J. Stuart Mill's System of Logic* (London: John W. Parker, 1849) and N. R. Campbell, *Foundations of Science: The Philosophy of Theory and Experiment* (New York: Dover, 1919).
7 See Bhaskar, *A Realist Theory of Science*, Chapter 3, Appendix, 'Natural tendencies and causal powers'.
8 Bhaskar, *The Possibility of Naturalism*, 47.
9 See William Outhwaite, *New Philosophies of Social Science: Realism, Hermeneutics and Critical Theory* (London: Palgrave Macmillan, 1987).
10 As I use the term 'voluntarism' it encompasses the views that (i) theory has a more or less immediate efficacy in practice, that is, *theoreticism*; or the converse, (ii), *practicism*: the collective decisions of people can ignore or readily reverse objective geo-historical tendencies and obstacles; or (iii) *strong social constructivism* and hermeneuticism: people make or create the social or their forms of life, which just are expressions of their beliefs and understandings; or (iv) *superidealism* or voluntarist superidealism (the counterpart of (iii) within the empiricist tradition): people change the world, including the natural world and its laws, along with their theories. 'Reification' is the process whereby human powers, social relations and products, or human beings themselves are transformed into (non-social, fixed, naturalised) things that appear to be independent of people's control, and dominate their lives.
11 Peter Winch, *The Idea of a Social Science and its Relation to Philosophy* (London: Routledge and Kegan Paul, 1958).
12 See Winch, *The Idea of a Social Science*, 114–15.
13 This helps to explain the oft-remarked primacy of the pathological; see Durkheim, Freud and my *The Possibility of Naturalism*, 48. More generally, unusual, freak and extreme, seemingly 'miraculous' events may reveal the existence, limits and possibilities (whether benign or malign) of structures.
14 'Thrownness' is a Heideggerian term I borrow and extend into a concept of *vehicular thrownness* to call attention to the fact, established by the TMSA, that philosophy, science and human life generally are pre-existing, ongoing social affairs. The concept highlights our arrival in the (pre-existing, pre-conceptualised) world as materially embodied beings as well as the spatio-temporality or processuality of our being and understanding (hence 'vehicular': we are hurled into life as if into an already moving vehicle). See Bhaskar, *Dialectic*, 76, 90.

15 Bhaskar, *Scientific Realism and Human Emancipation*, Diagrams 2.6 and 2.7, 126. See also *The Possibility of Naturalism*, 36; *Reclaiming Reality*, 94.

16 Archer, *Realist Social Theory*, esp. Chapter 5, 'Realism and morphogenesis', reprinted in *Critical Realism: Essential Readings*, eds Margaret S. Archer, Roy Bhaskar, Andrew Collier, Tony Lawson and Alan Norrie (London: Routledge, 1998) as Chapter 14, 356–82.

17 Archer, 'Realism and morphogenesis', 375; *Realist Social Theory*, 15, 154–8.

18 *Editor's note.* In Bhaskar's system of philosophy 'duality' signifies a totality or unity with real internal distinctions, whereas 'dualism' signifies split and diremption. Archer's 'analytical dualism' is not a philosophical or ontological dualism (Margaret S. Archer, 'Introduction: other conceptions of generative mechanisms and ours', in *Generative Mechanisms Transforming the Social Order*, ed. M. S. Archer (Dordrecht: Springer, 2015), 1–26, 10 n12); but it does acknowledge real distinctions as well as connections between people and society and so, considered from an ontological point of view, is deployed on the analysis of what in Bhaskar's terms is a duality.

19 Bhaskar, *Dialectic*, 158–60.

20 Bhaskar, *The Possibility of Naturalism*, 31 ff. 'Conflation' is Margaret Archer's term of art in this domain. See Margaret S. Archer, *Culture and Agency: The Place of Culture in Social Theory* (Cambridge: Cambridge University Press, 1988), 25–97.

21 Peter L. Berger and Thomas Luckmann, *The Social Construction of Reality: A Treatise in the Sociology of Knowledge* (Harmondsworth: Penguin, 1966/1991). Their model is critiqued in Bhaskar, *The Possibility of Naturalism*, 33.

22 See Bhaskar, *Scientific Realism and Human Emancipation*, 130 and *Dialectic*, 160.

23 Bhaskar, *Scientific Realism and Human Emancipation*, 130, Figure 2.10. The four planes comprise what I also call the *social cube*, which has six (not four) sides because it is 'open' at either end – a spatio-temporal stretch-flow or rhythmic (see Chapter 4.1). See also Bhaskar, *Dialectic*, 160.

24 Archer, 'Realism and morphogenesis', 375.

25 Anthony Giddens, *The Constitution of Society: Outline of a Theory of Structuration* (Cambridge: Polity, 1984), 26.

26 Bhaskar, *The Possibility of Naturalism*, 78.

27 cf. Bhaskar, *The Possibility of Naturalism*, 27–32.

28 Bhaskar, *The Possibility of Naturalism*, 40–1.

29 See Roy Bhaskar, 'Contexts of interdisciplinarity: interdisciplinarity and climate change', in *Interdisciplinarity and Climate Change*, eds Roy Bhaskar, Cheryl Frank, Karl Georg Høyer, Petter Næss and Jenneth Parker (London: Routledge, 2010), 1–34, 9–10.

30 The concept of geo-history, which I have used since the late 1970s, highlights that space and time, alterity and change are ontologically irreducible. In any enquiry, neither should be assumed in advance to be the more important. The term may refer either to specifically human geo-history or to the whole process of formation of the cosmos.

31 cf. Tobin Nellhaus, 'Signs, social ontology, and critical realism', *Journal for the Theory of Social Behaviour* 28:1 (1998), 1–24.

32 See Bhaskar, *The Possibility of Naturalism*, 44–53 and *Scientific Realism and Human Emancipation*, 123, 130–4.

33 It is important to distinguish those activities of agents that consist in the exercise of their intrinsic powers from those activities and powers that derive from their structural location or role.

34 A real definition captures the intrinsic structure or nature of a thing; for example, 'element with atomic number 79' is a real definition of 'gold'. See the discussion of the DREI(C) model of scientific discovery and development in Chapter 2. We can thus say that ideal types are attempts to grasp *real types*.

35 See Bhaskar, *Scientific Realism and Human Emancipation*, 113.

36 cf. Marx on the historically developed and socialised nature of biological functions and needs, such as eating. 'Hunger is hunger, but the hunger gratified with cooked meat eaten with a knife and fork is different from that which bolts down raw meat with the aid of hand and nail and tooth'. Karl Marx, *Grundrisse* (Harmondsworth: Penguin 1973), 42.

37 Bhaskar, *Plato Etc.*, 74, Figure 4.2.
38 See Bhaskar, *Scientific Realism and Human Emancipation*, 116.
39 See Bhaskar, The *Possibility of Naturalism*, Chapter 3, 'Agency', 80–120.
40 Bhaskar, *The Possibility of Naturalism*, 98.
41 See Bhaskar, *The Possibility of Naturalism*, 89–93.
42 For a fuller description and contextualisation see *Dialectic*, Chapter 2.9, from which Figures 3.4 and 3.5 are taken.
43 See Andrew Collier, *Being and Worth* (London: Routledge, 1999) and Margaret S. Archer, *Structure, Agency and the Internal Conversation* (Cambridge: Cambridge University Press, 2003). The concept of ultimate concern derives from Paul Tillich's existentialist theology.
44 See Chapter 2.10, Figure 2.3 and Bhaskar, *Dialectic*, 148–9.
45 See Margaret S. Archer, *Being Human: The Problem of Agency* (Cambridge: Cambridge University Press, 2000) and *Structure, Agency and the Internal Conversation*.
46 Bhaskar, *Dialectic*, 166, Figure 2.29.
47 Bhaskar, *Dialectic*, 167, Figure 2.30.
48 See Martha Nussbaum, *Creating Capabilities* (Harvard: Harvard University Press, 2011).
49 Archer, *Being Human*, 261 ff. The whole of the above paragraph is indebted to Archer's argument in this book, esp. Chapters 3, 7, 8 and 9.
50 Margaret S. Archer, 'How agency is transformed in the course of social transformation: Don't forget the double morphogenesis', in *Generative Mechanisms Transforming the Social Order*, ed. M. S. Archer (Dordrecht: Springer, 2015), 135–58.
51 See Christian Smith, *What Is a Person? Rethinking Humanity, Social Life, and the Moral Good from the Person Up* (Chicago: University of Chicago Press, 2010); and *To Flourish or Destruct: A Personalist Theory of Human Goods, Motivations, Failure, and Evil* (Chicago: University of Chicago Press, 2015).
52 The concept of efficient cause derives from Aristotle. In Aristotelian terms, human activity also has final causes (the ends it seeks to achieve), material causes (what the activity reproduces or transforms) and formal causes (the enabling and constraining powers of, for example, a social structure). See for example Bhaskar, *Scientific Realism and Human Emancipation*, 54–5.
53 See Chapter 5.3, below; Bhaskar, 'Theorising ontology', 200–3; and Bhaskar with Hartwig, *The Formation of Critical Realism*, 80–1.
54 See also Bhaskar, *Dialectic*, 55, 139 ff.
55 cf. Hans Despain, 'Karl Polanyi's metacritique of the liberal creed: reading Polanyi's social theory in terms of dialectical critical realism', *Journal of Critical Realism* 10:3 (2011): 277–302.
56 Bhaskar, *Dialectic*, 114.
57 'Centricity' refers to any dimension of ego-ethno-anthropo-centricity (or -centrism), including nationalism, europism and orientalism (which come under the umbrella of ethnocentrism), that is, the outlook of any human individuals or groups who take themselves to be at the centre of their/the world or cosmos. A crisis of centricity is ultimately a crisis of belonging. The various forms of centricity are discussed briefly in Chapter 7.
58 See Petter Næss and Leigh Price, eds, *Crisis System: A Critical Realist and Environmental Critique of Economics and the Economy* (London: Routledge, in press). *Editor's note*. Bhaskar was to have been one of the editors and contributors. The book will be dedicated to him and Karl Georg Høyer.
59 This generative separation involved the alienation of the immediate producers from their labour, their product, the means and materials of their production, each other and the nexus of social relations within which their production takes place, and ultimately from themselves. See Chapter 8.1, and Bhaskar, *Plato Etc.*, 240 and *passim*.
60 The Axial Age may be viewed either as a period of history from about 800–200 BCE that witnessed, relatively independently in a range of regions of the planet, a multifaceted cultural revolution, pivotal for the subsequent course of geo-history; or as a civilisational category that draws attention to the common features of this revolution and has an

open-ended historical field of application. These common features are widely held to have included the discovery of historicity and human unity and solidarity and the enhancement of reflexivity and agentiality. These momentous advances resonated, however, with the master–slave-type social contexts in which they occurred. Such societies are 'structurally unable to satisfy the need for legitimation that they themselves generate' (Jürgen Habermas, *Communication and the Evolution of Society* (Boston: Beacon Press, 1976/1979), 163). While the rise of master–slave-type societies was chronologically earlier, the Axial revolution is inconceivable in a pre-master–slave-type social context and occurred in societies that were witnessing both an increase in the mechanisms of social domination and the birth of organised protest, hence crises of legitimation. See Robert N. Bellah, *Religion in Human Evolution: From the Paleolithic to the Axial Age* (Belknap Press: Cambridge, MA, 2011), 573–6. The metaReal principles of axial rationality and universal solidarity are discussed in Chapters 4 and 7.

61 *Finality* is the relation or quality of being a final cause. *Counterfinality* (adapted from Sartre) refers to the accumulated unintended consequences (the presence of the past) that thwart or contradict the finality (purposes) of agents' intentional action in attempting to rationally change the world.

62 See esp. Bhaskar, *Dialectic*, 282–4. This argument is continued in Chapter 6.

63 cf. Bhaskar with Hartwig, *The Formation of Critical Realism*, Chapter 1 and *passim*.

64 See also Bhaskar, *Dialectic*, 129–31.

65 cf. Bhaskar, *A Realist Theory of Science*, Chapter 2.5 and *The Possibility of Naturalism*, 104–5.

66 cf. Bhaskar, *Dialectic*, 53.

67 Bhaskar, *A Realist Theory of Science*, Diagram 3.8, 198.

4

APPLIED CRITICAL REALISM AND INTERDISCIPLINARITY

4.1 Applied critical realism generally

If critical realism is to satisfy the criterion of seriousness (spelt out in Chapter 1), it must be applicable. Furthermore, it is in its applications that, on its own self-understanding, the whole point and value of critical realism as an underlabourer for and occasional midwife of good science lies. So much so that one could say that applied or practical critical realism – critical realism in action, so to speak – is, or should be the soul or heartbeat of critical realism.

The double specificity of applied critical realism

There is a double specificity of method in the research process in applied critical realism: first, with respect to *subject matter* (in the intransitive or ontological dimension) – thus, unless an object could talk, there would be no point in interviewing it; and second, with respect to the *location* of the particular activity *in the total research process or cycle* (in the transitive or epistemological/social dimension) – thus, if a generalisation is inductively well corroborated, there is little point in adding further confirming instances: instead, retroduction to possible explanatory mechanisms will be the order of the day.

Just as critical realism purports to be *ontologically maximally inclusive* in allowing, not just knowledge (and indeed epistemology, or the philosophical study of knowledge), but even false beliefs and illusions, at least when causally efficacious, to be real and so part of ontology, it also claims to provide a more general and *comprehensive epistemology* than its irrealist rivals. These typically remain fixated on a particular moment of the research process. Thus, if one defines a round of scientific enquiry as the movement of the research process from knowledge of one stratum of reality to knowledge of the next, then one can readily see how classical empiricism or Kantianism or Popper's falsificationism (for example) each derives their plausibility from a particular phase of scientific enquiry. By contrast, critical realism attempts to provide an account of the whole research cycle (for example, in the DREI(C) model of natural scientific discovery introduced in Chapter 2), so providing a fuller, rounder, more comprehensive epistemology.

The logic of the concrete: transcendental properties of applied critical realism in the social field

Critical realist research is characterised by the *primacy of ontology* in the research process, whereas for its irrealist rivals, such as positivism and social constructivism, epistemology is primary.

Accordingly, the interests of critical realists in empirical research are typically *exploratory*.[1] Indeed, they are characteristically to identify, discover, uncover (and in more engaged, participatory research, test the limit of and indeed unlock) structures, blocks and (generically) *causes*, and the particular sequences, combinations and articulations of them at work at specific times and places; whereas the interests of positivists and constructivists and others from the irrealist mainstream are typically to prove/disprove and justify *propositions*, theories and so forth.

Moreover, critical realism is primarily interested in *explanation* and only secondarily in prediction.[2] Furthermore, in critical realism our primary focus is on *structures* and *mechanisms*, not regularities or patterns of *events*; that is on the domain of the real, including the non-actual real, rather than that of the actual or empirical. Moreover, there is a mismatch between the domains of the real and the actual caused by the fact that almost everything we might want to study occurs in an open system, where we find causality without correlation and correlation without causality. It follows from this that for critical realism scientifically significant generality is not on the face of the world, but at a remove or distance, characteristically withdrawn from it; and that it is transfactual, not empirical or actual. Critical realism is interested in theoretical or transfactual rather than empirical generalisations.

Critical realism will thus necessitate specific research designs with distinct logics of enquiry. These logics will not involve centrally either induction or deduction (though both will continue to have a place, for instance in the Humean and Leibnizian moments in the process of scientific discovery (Figure 2.1, above)). Instead, *abduction* and *retroduction* come to the fore. Abduction involves redescription or recontextualisation, most usually (in critical realist research) in terms of a causal mechanism or process that serves to explain the state, condition or happening referred to (for example, redescribing a death as a murder). Retroduction involves imagining a model of a mechanism that, if it were real, would account for the phenomenon in question. (In practice, these two often shade into each other: there is only a relative difference between them.)

Retroduction features centrally in the DREI(C) model of theoretical (natural scientific) enquiry introduced in Chapter 2.4. I have differentiated this from the RRREI(C) model (involving both abductive redescription and retrodiction) of applied scientific research,[3] characterised as it is by a conjunctive multiplicity rather than a disjunctive plurality of causes.

In the DREI(C) schema, D stands for the *description* of some pattern of events or phenomenon; R for the *retroduction* of possible explanatory mechanisms or structures, involving a disjunctive plurality of alternatives (that is, *either* a *or* b *or* c, and so on); E for the *elimination* of competing alternatives; I for the *identification* of the causally efficacious generative mechanism or structure; and C for the iterative *correction* of earlier findings in the light of this identification. In the RRREI(C) schema, the first R stands for the *resolution* of the complex event or phenomenon into its components, involving a conjunctive multiplicity of causes (that is, a *and* b *and* c, and so on); the second R for the abductive *redescription* or recontextualisation of these components in an explanatorily significant way; the third R for the *retrodiction* of these component causes to antecedently existing events or states of affairs; E for the *elimination* of alternative competing explanatory antecedents; I for the *identification* of the causally efficacious antecedent (or antecedent complex); and C for the iterative *correction* of earlier findings in the light of this (albeit provisionally) completed explanation or analysis.

However, in addition to these general features, applied critical realism has some significant differentiating features in the social field. In Chapter 3 I have discussed the differences between the experimental natural and the social sciences. It will be remembered that these fall into four main types: epistemological, ontological, relational and critical. I have space here to discuss only the most significant implications for applied critical realism of these four types of difference.

A hugely important *epistemological difference* is that social phenomena only ever occur in *open systems*, in which events are determined by a multiplicity of mechanisms, perhaps of radically different kinds; that is to say, such open systems are characterised by both *complexity* and *emergence* (see Figure 4.1).

It follows from this that it will not in general be possible to specify how a mechanism operates independently of its context. Hence we must not only relate mechanisms back to explanatory or grounding structures, as in the theoretical natural sciences, but also to context or field of operation. This means that in the social field in principle we need always to think of a context-mechanism couple, C + M, and thus of the trio of context, mechanism, outcome (CMO), or more fully the quartet composed of context, mechanism, structure and outcome (CMSO). Now one problem with the application of the RRREI(C) schema in the field of the human sciences is that we do not have a body of independently validated theoretical knowledge of structures and mechanisms that we can apply straightforwardly, or at least unproblematically and without contestation, to retrodict antecedent states of affairs. And one reason for this is that very often in the social world, even if we know what the mechanism is, we do not know (or cannot be certain in advance of our investigation) how it will operate in the specific context concerned. It follows from this that discovery and application must often proceed in tandem and may be only analytically distinguishable. Hence we have the theorem of the contingent *duality (and simultaneity) of discovery and application*, together with that of

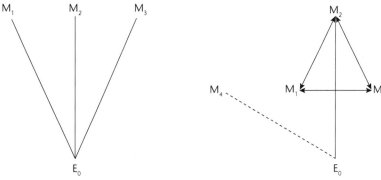

Case I: determination of events
in an open system

Case II: determination of events
within a system in an open system

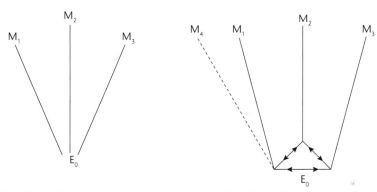

Case III: multiple determination
of events

Case IV: multiple determination of
events as a nexus in an open system

FIGURE 4.1   Determination of events in open systems[4]

Note: In Case II the mechanisms and in Case IV their effects are modified. Both may obtain
simultaneously.

the (again contingent) *co-incidence of retroductive and retrodictive moments* in research.
This means that every application of critical realism in the open-systemic world
potentially is (or at least readily begets) a creative process of discovery.

More formally, it is possible, by temporally separating the retroductive and
retrodictive moments, to develop *a unified general model* applying properties of
both schemas. We would then have the following, more complex pattern of
development:

> *Resolution, abductive redescription, retroduction* (RRR)
> *Inference* to the best explanation – most plausible mechanism or complex (I)
> *Retrodiction, elimination, identification* of antecedents and *correction* (REI(C)).

This would be the RRRIREI(C)[5] model of exploratory investigation.

The most important *ontological differences* are the activity- and concept-dependence of social, in contrast to natural, structures, which can be taken together with the important relational difference that the social sciences are internal to their subject matter, that is, part of their own field of enquiry.

Ontologically, the social world is an emergent, concept- and activity-dependent, value-drenched and politically contested part of the natural world. In it, social structures pre-exist and enable or constrain human activities, which are in turn (through the intentional causality of reasons) causally efficacious in the material world. The fact that we are *material*, as well as *conceptual* beings means that social life, though concept-dependent, is never exhausted by its conceptuality and that our conceptualisations of it are always potentially subject to critique, including explanatory critique, in the context of practical and hermeneutical struggles over (among other things) discursively moralised relations of oppression (power$_2$ or master–slave-type relations).

Finally, there is the *critical difference*. It is the necessity for, and contingently critical character of hermeneutics in the social sciences that, taken together with its internality to its subject matter, generates the model of explanatory critique; just as the value-drenched and politically contested nature of a relationally defined social world means that the exploratory conception of social research readily transmutes into an action-oriented research model and to a transformative model in which 'learning about' and 'changing' the world are two moments of what I have called 'depth struggle'[6] in emancipatory axiology (see Chapters 5 and 6).

We are then equally and irreducibly materially embodied and part of nature, and emergent conceptualising, reflexive and self-conscious beings. It is the fact that social life has an interior, at least partially conceptualised and reflexively accessible, that makes possible the rich, thick descriptions of qualitative research. Many of these hermeneutical features can, however, be seen to be complexly interwoven with the extensive materially embodied features of social life, amenable to quantitative research. Social research involves a constant toing and froing, a moving back and forth between the inner and outer, the internal and extensional, the intensive and extensive.

Antireductionism and laminated systems (LS)

The condition of possibility of actualism and monocausality is closed systems. But outside the artificially created laboratories of natural science and a very few naturally occurring closed contexts we are always confronted by open systems where the determination of phenomena by a multiplicity of mechanisms, perhaps of radically different kinds, is the rule. In order to guard against the constant tendency of mainstream-influenced thought to actualising reductionism, that is to flatten or one-dimensionalise, to de-stratify or un-differentiate reality, Berth Danermark and I[7] purloined our colleague Andrew Collier's notion of a *laminated system*[8] to mark the irreducibility of the mechanisms at the levels specified. Since the publication of our article in 2006, various concepts of laminated system have come into circulation.

Our first or original kind of laminated system was one constituted by a number of ontological levels, in the original case seven: namely, physical, biological, psychological, psycho-social, socio-economic, sociocultural and normative, earmarked for the understanding of a specific problem, in this case a type of disability. This model is similar to the World Health Organisation's notion of a human being as, for health purposes, a bio-psycho-social mix, and to critical naturalism, where psychology is seen as always and inexorably bounded and conditioned by, on the one hand, sociology and, on the other, biology.[9] Gordon Brown employed a similar kind of laminated system for education[10] (positing physical, biological, psychological, [we should perhaps add, socio-economic], sociocultural, and curricular or normative levels), and others have developed kindred laminated systems for ecology, social work and elsewhere.

LS1. An irreducible ontological level

This type of laminated system, *LS1*, is composed, *in a case-specific way*, of irreducible ontological levels (for the case at hand).

However, in our article, we had already mentioned two other types of laminated system.

LS2. Four-planar social being

This model (see Figure 3.2), first introduced in *Scientific Realism and Human Emancipation*,[11] was an elaboration of the transformational model of social activity and sees social life and in principle every social event as occurring simultaneously at each of four planes of social being. These are constituted by

(a)   material transactions with nature;
(b)   social interactions between people;
(c)   social structure *sui generis*; and
(d)   the stratification of the embodied personality.

This model, like the first type of laminated system, highlights the irreducibility of planes of being that the researcher or analyst might be inclined to overlook. One obvious immediate virtue of the four-planar model is that it pinpoints the ecological dimension of social being that social theorists have been prone to ignore.

LS3. Seven-scalar social being

This is a laminated system based on levels of scale. These range between

(i)   the sub-individual level of motives and depth psychology;
(ii)   the individual level of the biography of the individual personality;
(iii) the micro-level of small-scale interaction;

(iv) the meso-level of functional roles and structural positions, defined in relation to ongoing practices and institutions;

(v) the macro-level, concerned with the properties of large wholes, such as the UK economy or contemporary Norway;

(vi) the mega-level, occupied with long geo-historical stretches or swathes of space–time such as mediaeval Christianity or feudalism;

(vii) the global or planetary whole; or even

(vii*) the planetary whole of world geo-history (of course itself embedded in cosmic geo-history).

In articulating such a laminated system, it was not my intention to suggest an exhaustive taxonomy. Clearly the pie can be carved in other ways and, for example, various regionally specific classifications inserted. However, one virtue of the seven-scalar model I have articulated is that with it we are less likely to abstract illicitly from levels of causation that are practically indispensable for, but different from the analytical focus of the study.[12]

However, following the publication of our 2006 article, another kind of laminated system quickly hove into view. In looking at emergent spatio-temporalities in my book on dialectic, I had argued for the reality of intersecting or overlapping spaces and times or more generally *rhythmics*, as illustrated in Figure 4.2.[13] This raised the possibility of a fourth type of laminated system constituted by co-present spaces, times, spatio-temporalities or rhythmics (understood as spatio-temporalising causal processes), forming so many condensed geo-historical layers, as in the *pentimento* or layered levels of drawing or painting found on the canvas of an old work of art.[14] So we have:

LS4. Co-existent emergent space-temporalities (rhythmics), or pentimented social being

However, it was now becoming clear that in principle the idea of a laminated system could be used in any case where it was important not to leave out an irreducible and necessary but causally variable element in the non-reductionist explanation of a phenomenon. Thus, one could extend the idea to include the members of a set where each member is irreducible and necessary for the set as a whole; that

Intersecting spaces:	pavements used for sleeping; sofa-beds; table/desks
Intersecting times:	the Queen's speech written by the Prime Minister's press officer (with advice from an advertising firm) opening Parliament in the House of Lords
Overlapping spaces:	residencies, offices and factories within the same locale
Overlapping times:	constitutional procedure ——————————————— political power ————————————- - - - - - economic process ————————— - - - - - - 'fashion' ————

                                    1690   1790   1890   2010

FIGURE 4.2 Intersecting and overlapping spaces and times[15]

is, one could specify a multiplicity of different components where each component is irreducible and necessary, for example, the elements of a diet, the components of a curriculum, the aspects of a good education or hospital or government, and so on.[16] Thus a further level is:

LS5. Irreducible and necessary components in a complex whole

While I have hitherto mainly presented laminated systems as a heuristic for inter-disciplinary research,[17] a laminated system may be useful even where the distinct mechanisms at work are known under the descriptions of a single discipline; that is, and more generally, whenever one is dealing with cases of both complexity and emergence or qualitative novelty, and/or whenever one needs to guard against the inherent tendency of mainstream-influenced thought to actualism, and thence to the illusory and fateful couple of interactionism and reductionism.

4.2 Interdisciplinary research

When I began work some ten years ago on the topic of interdisciplinarity with my colleague Berth Danermark as a guest professor at the Swedish Institute for Disability Research, we embarked on a lengthy review of the existing literature on interdiscipli-narity. We were shocked by the almost complete absence of any ontological discus-sion, that is, any discussion about what there was in the world that necessitated recourse to interdisciplinary as distinct from disciplinary research. This absence, of course, parallels the more general absence of ontological discussion, at least in the philosophy of science, before the critical realist revindication of ontology in the mid-1970s. Nor, as in that context, was there any differentiation of epistemological from ontological questions. By contrast, a critical realist approach to interdisciplinarity will presuppose that ontological questions can be disambiguated from epistemologi-cal ones and that there are ontological, not just epistemological, grounds for interdis-ciplinarity in scientific research (and for inter-professional co-operation generally).

Indeed, a critical realist approach to interdisciplinarity will be distinctive for two main reasons. First, in so far as it focuses on ontological as well as epistemological considerations and grounds for interdisciplinarity. This follows from the critical realist revindication of ontology and differentiation of ontological from epistemo-logical concerns and the critique of the reduction of the former to the latter as the epistemic fallacy. Second, it brings to the fore a non-Humean, differentiated and stratified, non-actualist and non-reductionist view of the world. On this, the move from manifest phenomena to underlying generative mechanisms and structures lies at the heart of scientific discovery and the scientific enterprise generally. Indeed, it is precisely this move that provides the rationale for *disciplinarity* in science.

The argument for *interdisciplinarity* builds on the basis or foundation of the argu-ment for disciplinarity, but involves a series of additional ratchets or steps. These can be set out most fruitfully by differentiating ontological from epistemological considerations. I will accordingly frame my discussion of interdisciplinarity using these two optics seriatim.

The ontology of interdisciplinarity

1. Multi-mechanismicity

The ontological case for interdisciplinarity begins with the consideration that, outside a few experimentally (and even fewer naturally occurring) closed contexts a multiplicity of causes, mechanisms and, potentially, theories is always involved in the explanation of any event or concrete phenomenon. This is an index of the *complexity* of the subject matter of any science.

2. From multi-mechanismicity to multidisciplinarity

However, to get from multi-mechanismicity to multidisciplinarity, we have to add considerations of *emergence* to those of complexity. We can broach this topic by revisiting the three forms of *stratification* discussed in Chapter 2:

   (i) the stratification implicit in the movement from a manifest phenomenon to an underlying mechanism or structure;
  (ii) the multi-tiered nature of such stratification revealed in the development of any one branch of science, for example, the fact that solid material objects such as tables and chairs are constituted by molecules which are in turn constituted by atoms which are in their turn constituted by sub-atomic particles;
 (iii) emergence: briefly, an emergent level of reality is (as we have seen in Chapters 2.4 and 3.4) one that is:

   (a) unilaterally dependent on a more basic one; and
   (b) varies along with it; but is
   (c) taxonomically irreducible to the more basic one; and additionally
   (d) causally irreducible to the domain of the more basic one.

If such emergence is involved, then the characteristic multi-mechanismicity of open systems will have to be studied in a multidisciplinary way, that is, by (or from the perspective of) a multiplicity of disciplines.

3. From multidisciplinarity to interdisciplinarity

If in addition to an *emergent level*, a qualitatively new or *emergent outcome* is involved in the causal nexus at work, then the knowledge required can no longer be generated by the additive pooling of the knowledges of the various disciplines concerned, but requires a synthetic integration, or genuine interdisciplinarity.

4. Intradisciplinarity

If in turn the *mechanisms* are themselves emergent, then we have the case of what may be called *intradisciplinarity*.

5. Anti-reductionism, laminated systems and the axiom of methodological specificity

After our review of the general literature on interdisciplinarity, Danermark and I undertook a critique of the existing literature in disability studies, which had witnessed the successive dominance of three forms of reductionism since the mid-1960s. First was a reductionism, espoused by the adherents of the so called *medical* or *clinical model*, which had reduced everything to neurophysiological or related considerations. This was displaced by a second form of reductionism, which sought to explain the phenomena in socio-economic terms, as arising from the existing distribution of socio-economic forces (thus it was now argued that if sufficient resources were put into providing accessible facilities for the disabled, the problem would go away). This reductionism of the so called *social model* was in turn replaced by that of the cultural or *social constructivist model* from the 1980s onwards. Here it was assumed that the problem arose from the particular language used to describe it. Each form of reductionism made good criticisms of the other reductionist positions, but failed to see how similar criticisms applied to their own position. Clearly, Danermark and I felt, what was needed was an approach to the study of phenomena such as disability that could make use of biological or neurophysiological, socio-economic and cultural (or psychological) considerations alike, without assuming that any one of these sets of considerations would be sufficient for a complete analysis of the phenomenon in hand. This was the origin of our invocation of the idea of a laminated system, which (as we have seen in the previous section) we introduced as a device to guard against the reductionism encouraged by actualism and in relation to phenomena where it was vital to take the mechanisms at different levels together, that is, where they were each irreducible and necessary components of a whole.

It should be noted that the different levels of a laminated system may, and in general will require different methodologies for their study. As discussed in section 4.1 of this chapter, in general method will always be specific to both the nature of the relevant subject matter and the place of the particular research project in the total research process in the field in question. (Thus one would not expect the methods used by a sociologist in an interdisciplinary research project to be the same as those used by a geographer in a similar project.) This may be called the *axiom of methodological specificity*.

6. Special features of social systems

Open systems in which human beings act will be characterised not only by emergence but by some other special, categorially distinctive features.

(a) The first of these relates to the *irreducibility and co-implication of social structures and human agency*. Social structures stand to human agents as something that they never create, but that always effectively pre-exist them and their agency: as something that they reproduce or transform, and as something that exists only in virtue of such present or past (reproductive or transformative) agency.

This first feature of social life, can in turn be set in the more general context of four-planar social being; that is, the conception that sees every social event or phenomenon as occurring necessarily in the four dimensions of material transactions with nature; social interactions between people; social structure proper; and the stratification of the embodied personality.

(b) The second relates to the characteristically *relational quality of social life* and the fact that the agency involved, although always mediated by human intentionality, may occur at several different *orders of scale*, ranging from the sub-individual, such as personal motivation, to the global.
(c) The third relates to the characteristic conceptuality of social life. Conceptuality is a distinctive and essential feature of social being, but it does not exhaust it. It follows from this that the conceptualisations of agents are always in principle corrigible and that the conceptual component of social being will be both causally conditioned by and causal efficacious on the extra-conceptual (-discursive, -linguistic) aspect of social being. This third feature of social life, namely its *corrigible conceptuality*, renders it contingently subject to critique.

I turn now from ontological to epistemological considerations.

The epistemology of interdisciplinarity

7. Transdisciplinarity

The generation of the knowledge of an emergent outcome (or mechanism) will depend upon a species of *transdisciplinarity*. This involves drawing on the resources of pre-existing knowledge, which may be exploited in myriad different ways, including the creative – often lateral, occasionally oblique – use and development of analogies, metaphors and models from a whole variety of different cognitive fields (and even eras).

8. Cross-disciplinary understanding, immanent critique and effective epistemic integration

The successful integration of knowledge of the workings of the laminated system to produce an integrated result or field will also necessarily depend on *cross-disciplinary understanding* between the members of the research (or inter-professional) team. I have argued that the possibility of such cross-disciplinary (or cross-professional) understanding and interdisciplinary (or inter-professional) integration presupposes principles, or are grounded in axioms or postulates of universal solidarity and axial rationality.[18]

However, the irreducibility of structure to agency and the corrigibility of agents' conceptions mean that, in addition to the limitations on the ability of practitioners to successfully practice hermeneutic encounter and understanding with members of the other disciplines and the limitations on their ability to successfully integrate their respective findings epistemically in a unified explanatory account, the nature of the cognitive structures at work in the various disciplines may play an independent role in constituting blocks within interdisciplinary research.

Thus, characteristically, economics does not allow a space for the social presuppositions of economic activity; nor does medicine typically specify all the components of the holistic 'chain of care' necessary for healing. In such cases, hermeneutic encounter with the practitioners in a research team must be supplemented by immanent critique of one or more of those disciplines for any effective epistemic integration to be possible. Another possibility is that the substantive scientific ontology of the disciplines may be so discrepant that there is no referential overlap between them and the mechanisms they postulate or describe. In this case, one or both of them will need to be immanently developed or extended until some commonality of object or reference frame is obtained, possibly with the help of a mediating discipline or discourse.

The order of these processes will typically be:

(i) hermeneutic encounter with the practitioners of the other disciplines in a research team whose expertise is necessary for the construction of an adequate articulated laminated system;
(ii) immanent critique or development (or extension) of one or more of the other disciplines involved in the research, if necessary;
(iii) effective epistemic integration.

For such integration to become possible in an open-systemic world we will often have to reconsider the question of the education and training of the relevant researchers or professionals to ensure that they are fit and primed to work in an interdisciplinary team, that is, with others from different backgrounds and with different disciplinary concerns.

The practical goal is an integrated policy response to an integrated problem

The real-world problems with which the researcher or professional is faced come to their attention as integrated, not broken up into distinct disciplines. The end of successful interdisciplinary research – or inter-professional work generally – will achieve a similarly integrated understanding of the problem, epistemologically and axiologically, to achieve the formulation of an equally integrated policy response.

We can sum up the conditions for successful interdisciplinary research as follows.

(i) the *disambiguation* of ontology from epistemology, and the concomitant acceptance and understanding by practitioners of the tri-unity of ontological realism, epistemological relativism, and judgemental rationality, that is, of the holy trinity of critical realism;
(ii) *anti-reductionism*;

(iii)   the idea of explanation in terms of a *laminated system*;
(iv)   what I have called the *holy trinity of interdisciplinary research*, consisting in:

  (a)   *metatheoretical unity*, comprising minimally points (i)–(iii), above;
  (b)   *methodological specificity* as the norm of the different levels of components of the laminated system; and
  (c)   *theoretical pluralism and tolerance*;

 (v)   the achievement of:

  (a)   sufficient and generalised *cross-disciplinary understanding*; and
  (b)   *epistemic integration* to enable a unified explanation and/or policy response (which may need to be mediated by immanent critique of one or more of the disciplines involved);

(vi)   the *dissolution* of career, administrative and financial barriers to interdisciplinary research;
(vii)   a *dialectic of disciplinarity and interdisciplinarity* (both occasionally requiring transdisciplinarity) in the research process and in the education or training and nourishment or support of putative interdisciplinary research workers. Disciplinarity is required for *depth explanation* and, pedagogically, for familiarity with the move from manifest phenomena to explanatory structure, whereas interdisciplinarity is required to integrate the knowledge of the different mechanisms at work at the various levels of the laminated systems. In other words, successful interdisciplinary work requires both *depth* and *integration*.

As research on interdisciplinary research has itself made clear, one of the biggest blocks to successful interdisciplinary research is the non-understanding and non-communication between those trained in the 'hard' natural sciences and those trained in the 'soft' social sciences. We still seem to be living in the world of C. P. Snow's 'two cultures', in which many researchers with a natural science background find great difficulty in understanding reason explanations or reference to social structures, and in which many arts and humanities graduates freeze at the sight of anything mathematical. Indeed, it seems that we still suffer from too early and too complete 'specialisation', especially perhaps in the UK. For successful cross-disciplinary understanding, the prerequisite for effective epistemic integration, our educational system would seem in dire need of reform. It is important to move to a situation in which graduates in the social sciences feel at ease in at least one of the natural sciences, and vice versa.

However, there is a further problem, which showed up in some research done on the graduates of the Swedish Institute of Disability Research. Research on those graduates who went on to do interdisciplinary research revealed a widespread malaise with it, a feeling that the researchers reported of 'being strays', being not entirely at home, to some extent definitely alienated in their interdisciplinary research environments. What was missing was the common background and shared assumptions of a regular disciplinary home. Perhaps one way around this is an educational and social research context in which interdisciplinary research workers can readily acquire a second or third home, especially in subjects or disciplinary fields drawn from the other side of the cultural divide.

4.3 Utilising further developments in critical realism in applied critical realist research

Ultimately I hope it will be possible to regard critical realism as, among other things, a box of tools for applied critical realist research without differentiating the toolkit into compartments marked 'basic critical realism', 'dialectical critical realism' and 'the philosophy of metaReality'. However, at present the uneven reception of non-basic critical realism means that this is how we must proceed. I want to illustrate the rich potential of dialectical critical realism and the philosophy of metaReality in applied critical realism with just a few concepts or figures, drawn mainly from dialectical critical realism.

Negativity

Absence

Absence is a hugely valuable diagnostic category. Looking at what is missing in a social context/situation or entity/institution/organisation will often give a clue as to how that situation and so on is going or needs to change. The absence of rain presages shortages, inflation and food riots; of free speech, the demand for civil society; of a public sphere, constitutionality and democracy.

Epistemological dialectic

In the epistemological dialectic we start with some relevant absence or incompleteness. This generates aporias or problems that become increasingly troubling, as inconsistencies and contradictions in the cognitive or practical situation proliferate. These contradictions act as a signalling device to the relevant community, telling them that something is radically wrong, and in particular that they have left something out of the theoretical or practical mix. This entropic degeneration can only be halted (and consistency restored to the situation) by repairing the omission, namely by incorporating what had been excluded in a more comprehensive, inclusive totality. Such a totality may in turn again leave out something relevant, triggering a further round of this dialectic. It is largely this scheme that (I have argued) Marx hailed as the 'rational kernel' of Hegelian dialectic.[19]

Rhythmic

We have already encountered this concept in section 4.1. It connotes some tensed spatialising process that consists in the exercise – in space and time – of the causal powers of a structure or thing. Thus for many purposes we may want to take the causal, spatial and temporal properties of a process together. The seasons, agriculture, industry, the university term, Kant's daily stroll around Königsberg, the office Christmas party, each have their own rhythmics. Rhythmics may clash, coalesce, reinforce or undermine one another or other processes in a variety of different ways.

Totality

Concrete universal (or singular)

Universals in the real open-systemic world are not abstract universals specifying that a is always b; rather they specify that this particular a, while sharing

(i)   the universal tendency of a to b (whether it is actualised or not in this case), is also characterised by
(ii) distinctive mediations, $Xi....Xn$,
(iii) a specific geo-historical trajectory, $GxHy$ and
(iv) an irreducible (concrete) singularity.

It is the concrete universal that allows an English soccer fan to say: 'Though I was born in Chelsea, I support Arsenal.' Every universal in the world is of this type and every particular thing has these four aspects (universality, mediations, geo-historical trajectory and singularity).[20] In applied critical realist research, we must move both from the empirical to the transfactual (theoretical) and from abstract to concrete universality.

Holistic causality

Holistic causality presupposes internal relations between the members of a complex, such that what happens to one element affects the other, so that for explanatory and research purposes they cannot be treated separately or individualistically but must be taken *together*. This is clearly a widespread condition in the social world. This sentence is internally related to the last, your well-being is affected by that of your family and friends. Generally in holistic causality, the form of the combination of elements causally co-determines the elements; and the elements causally co-determine each other and so causally co-determine the form of the whole.

Constellationality

This is a figure that describes the relationship between two terms that are distinct and initially defined in relation to each other, but where one term overreaches and contains the other. Thus being may be said to constellationally contain thought or knowledge, while at the same time the distinction between knowledge and its object or the existential intransitivity of the object in relation to its knowledge is maintained. So epistemology is both a part of ontology and distinct from it. (See further Chapters 2.10, Figure 2.3, and 6.5.).

Transformative agency

Four-planar social being

We have already discussed this notion in Chapter 3.3, but it is interesting to note that, like holistic causality, it was already introduced in basic critical realism, as was the next concept.[21]

TINA compromise form

This is the theory/practice compromise that results from the combination of a theoretical falsity and a practice that, in accordance with axiological necessity, nevertheless upholds or respects the categorical truth theoretically denied. Understanding TINA compromise formation enables us to see how ideologies can render themselves plausible. More on this in Chapter 6.4 and 6.6.

Concrete utopianism

This is an exercise that invites us to think how we could better deal with a constraint or a necessity with a given set of resources. It is grounded in dispositional realism, the idea that possibilities as well as their actualisations are real. From this perspective the actual is only one (contingent) instance or manifestation of the real, and other, different and better manifestations of it are possible. Concrete utopianism is a key figure for thinking about how to effect a *transition* to the good society. This will be explored further in Chapters 5, 6 and 9.

The philosophy of metaReality

Universal solidarity and axial rationality

Among its many uses, the philosophy of metaReality can sensitise us to levels or aspects of social reality of which we may not normally be aware. Thus the axioms of universal solidarity and axial rationality can be used to show the limiting conditions under which the participants in a conflict situation would no longer be disposed to give radically incommensurable descriptions; while the identification of a metaReal sub-stratum in some particular instance of demi-reality can indicate a level of human goodness (or neutrality) on which some social horror or evil depends, a level that, once recognised and mobilised, can begin the process of transforming the source of that evil.[22]

Notes

1 cf. Stephen Ackroyd and Jan Ch. Karlsson, 'Critical realism, research techniques, and research designs', in *Studying Organisations Using Critical Realism: A Practical Guide*, eds Paul K. Edwards, Joe O'Mahoney and Steve Vincent (Oxford: Oxford University Press, 2014), Chapter 2, 21–45.

2 See Bhaskar, *A Realist Theory of Science*, appendix to Chapter 2. However, for the importance of prediction see also Petter Næss, 'Predictions, regressions and critical realism', *Journal of Critical Realism* 3:1 (2004): 133–64.

3 See for example Bhaskar, *Dialectic*, 133.

4 Bhaskar, *Scientific Realism and Human Emancipation*, 110, Diagram 2.2.

5 cf. Berth Danermark, Mats Ekström, Liselotte Jakobsen and Jan Ch. Karlsson, *Explaining Society: Critical Realism in the Social Sciences* (London: Routledge 2002), 109–11; and George Steinmetz, 'Critical realism and historical sociology', *Comparative Studies in Society and History* 40:1 (1998): 170–86.

6 Bhaskar, *Scientific Realism and Human Emancipation*, Chapter 2.5–2.7. The concept of 'depth struggle' is strongly implicit rather than explicit in these pages, which explore the implications of 'depth enquiry' or 'depth investigation' for social transformation.

7 Bhaskar and Danermark, 'Metatheory, interdisciplinarity and disability research'.

8 Andrew Collier, *Scientific Realism and Socialist Thought* (Hemel Hempstead: Harvester Wheatsheaf, 1989), 98 f.

9 Bhaskar, *The Possibility of Naturalism*, Chapter 3 and *Scientific Realism and Human Emancipation*, 115 ff.

10 See Gordon Brown, 'The ontological turn in education', *Journal of Critical Realism* 8:1 (2009): 5–34.

11 Bhaskar, *Scientific Realism and Human Emancipation*, 130.

12 For an example of this third type of laminated system, which looks at the laminated system of women's oppression in southern Africa, see Leigh Price, 'Critical realism versus mainstream interdisciplinarity', *Journal of Critical Realism* 13:1 (2014), 52–76.

13 See Bhaskar, *Dialectic*, Chapter 2.2 and *passim*.

14 For a development of this idea in relation to mental health practice, see Rich Moth, 'How do practitioners in community health teams conceptualise mental distress? – the pentimento model as a laminated system', unpublished discussion paper.

15 Bhaskar, *Dialectic*, 55, Figure 2.2.

16 For an example of this kind of laminated system see Matthew L. N. Wilkinson, 'Towards an ontology of educational success: Muslim young people in humanities education', in his *A Fresh Look at Islam in a Multi-Faith World: A Philosophy of Success through Education* (London: Routledge, 2015), Chapter 6, 117–50.

17 See for example Bhaskar, 'Contexts of interdisciplinarity' and Roy Bhaskar, Berth Danermark and Leigh Price, eds, *Interdisciplinarity and Well-Being* (London: Routledge, in press).

18 A full discussion of this raises questions of scientific and cultural (in)commensurability in the field of conflict resolution and peace generally, which will be revisited in Chapter 7. On this see also my 'Theorising ontology', 200–3, 'Contexts of interdisciplinarity', 20–1, and Bhaskar with Hartwig, *The Formation of Critical Realism*, 196–9.

19 See Chapter 6.3 and Bhaskar, *Dialectic*, Chapters 1 and 2.

20 See Chapter 6 and Tables 6.2 and 6.3 and Bhaskar, *Dialectic*, 130–2.

21 In Bhaskar, *Scientific Realism and Human Emancipation*, 9–10, 130.

22 See Chapter 7, and Bhaskar, *Reflections on MetaReality*.

5

ETHICS AND LANGUAGE

Explanatory critique and critical discourse analysis

In this chapter I am concerned to do two things, which will turn out to be closely related. The first is to outline the critical realist approach to ethics, focusing especially on the critical realist development of a form of ethical naturalism known as the *theory of explanatory critique*. This is oriented against 'Hume's Law', namely that the transition from factual to evaluative statements, although frequently made (and perhaps even psychologically necessary), is logically inadmissible. The second is to go a little more deeply into the critical realist take on language, and in particular to look at a CR-compatible and to a degree CR-influenced approach to the analysis of discourse: *critical discourse analysis*.

5.1 Explanatory critique and ethics

The idea that one cannot derive values from facts could well be called the second big shibboleth of orthodox or mainstream philosophy of the social sciences, the first being the Humean theory of causal laws, the lynchpin of the deductivist account of science. Together they render social science irrelevant to the explanation of real-world phenomena and to debates about social policy, since social science must deal with open systems; and any explanations that did happen to be generated would be irrelevant to social debates about values, since (by Hume's Law) one cannot derive values from facts.

In this chapter I show how the criticality of discourse establishes a basic argument for the evaluative implications of factual discourse. This is further developed in the critical realist theory of explanatory critique, on which we can pass from negative evaluations of beliefs, to negative evaluations of actions informed by them, and thence to negative evaluations of their causes and to positive evaluations of action rationally directed at the removal of their causes. This model of *cognitive explanatory critique* can both be generalised to embrace *non-cognitive* and non-communicative *ills* and be embedded within a *depth-emancipatory practice*. At the heart of this extended model lies an ontology of human being, in which our desires, needs and unfulfilled potential depend on the understanding and actions of others and in which freedom and solidarity are interdependent. This is an ontology that will be further developed in subsequent chapters.[1]

In Chapter 3.3 we identified ontological, epistemological, relational and critical types of difference between the social and natural sciences. The fourth *critical* type of difference depends upon the third or relational kind of difference, which stems from the fact that the subject matter of social science is both about social objects and about (social) beliefs about those social objects (or to put it another way, that social objects include beliefs about themselves). This makes possible the *explanatory critique* of consciousness (and being), which entails judgements of value and action without parallel in the domain of the natural sciences, so vindicating a modified form of substantive *ethical naturalism*, that is, the absence of an unbridgeable logical gap between statements of facts and values of the kind maintained by Hume, Weber and G. E. Moore. Indeed the theory of explanatory critique is most economically presented as a refutation of the philosophical orthodoxy known as Hume's Law.[2]

It need not be denied by the advocate of Hume's Law that causal relations exist between factual and evaluative statements such that they motivate, predispose or *causally influence* each other, but it is asserted to be the case that facts do not *logically entail* values. Doubt is immediately cast upon this by the value-impregnated character of much social discourse. This seems closely bound up with the value-impregnated character of the social reality that the social sciences are seeking to describe and explain, which is such that the best (most precise or accurate or complete) description of a social situation will very often be evaluative, that is, possess evaluative implications. Thus to take a famous example offered by Isaiah Berlin, compare the following accounts of what happened in Germany under Nazi rule:[3]

(α) 'the country was depopulated';
(β) 'millions of people died';
(γ) 'millions of people were killed';
(δ) 'millions of people were massacred'.

All four statements are true, but (δ) is not only the most evaluative, it is also the best (that is, the most precise and accurate) description of what actually happened.

However, the defender of Hume's Law can still argue that one is free to reject the value in the so to speak re-enchanted[4] social reality that necessitates such a description. It is for these kinds of reasons that the arguments, prevalent in the mid- and late 1960s, of John Searle from institutional facts, Anthony Prior, Philippa Foot and others from functional facts and Elizabeth Anscombe's generalisation of their arguments through to the notion of flourishing are less than logically compelling. For it is always logically possible to deny that watches, knives or guns or the flourishing of some particular species (including human beings) are themselves good things.

The definitive critique of Hume's Law begins to get off the ground when we refuse to *detotalise* or extrude (for example, by hypostatisation) social beliefs from the societies in which they are formed, that is, when we understand societies as including or containing beliefs and the processes of their formation. Such beliefs may patently be logically contradictory, or in some other way false to the subject matter that they are about. And it is clearly within the remit of factual social science, which includes in its subject matter not just social objects but social beliefs about those objects, to show this. If and when it has done so, we can pass immediately to a negative evaluation of those beliefs and of action based on them and, *ceteris paribus* to a positive evaluation of their rejection (and thence, I will argue, *ceteris paribus* to a removal of their causes).

Hume provides an example of gratuitous detotalisation, as we saw in Chapter 1.1, when he avers that he has no better reason to prefer the scratching of his finger to the destruction of the whole world.[5] What he is doing here is assuming that he is not a part of the world; that is, he is extruding himself from the totality. Because if he were to choose the destruction of the world, then since his finger is clearly part of the world, he would lose that too! What Hume is tacitly doing is extruding himself (and philosophy) from the rest of the world, which of courses includes himself and philosophy (and science, including social science). This is an error characteristic of Western philosophy, and indeed the academy generally.

If the value-impregnated character of social reality and hence of factual descriptions of it cast doubt on Hume's Law, then the definitive critique of it stems from the inclusion of belief and values in society, together with rejection of the idea that such beliefs cannot be causally explained. Then, if we have a true account of the causes of such false beliefs, we may – and must – pass immediately to a negative evaluation of those causes, and thence to the conditions, structures or states of affairs found to be responsible for them, and thence, *ceteris paribus*, to a positive evaluation of action rationally directed at removing or transforming those causes and conditions. Thus, if a social structure is generating for example false racist or sexist ideas we should act to change it, *ceteris paribus*. Opponents of the theory of explanatory critique sometimes aver that it lacks real-world examples but, to look no further than the example of racism, in the second half of the twentieth century formal segregationist structures were dismantled around the world on the grounds, among other things, that they were generating ideas that had been demonstrated by science to be false. The theory of explanatory critique thus opens up the exciting possibility that social science (more generally science) may be able to justify social policies rationally and indeed, in the last instance, *determine* and even *discover* true and well-grounded values – in particular by undermining beliefs that prove to be *incompatible* with their own true explanation.

Let me rehearse the argument for this result more simply.

Step one
The first step is to see that all discourse is implicitly or explicitly critical or at least has a critical component. We can perhaps see this most clearly in the

context of education, which consists largely in the process of learning truer, more accurate and rounded or coherent beliefs about a subject matter. To acquire a new belief about a subject matter normally means to reject an old, less adequate belief about it. Acceptance of the truth of the statement that the earth is spherical implies rejection of the belief that it is flat, and the rejection of that false belief is already an evaluation, and an action.

Step two

Once we have rejected a belief as false, then we are logically committed to rejecting any action informed by that belief. All intentional action is informed by beliefs, together with desires, values, and a variety of other components of one sort or another. And as we come to improve our understanding and knowledge of the world then we need to modify our actions accordingly; or rather (this is to say that) our actions will be modified if informed by the new, more adequate, beliefs. Thus to reject the idea that there are witches is to reject practices informed by such a belief.

Step three

The third step is to see that, once we form a new belief, we must not only reject action informed by the old false belief, but we must also be committed in principle to an enquiry about the causes of that false belief, especially if that false belief is persistent or widespread and insusceptible to rational criticism.

Let us now consider some possible rejoinders. First, it might be objected that this refutation depends upon our acceptance of the value that truth is a good and falsity is an ill. But that this is so is a condition of factual discourse (an aspect, as it were, of the logical geography of the concept of a belief) and so it does not involve anything other than considerations intrinsic to factual discourse to legitimate the deduction of values, which is denied by Hume's Law. It should be noted that this recasts the positivist understanding of what a fact is: a fact is not value-free but incorporates a commitment to truth. The positivist account of a fact was always in fact false. Other values and interests besides truth do enter into the constitution of facts, but my claim is that commitment to truth is the only value that *necessarily* does so. This is at one with our everyday intuitions. Thus we do not suppose that the science that discovered the Ebola virus is *necessarily* contaminated by the desire of scientists to attract more research grants or of funding corporations to make profits.

It is not an objection to point out that truth is not the only social good, or falsity the only social ill, so that the inference schemes[6] of explanatory critique may be *overridden* by other considerations. Science is only one amongst other social institutions and truth is only one amongst a number of values, but this does not gainsay the fact (and condition of factual discourse) that, other things being equal, truth is a good and falsity an ill.

Third, it is the case that the inference from the negative evaluation of a structure or state of affairs accounting for the falsity of a belief to a positive evaluation of action rationally directed at transforming it is contingent upon both substantive theory and concrete practical judgements. *That* something should be done *ceteris paribus* is however undeniable; *what* should be done is a different matter.

Finally, the inference schemes of explanatory critique hold only *ceteris paribus*, other things being equal. But this has an exact parallel in ordinary scientific discourse. To invoke a causal law is not to say what will happen, but rather what tends to happen or what would happen *ceteris paribus*. The *ceteris paribus* clause is the condition for moving from fact to fact in the open-systemic world to which the laws of nature transfactually apply (the best-designed building or bridge will stay up only *ceteris paribus*), as much as it is to moving from fact to value in the practical social world of beliefs, judgement and action. Where philosophical orthodoxy posits radical dichotomies, critical realism finds instead exact parallels.

In *Scientific Realism and Human Emancipation* I generalise the argument for explanatory critiques from cognitive ills, such as falsity, to non-cognitive and non-communicative ills, such as poverty and ill health. This is something that will prove important when we turn to the appropriation of explanatory critique in discourse analysis. I also show how the model can be embedded within a depth-emancipatory praxis.[7] In doing so we logically presuppose:

(a) a theory of a feasible better state; and
(b) a theory of transition to it.

In dialectical critical realism these two become *concrete utopianism* and the *theory of transition* and, added to explanatory critique, this package becomes the *explanatory critical theory complex*, to be related to a depth-emancipatory practice in the *ethical tetrapolity* (see Chapter 6.7).[8] Concrete utopianism involves the imaginative working out of the way in which a person or a social entity, such as a family or university department, could better deal with a constraint. It is philosophically grounded in dispositional realism, especially the idea that possibilities, as much as actualities, are real, and indeed ontologically prior to them.[9]

I now want to recapitulate the part of the argument for explanatory critique in *Scientific Realism and Human Emancipation* that moves through *seven levels of rationality*.[10] The first two levels involve merely *instrumental rationality,* specifically technical rationality and what I will call contextually situated instrumental rationality. Thus

(i) *technical rationality*
    involves the use of the social sciences as sheer technique, and no interesting normative conclusions are entailed; but at level
(ii) of *contextually situated instrumental rationality*
    social science is no longer neutral in the context of power$_2$ relations. For the oppressed have an *interest* in knowledge that their oppressors may, and perhaps must lack.[11]
    Moving on to *critical rationality*, at level
(iii) we have *intra-discursive (non-explanatory) critical* or *practical rationality*

To say that a belief is false is to apply a negative evaluation of actions sustained or informed by the belief in question. All the sciences are intrinsically critical and so evaluative, since they all make judgements of truth or falsity on beliefs about their object domain. But the human sciences, in virtue of the distinctive nature of their domain, that it includes, among other things, beliefs about social objects, also make (or at least entail) judgements of truth or falsity on aspects of that domain in pursuing their explanatory charter.

At level

(iv) we have *explanatory critical rationality*
We have that if we possess:

    (a) adequate grounds for supposing that proto-scientific[12] theory, P, is false or misleading; and
    (b) adequate grounds for supposing that structure, S, co-explains P.

Then we may, and must, pass immediately to

    (c) a negative evaluation of S (CP); and
    (d) a positive evaluation of action rationally directed at the removal of S (CP)

The next two levels are of *emancipatory rationality*. At level

(v) of *depth explanatory critical rationality*

simple models of psychological rationalisation and ideological mystification may be sketched.[13] Such mystification results in constraints on human well-being or free flourishing (which includes the satisfaction not just of needs but of the conditions of possibility of development). In any situation of constraint on flourishing what is required is *diagnosis, explanation* and *action*. This is the *DEA model of practical problem resolution*. In so far as this involves normative change, what will be needed is *description, explanation* and *transformation* of some normative consensus or actually existing morality. This is the *DET schema* represented in Figure 5.1. This model may be regarded as successively combining Humean, explanatory-critical and Spinozan moments. At the first, Humean moment some widely shared set of values is described; at the second, critical realist moment the genesis or maintenance of the

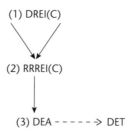

FIGURE 5.1 The DEA --> DET model of practical problem resolution[14]

consensus is explained, and at the third, Spinozan, moment cognitively inappropriate (false or otherwise inadequate) values are transformed or eliminated in the praxis of the agents concerned as the agents come to see that their values are no longer appropriate in the light of the explanatory structures revealed.[15]

At level

(vi) of *depth investigation* (proceeding from depth explanation)

the internal relations between explanatory theory and emancipatory practice come into their own. Here the DEA --> DET model comes fully into its own: *diagnosis, explanation* and *action/transformation* follow each other in rapid succession.[16]

Discussion of

(vii) *geo-historical directional rationality*

is postponed until the next chapter (6.7).

Five general conditions for the possibility of emancipatory practices may be indicated:[17]

(a)   the causality of reasons;
(b)   the immanence of values;
(c)   the internality of critique to its object, together with the engagement and reflexivity of social theory;
(d)   a coincidence of objective needs and subjective possibilities;
(e)   emergent powers must operate for qualitative change to be possible.

A stark contrast with critical theory now heaves into view. For critical realism explanatory theory *implies*, rather than (as in Horkheimer and Habermas) *presupposes*, a commitment to emancipation.[18] Thus we need not preface our search for explanatory mechanisms with our interest in emancipation; on the contrary, our interest in emancipation can flow from the search. The error of critical theory comes from acceptance of a fundamentally positivist conception of natural science. For once the natural world is so described there is no room for human action to make any difference to it.

The theory of explanatory critique does presuppose a definite view of human nature and human possibilities in four-planar social being. This *philosophical anthropology* or more generally ontology that it presupposes is argued for in *Scientific Realism and Human Emancipation* and developed further in dialectical critical realism (see Chapter 6). It is one in which the satisfaction of our desires, needs and our meta-desire to remove constraints on their satisfaction depend irreducibly upon the actions of others, in the *dialectical interdependence of freedom and solidarity*, discourse and praxis and the *dialectics of discourse and praxis*. Here there are two fundamental mechanisms or dialectics, one involving discourse and the other desire and action generally. What links freedom and solidarity and these two dialectics is the *logic of dialectical universalisability*.

The practical presupposition of discourse is given by the assurance: 'trust me, act on it'; and the discursive presupposition of action is given by the assurance: 'my action is justified because it seeks to remove a constraint on my freedom, and I am committed to the removal of such constraints in all dialectically similar circumstances'.

Thus I am saying or presupposing that 'there is something about this case, a specific difference, that entails a commitment to act in the same kind of way in all dialectically similar circumstances'. This is because for any act there must be a ground or justification, and the same action must be performed in exactly the same circumstances, unless there is a relevant difference between the cases. So the *process of rationally grounding* or of reflexively deliberating *implies a commitment to dialectical universalisability*. This itself may be seen as an application in the moral realm of the principle of ubiquity determinism (which I introduced in Chapter 2.7).[19] This principle needs to be suitably concretised and dialecticised, and this, together with the force of the 'dialectical' in the idea of dialectical universalisability will be discussed in Chapter 6. Here it is important to note that universalisability is subject to the *ceteris paribus* clause and a number of side constraints, such as feasibility, which will also be discussed in the next chapter.

5.2 Critical discourse analysis and language

Critical discourse analysis (CDA) is concerned with the analysis of value-impregnated and ideologically saturated discourse, relating such discourse back to its conditions of production in such a way as to bring out the practical implications and presuppositions of the discourse. Such conditions are both discursive and extra-discursive, and they include power$_2$ relations. Notwithstanding the fact that critical realism justifies a strong, and even ontological (alethic) sense of truth (see Chapter 6.4), critical discourse analysts typically fight shy of analysing discourse in relation to its truth or falsity, that is, in relation to cognitive ills, preferring to show how the discourse reinforces, or at any rate fails to challenge, gross inequalities of income, wealth or opportunity or power$_2$ relations. No doubt this is partly explained by the widespread scepticism in the academy, dominated by postmodernist epistemic and judgemental relativism, concerning the possibility of using strong epistemic criteria. But it is a shame, since it has served to prevent discourse analysts from making full use of the resources of the theory of explanatory critique, while at the same time critical realists have often fallen back on the textbook examples of Marx and Freud, effectively ignoring the huge number of contemporary texts and actions, discourses and policies susceptible to an explanatory critique informed by CDA.

The leading proponent of CR-compatible and -influenced CDA is Norman Fairclough.[20] Critical discourse analysis is concerned very generally with looking at the meanings of texts. This clearly involves both *semiosis*, the study of meaning-making; and *hermeneutics* or the interpretation of texts.

The minimum necessary unit for semiotic analysis is the *semiotic triangle*, constituted by the signifier (word), the signified (concept, sense or intension of the signifier) and the referent (the object or thing referred to by the signifier) (see Figure 2.2, above).[21] The referent is an absolutely indispensable part of this ensemble; it is existentially intransitive and depends upon its detachment from the act of referring. As such the referent is, in respect of any production of meaning, extra-discursive, something outside the discourse of which it is the referent.

Elsewhere I have differentiated four hermeneutical circles:[22]

C1: the circle of enquiry;

C2: the circle of communication;

C3: the circle of enquiry or investigation into other existing societies, cultures, traditions (which may be written as 'C of I (C)') and

C4: a circle of investigation into meaningful objects or products, including texts (which can be represented as 'C of I (T)').

Critical discourse analysis is a form of the fourth hermeneutical circle.

A discourse is a collection of texts that have been pressed into service by an individual, group or institution for a particular purpose or end. Critical discourse analysis is a method of analysis that examines the meaning-making (or semiosis) and the circulation of systems of meaning (discourses) and their imbrication in relations of power (especially power$_2$) and ideology.

In Chapter 2 we saw that critical realism established its break from mainstream philosophy by revindicating ontology and establishing a new ontology, which will be further developed in Chapters 6 to 9. A question therefore arises about language: Does it have an ontology? And can the new critical realist ontology be applied to it? The answer to both questions is yes. The new ontology, pivoting initially on the distinctions between the domains of the real, the actual and the empirical, can certainly be applied to language. Thus, corresponding to this general distinction we have the distinctions between

d_r: discourses at the level of the real;

d_a: texts at the level of the actual; and

d_e: interpretations at the level of the conceptual, which corresponds in this field to the empirical.

However, a further set of questions immediately arises: Given that language use is a social activity, and therefore necessarily part of social ontology, does it exhaust social ontology or is there an extra-conceptual component of social ontology?

We have already noted (in Chapters 2.2 and 3.3) how in the twentieth century a growing concern with language resulted in an exaggeration of its role in two distinctive ways, which it is important to differentiate here. In both cases, *inflation of the role of language* served to eliminate any Other to language in the relevant domain. The first form of the *linguistic fallacy* consists in the supposition that one can analyse being in terms of the language used to describe it (or in a more mediated way, used to express our knowledge of it). This form of the linguistic fallacy, which I shall write 'LF_1', is clearly a variant of the *epistemic fallacy*. As such it represents a form of the *anthropic fallacy* and, together with the reciprocating *ontic fallacy*, establishes a characteristic form of *anthroporealism*, necessitating (as we will see in Chapter 6) a complementary transcendent realism. This form of the linguistic fallacy can be refuted by reference to the arguments we used to establish ontology in Chapter 2, arguments turning on the conditions of possibility of experimental and applied activity. But it can also be refuted by reference to the material practices of ordinary life. For all language use presupposes the semiotic triangle, constituted by signifier, signified and referent. And any use of language presupposes the characteristic activity of referential detachment, which is the process whereby the referent is detached from the human activity of referring.

The second form of inflation of the role of language serves, not to identify language with the whole of knowable reality (as in LF_1), but rather to identify it with specifically *social* reality. I shall write this fallacy 'LF_2'. This is a characteristic position of hermeneuticists, social constructivists and most so called poststructuralists, at least in their strong or exclusivist form. It can be refuted by consideration of the role of the material, including the materially embodied, alongside the conceptual part of social reality. It follows from this that conceptuality, though a defining and necessary feature of social reality, does not exhaust it. Thus, as we saw in Chapter 3, fighting a war, or homelessness, or hunger cannot be explicated solely in terms of the satisfaction of criteria for the application of a concept, but constitutes material states of being. It follows from this that social reality, though concept-dependent, is not exhausted by conceptuality.

There is a close interdependence between hermeneutical and constructivist accounts of the social world and social science and the positivist account of natural science, which we have already noted in Chapter 3. The arguments of these accounts for the distinctive character of social science often turn on a contrast with an account of nature and natural science as misdescribed by positivism. Thus in *The Idea of Social Science*, Peter Winch has two main arguments for the hermeneutical position. The first is that social science, unlike natural science, seeks out intelligible connections in its subject matter. But of course, on a critical realist understanding, this is just what natural science, indeed any science, does. The legacy here of the Humean, positivist idea that events are conjoined, but never connected, is only too clear. (From a critical realist standpoint, the connection is provided by an in principle (fallibly) knowable generative mechanism or structure at work; this is the *principle of intelligibility*: nature, like society, is intelligible.) Winch's second main argument is that things in the social world have, if they are not to be reduced to their physical manifestation, only a conceptual existence. This argument betrays the heavy legacy of the empiricist doctrine that *esse est percipi*. But of course, if we reject this, then the possibility of a causal criterion for establishing existence is opened up; and we can allow that, although unperceivable, reasons and social structures may function as causes in the social world, just as magnetic or gravitational fields do in the natural one.

Very often the two forms of the linguistic fallacy are combined. With this in mind, critical realists should rather talk about the *construal* of social reality than its *construction*, because the idea of construal allows for the notion of an independently existing intransitive domain that is described or interpreted one way rather than another. The voluntaristic implications of 'construction' are also objectionable on the grounds that they ignore the pre-existence of a social object, a pre-understanding, a nominal definition, and so on, that is always presupposed, on the transformational model of social activity (TMSA), when we arrive at a new conceptualisation of a thing. And the idea of a 'construction' is further objectionable in that it scouts the fact that social things are always at least partly materially embodied. In sum, social reality is always existentially intransitive to any 'construction', and in so far as it is social it is also at least in part pre-formed (in virtue of the TMSA) and at least partially materially embodied.

Despite the inflation of the role of language by hermeneuticists, critical realism accords the activity of hermeneutics an absolutely indispensable role. Indeed, it will typically form the starting point of a critical realist investigation, because we must at least know what agents think they are doing, and why they are (in their opinion) doing it when we set out to describe and explain a social form of life. However, critical realism will insist of course that all such conceptualisations are fallible and subject to critique, including explanatory critique.

In the social world language/discourse cuts across four-planar social being, and there are crucial linguistic/conceptual components at all four planes. Furthermore, in considering discourses we may differentiate *order of discourse* from a *discourse*, and in considering the operationalisation of discourses we may distinguish *genres* (ways of acting communicatively) from *styles* (ways of being) and their objectification, for example, in bodily gesture or the built environment. We may focus on the production or emergence of meaning in *texturing*, which will often occur at the intersection of two (or more) discourses, or involve the interlacing of several different discourses, in *intertextuality*.

Discourse operates at three levels simultaneously:

(i) as text;
(ii) as discourse practice (the process of producing and interpreting texts); and
(iii) as sociocultural practice, with the discursive activity occurring in a particular immediate situation, a specific social institutional locale and a more general societal context.

Any of these three may then be described and analysed in their complexity, using any of the laminated systems introduced in Chapter 4 (for example, using seven-scalar social being).

A typical discourse analysis might take the form of the following three phases:

(a) description of the text, including its formal linguistic properties;
(b) interpretation, in terms of the relationship between the (productive and interpretive) discursive processes and the text; and
(c) explanation of the production, role, intended effect and force of the text in terms of the relationship between the social and discursive processes.

The text can in turn be regarded as constellationally contained or embedded in the context of the discursive processes of its formation and interpretation, which are in turn embedded in the wider (including extra-discursive) social and cultural reality. Let us call this *CDA Schema 1*.

In social explanation we must in principle understand the relationship between language and the extra-discursive part of social reality as a causal one, with the causality being two-way. Thus we see language and discursive processes as being *causally conditioned by* extra-discursive aspects of the social reality (including power$_2$ relations, the pre-existing distribution of resources, and so on); and at the same time as *causally efficacious on* the rest of social reality.

A good example of the use of CDA Schema 1 is provided by the first eight paragraphs of Will Hutton's article in *The Observer* (London), 29 June 2013, which analyses UK Chancellor George Osborne's financial statement of the week before – see textbox.[23] (The text as a whole – ten paragraphs – also illustrates many aspects of *CDA Schema 2*, below.) Phase one of the process is the description of the text, Osborne's speech. This is accomplished in paragraphs 1–5. It is then, in phase two, interpreted in terms of 'political positioning' in the context of the discursive processes of the production and intended effect of the text. This occurs in the first two sentences of paragraph 6, where it is interpreted as a party political stratagem. It is then explained in the rest of paragraph 6, which relates these discursive processes back to the state of the British economy and society, that is, to the social context that generates them and in which they are intended to play a role. This corresponds to phase three of the schema. In paragraphs 7 and 8 Hutton expresses doubts about whether this stratagem will be as successful as the author of the text (George Osborne) supposes.

In language and action, there's a new brutalism in Westminster

Will Hutton

1. It was a litany of nastiness couched in the language of reform, fairness and helpfulness. A series of measures to bring the spending review speech to a triumphant political finale, appealing to poisonous prejudice but framed to minimise any such suspicion. In order to 'change lives for the better' and reduce 'dependency', George Osborne introduced the 'upfront work search' scheme. Only if the jobless arrive at the jobcentre with a CV, register for online job search, and start looking for work will they be eligible for benefit – and then they should report weekly rather than fortnightly. What could be more reasonable?

2. More apparent reasonableness followed. There will now be a seven-day wait for the jobseeker's allowance. 'Those first few days should be spent

looking for work, not looking to sign on', he intoned. 'We're doing these things because we know they help people stay off benefits and help those on benefits get into work faster.' Help? Really? On first hearing, this was the socially concerned chancellor, trying to change lives for the better, complete with 'reforms' to an obviously indulgent system that demands too little effort from the newly unemployed to find work, and subsidises laziness. What motivated him, we were to understand, was his zeal for 'fundamental fairness' – protecting the taxpayer, controlling spending and ensuring that only the most deserving claimants received their benefits.

3. Osborne has taken the Orwellian misuse of language to new levels. Losing a job is traumatising: you don't skip down to the jobcentre with a song in your heart, delighted at the prospect of doubling your income from the munificent state. It is financially terrifying, psychologically mortifying and you know that support is minimal and extraordinarily hard to get. You are now not wanted; you are now excluded from the work milieu that offers purpose and structure in your life, along with the company of others. Worse, the crucial income to feed yourself and your family and pay the bills has disappeared. Of course you want to find a job as fast as you can. The sooner the whole experience is behind you the better. Ask anyone newly unemployed what they want and the answer is always: a job.

4. But in Osborneland, your first instinct is to flop into dependency – permanent dependency if you can get it – supported by a state only too ready to indulge your mendacity. It is as though 20 years of ever-tougher reforms of the job search and benefit administration system never happened. The principle of British welfare is no longer that you can insure yourself against the risk of unemployment and receive unconditional payments if the disaster happens. Even the very phrase 'jobseeker's allowance' – invented in 1996 – is about redefining the unemployed as a 'jobseeker' who has no mandatory right to a benefit he or she has earned through making national insurance contributions. Instead, the claimant receives a time-limited 'allowance', conditional on actively seeking a job; no entitlement and no insurance. Britain has led the world in linking the administration of benefits to the job search. What's more, at £71.70 a week, the jobseeker's allowance is one of the least generous in the EU.

5. In this context, it's insane to describe as 'help' making an unemployed person wait seven days for a mean benefit they need at a moment of crisis in their lives. And to present 'upfront work search' as a pioneering transformation of the jobcentres' operations, already entirely based on making benefit conditional on actively applying for jobs, is to compound the felony.

6. Osborne was not interested in help. His purpose was political positioning: to locate the Conservative party as the friend of the taxpayer, Labour as the welfare party and to make his 'reforms' the baseline normal. It is a big

bet: that those at the receiving end of the punishment will remain voiceless and illegitimate while the majority will continue to see welfare as a burden and the breathtaking rollback of the state as an unavoidable necessity. To succeed, there must be no big questions asked about the operation of the British economy and its management, none about the impact on British society, and widespread acceptance that the state in any guise is useless. We are all conservatives now.

7. I am not so sure. The evidence of growing hardship is all around. The Children's Commissioner has reported that the number of children living in poverty will have risen from 2.3 million in 2010 to 3 million in 2015. Two million people survive from week to week courtesy of payday loans. The Resolution Foundation found that the numbers of people working on zero-hour contracts has risen to 208,000 – a figure it considers a massive underestimate because 150,000 domiciliary care workers alone are known to be on zero-hour contracts. The use of food banks is exploding.

8. The TUC austerity bus, on a national tour, features harrowing personal stories of how the new bedroom tax is forcing councils – themselves under enormous pressure – to move tenants from their homes. The Joseph Rowntree Foundation says that over the last five years social housing rents have risen 26%, energy costs 39% and transport costs 30%. Yet benefits for both those in and out of work are being cut in real terms for the first time since the 1930s. As need becomes acute, provision of services at the local level is being emasculated. Sir Merrick Cockell, Tory chair of the local government association, says the further 10% cut in local government budgets, on top of the existing cut of a third, will stretch services to breaking point. When he also accuses the whole top-down approach as 'feudal', take note. This is civil society beginning to stir itself.

9. There is a plausible alternative – a slower pace of cuts, more revenues from a wider tax base, a new social settlement, a recasting of the relationship between the centre and locality and, above all, a dramatic reshaping of British capitalism to make it more innovative and productive. Osborne believes his bet will succeed because no coalition can be constructed to argue for a contrary position: that while Sir Merrick and the children's commissioner may fulminate, there is no possibility of their becoming part of a broad-based coalition arguing for change, including, say, both unions and business.

10. But nastiness disguised as help, and coming with no promise of anything but more of the same, is not the way to a majority coalition either, and the social impact is desperate. The spending review looked clever for 24 hours, but discomforting Ed Balls on the *Today* programme is not a long-term political strategy. Instead, it may prove the catalyst for an effective opposition coalition. The chancellor has gone a step too far.

Norman Fairclough has developed a methodology for doing critical discourse analysis (CDA) modelled on my conception of explanatory critique:[24]

Stage 1: Focus upon a social problem that has a semiotic aspect

This corresponds to the initial focus in a basic explanatory critique on a false belief, or more generally, a social ill. The point of focusing on the problem or the ill is to produce explanatory knowledge of it which can inform emancipatory change.

Stage 2: Identify obstacles to its being tackled through an analysis of

(a) the network of practices within which it is located;
(b) the relationship of semiosis to other elements within the particular practices concerned; and
(c) the discourse (or semiosis) itself.

(a)–(c) correspond loosely to 1–3 in CDA Schema 1 and so to the first eight paragraphs of Hutton's article. The objective at (c) is to understand how the problem or ill arises, and how it is rooted in the way social life is organised, by focusing on the obstacles to its resolution, on what makes it more or less intractable.

Stage 3: Consider whether the social order (network of practice) in a sense 'needs' the problem. Why if at all is the problem 'needed'? What are the mechanisms (somehow) producing and reproducing it? The point here is to ask whether those who benefit most from the way social life is organised have an interest in the problem not being resolved.

Stage 4: Identify possible ways past the obstacles. This stage is a crucial complement to stage 2 – it looks for hitherto unrealised possibilities for change in the way life is currently organised. This is where concrete utopianism, a theory of transition and a relationship to an on-going depth struggle becomes crucial. We can now define a notional.

Stage 5: These unrealised possibilities become the object of an emancipatory practice oriented to the definitive resolution of the social problem or ill, in the context of concrete utopianism and a coherent theory of transition. This will in principle include a moment of self-reflexivity defining a notional.
Stage 5* in which we self-reflect critically on our analysis (1–4), including considerations as to the interests and social positionality of the analyst.

We may call this five-stage schema *CDA Schema 2*. Its last two stages are partially exemplified by paragraphs 9 and 10 of Hutton's article. Another example of its use might be in relation to the text normally provided by 'experts' on news and current affairs programmes when the topic of anthropic climate change comes up. The context may be that of a sudden freak storm or unusually hot or cold or wet weather. The expert will be asked whether humanly driven climate change has anything to do with it. They will reply that they cannot say because of the huge number of factors impinging on this particular event or period.

From a critical realist meta-perspective this is very unsatisfactory. For, of course, any event or sequence of events in an open system will be determined by a multiplicity of factors, and as such it will not be deductively predictable or completely explicable in terms of a single factor. However, there is a clearly established main mechanism relating to the burning of fossil fuels that is causing the rise in global temperature, and empirically verified measurements of both suggest that they are rising at alarming rates. Clearly, to say this one needs to differentiate, as critical realism does, open from closed systems, with empirical regularities only being a decisive indicator in the latter; and between structures or mechanisms and events or their patterns, that is, between the domains of the real and the actual.

The discursive processes in relation to climate change include those of newsworthiness, the prevention of media bias and the generation and maintenance of an empiricist-deductivist conception of science. The social processes in terms of which one might want to explain texts of this particular kind include the large amount of oil and other corporate money poured into right-wing think tanks and research specifically designed to produce scepticism about or denial of anthropic climate change. This can be taken together with the fear on the part of those in the media and in the climate science community or its periphery of suffering the same kind of fate (vilification in the media) that the climate scientists in the University of East Anglia experienced just before the Copenhagen Summit on climate change in December 2009.[25]

How might critical realism intervene in this discursive process? Clearly by critiquing, among other things, the deductivist ideology at work in and underpinning these discursive practices. Note that critical realism can become immediately liberating here at level two of the seven levels of rationality sketched earlier in this chapter, that is, at the level of intra-discursive, contextually situated instrumental rationality. For we can see clearly that the general public have an interest in knowledge, here of these critical realist distinctions, that the oil corporations and those funded by them do not have (see section 5.1).

Notes

1 The theory of explanatory critique is first developed in my *The Possibility of Naturalism*, 55–71. It is elaborated and related to a dialectic of human emancipation in Bhaskar, *Scientific Realism and Human Emancipation*, Chapter 2.4–2.7, 154–211, which is then further developed in dialectical critical realism and the philosophy of metaReality. See also Reeves, *The Idea of Critique*.

2 Whether Hume himself held that values cannot be derived logically from factual statements is eristic (see for example Bhaskar, *Scientific Realism and Human Emancipation*, 179 n95; Smith, *What is a Person?*, 388 f; and Charles R. Pigden, ed., *Hume on Is and Ought* (Basingstoke: Palgrave Macmillan, 2010)). However, this is not a controversy that need concern us here. The target of my critique is the philosophical orthodoxy that has

come to be known as Hume's Law, namely that conclusions about values cannot be deduced validly from factual premises.

3 Bhaskar, *The Possibility of Naturalism*, 59.

4 As explained in Chapter 1, to understand being as re-enchanted is to see that, contrary to the philosophical discourse of modernity, it is intrinsically valuable and meaningful. Here social being is said to be 're-enchanted' because it is acknowledged to contain values. The dominant view *disenchants* the world (the transitive dimension), which however is always already *enchanted* (intransitive dimension). See also Chapters 7 and 8.

5 Hume, *A Treatise of Human Nature, Vol. II*, 128.

6 See Bhaskar, *Scientific Realism and Human Emancipation*, Chapter 2.5–2.7.

7 See Bhaskar, *Scientific Realism and Human Emancipation*, 207 ff.

8 See also Bhaskar, *Dialectic*, 262–5.

9 Critical realist metatheory thus opens up the exciting prospect of underlabouring for the burgeoning new field of transitions studies, and in particular sustainability transitions.

10 Bhaskar, *Scientific Realism and Human Emancipation*, 180–211.

11 See Bhaskar, *The Possibility of Naturalism*, 60 n84, 177; *Scientific Realism and Human Emancipation*, 182; and *Reclaiming Reality*, 6.

12 See Chapter 2.8.

13 See Bhaskar, *Scientific Realism and Human Emancipation*, 194 ff.

14 Bhaskar, *Plato Etc.*, 112, Figure 5.13.

15 See Martin Evenden, 'Critical realism in the personal domain: Spinoza and the explanatory critique of the emotions', *Journal of Critical Realism* 11:2 (2012), 163–87.

16 See also Tim Rogers, 'The doing of a depth-investigation: implications for the emancipatory aims of critical naturalism', *Journal of Critical Realism* 3(2) (2004), 238–69.

17 Bhaskar, *Scientific Realism and Human Emancipation*, 210–11.

18 See Bhaskar, *The Possibility of Naturalism*, 56 f.

19 See also Bhaskar, *A Realist Theory of Science*, 70.

20 See Norman Fairclough, *Critical Discourse Analysis: The Critical Study of Language* (Harlow: Pearson 1995/2010). See also Norman Fairclough, 'Critical discourse analysis' in *Dictionary of Critical Realism*, ed. M. Hartwig, 89–91. Here Fairclough differentiates six versions of CDA: (i) French discourse analysis of an Althusserian cast; (ii) critical linguistics; (ii) socio-cognitive approach to CDA; (iv) a discourse historical approach; (v) a social semiotic approach; and (vi) a dialectical approach.

21 See also Bhaskar, *Dialectic*, 222–4.

22 Bhaskar, *The Possibility of Naturalism*, Chapter 4, 152 ff.

23 Numbering of paragraphs has been added.

24 Norman Fairclough, *Analysing Discourse: Textual Analysis for Social Research* (London: Routledge, 2003), 209–10.

25 See Wikipedia contributors. 2015. 'Climatic Research Unit email controversy', 30 September. *Wikipedia, The Free Encyclopedia*, retrieved on 25 February 2016 from https://en.wikipedia.org/w/index.php?title = Climatic_Research_Unit_email_controversy&oldid = 683477293.

6

THE FURTHER DEVELOPMENT OF CRITICAL REALISM I

Dialectical critical realism

6.1 The development of ontology

If there is a single big idea in critical realism it is the idea of *ontology*. Thus in Chapter 2 we saw how critical realism began with a double argument about ontology: an argument for ontology, revindicating ontology, in which the epistemic fallacy was isolated; and an argument for a new, stratified and differentiated, non-Humean ontology that critiqued the actualism of existing accounts of science. In this chapter and the next I will be concerned with the further development of critical realism, and in particular of ontology, in a process by which our understanding of being is successively enhanced and refined.

There are seven levels in this development, the first four of which are mapped by dialectical critical realism, and the last three by the philosophy of metaReality. In this chapter, I will be concerned with dialectical critical realism.[1] By way of anticipation and overview I will list all seven levels here, the names of which (1M, 2E, and so on) form the acronym MELDARZ or MELDARA when the numerals are omitted.[2] They are set out, together with their characteristic figures and themes, in Table 6.1.

1. Being as such, and as involving non-identity, difference and structure (1M or 'first moment');
2. Being as process (2E or 'second edge');
3. Being together or as a whole (3L or 'third level'); and
4. Being as incorporating transformative practice (human agency) (4D or 'fourth dimension').

These are the four moments or levels (MELD) of dialectical critical realism. The philosophy of metaReality incorporates the further understanding of:

5. Being as incorporating reflexivity, inwardness (or interiority) and, in a certain sense, spirituality (5A or 'fifth aspect');

TABLE 6.1 The moments of the philosophy of critical realism and metaReality mapped to the stadia of the ontological–axiological chain[3]

Stadion/Moment	1M Non-identity	2E Negativity	3L Totality	4D Transformative agency	5A Spirituality	6R (Re-)enchantment	7 Non-duality
CR as a whole: thinking being	as such and in general	processually + as for 1M	as a totality + as for 2E	as incorporating human praxis and reflexivity + as for 3L	as incorporating spirituality + as for 4D	as incorporating enchantment + as for 5A	as incorporating non-duality + as for 6R
Form of reflexivity – immanent critique of TR: thinking being as	philosophical discourse of modernity (PDM)	PDM + 1M	PDM + 1M, 2E	PDM + 1M, 2E, 3L	PDM + 1M, 2E, 3L, 4D	PDM + 1M, 2E, 3L, 4D, 5A	PDM + 1M, 2E, 3L, 4D, 5A, 6R
CN inflection: thinking being as	structured and differentiated containing mind and concepts	negativity, contradiction, emergence (social relationism, transformationalism)					
EC inflection: thinking being as	intrinsically valuable	negativity qua absenting constraints (ills)	totality, understood as including values (retotalisation)				

(Continued)

TABLE 6.1 (Continued)

Stadion/Moment	1M Non-identity	2E Negativity	3L Totality	4D Transformative agency	5A Spirituality	6R (Re-)enchantment	7 Non-duality
DCR inflection: thinking being as	alethic truth (reality principle, axiological necessity)	negativity qua (determinate) absence, generalised to the whole of being as real and essential to change	totality, understood as maximised by praxis (which absents incompleteness)	transformative praxis and reflexivity (emancipatory axiology)			
TDCR inflection: thinking being as	underlying non-duality (God, transcendentally real self)	transcendence co-presence creativity	totality, understood as incl. unconditional love	spontaneous right-action	spiritual		
PMR inflection: thinking being as	underlying non-duality (cosmic envelope, ground-state)	transcendence co-presence creativity	totality, understood as incl. unconditional love	spontaneous right-action	spiritual	enchanted	non-dual

6. Being as re-enchanted (6R or 'sixth realm'); and
7. Being as incorporating the priority of identity over difference (and unity over split), or as non-dual (7Z/A or 'seventh zone' or 'awakening').

The key concept of dialectical critical realism, which necessitates its formation as a distinct, systematic structure of concepts, is that of *absence*. What this concept makes possible above all else is the understanding and analysis of *change*. It is therefore to situating absence and change that I turn first.

6.2 Absence and change

Absenting and presencing

Our ordinary understanding of change involves the *absenting* of something that was there and/or the *presencing* of something that was not there. This presencing can also be understood as 'absenting the absence' of what was not there. This understanding of change incorporates two concepts, namely those of absence and negativity, that have been anathema to mainstream philosophy since the time of Parmenides (*c.* 515–460 BCE). Consequently there has been a taboo against their use, a taboo that has had (or so I will argue) momentous and extremely undesirable effects. The doctrine that philosophy must eschew the use of negating concepts, and therefore of change in our ordinary understanding of it, I call *ontological monovalence*.[4] Because the world evidently contains change, or at least appears to do so, there is a prima facie implausibility about this approach. It was Plato who rescued Parmenides' injunction 'not to speak the not' (in itself a self-referential paradox, because any denial that 'the not' can be said necessarily says it). He did so by analysing change in terms of *difference*.[5] And the idea that change can always be reparsed in terms of difference is fleshed out substantively by the understanding of difference as involving the *redistribution* of unchanging parts, be they Platonic forms, atoms or whatever.

In a moment I will show why the category of absence is necessary for the coherent understanding of change. But first we might reflect on why and how absence is necessary for being. Consider for a moment the articulation of sounds or marks in a sentence. They would be unintelligible without their boundaries and the spaces within and between them. If we were packed together, with no space between us, we couldn't breathe. We know in fact that we are, like other solid, material objects and like the universe generally largely constituted by absence: empty space.[6]

We might also want to reflect on the consideration that absence is equally necessary for intentional agency. Intentional agency always presupposes a lack, want or need that it is precisely the point of the action to remedy.

Absence as a presupposition of basic critical realism

Pre-dialectical critical realism had not thematised absence as such.[7] But it had, of course, presupposed it. Thus the distinction between (i) that part of the real which is actual and (ii) that part which is not (and which grounds the distinction between the domains of the real and the actual), involves centrally the idea of absence in the shape of the absence from actuality or the non-actualised character of a part of the real.

Of course, one of the initial motivations for basic critical realism was precisely to ground the possibility of change. Thus, once we differentiate clearly between the transitive and intransitive dimensions, change (in both) can be coherently described. But what such change means or involves remains unanalysed. Moreover, emergence plays a crucial role in the basic critical realist argument, and diachronically it too clearly involves change. Similarly, in critical naturalism the transformational model of social activity puts transformation, thence change at the heart of the social process, but the concept of change remains unanalysed, that is to say, change, unlike say structure or difference is taken for granted: not analysed, but merely presupposed.

The analysis of change

Prima facie, *change*, involving absenting, and *difference* are distinct concepts. Thus if Sartre is waiting in a café for his friend Pierre to turn up, then we would say that Pierre is absent from the café. And this is different from saying that he is somewhere else. On the other hand, when Pierre arrives in the café, then we can describe his presence in the café as the absenting of his absence from it. Change presupposes a continuous something (in this case the space of the café) that has or undergoes the change.[8]

It is important here to differentiate absence and negativity at the level of the intransitive dimension from absence and negativity at the level of the transitive dimension; that is, to distinguish clearly negativity in the world from negativity in our understanding and description of the world. The Western philosophical tradition has been prepared to countenance transitive change, as of course it must do if it is to talk about our changing beliefs or knowledge or to situate the possibility that some claims to knowledge are false. But it has always fought shy of allowing negativity in being itself.

Now I want to differentiate clearly three levels of negation, and to do so making use of the terminology of R. M. Hare.[9] Hare distinguished the *phrastic* or ontic content of a proposition from its affirmation or denial, which is an operation on the *neustic*. He differentiated this, in turn, from an operation on the assertion or denial of the ontic content, such as imagining, entertaining, or hypothesising it, which is an operation involving the *tropic*. *Tropics* (Greek *tropos*, mode) designate a domain of discourse, for example, the fictional as distinct from the factual. *Neustics* (Greek *neuein*, to nod or give a sign of assent) convey attitudes such as acceptance, rejection or indecision. *Phrastics* (Greek *phrasein*, to declare, propose) denote the ontic content of propositions, what they are about, which may be positive or negative. Thus we can distinguish between the following kinds of statement:[10]

S1. 'It is raining (or not raining) in Manchester.' This expresses the presence or absence of rain in Manchester, which involves an operation on the *phrastic* (and is a statement or claim about Manchester).

S2. The affirmation or denial of the proposition that 'It is raining (or not raining) in Manchester', which is an operation on the *neustic*, affirming or denying the claim about Manchester.

S3. The invitation to imagine, or pretend, or to investigate whether, or to adopt some other meta-epistemic attitude to the assertion that 'It is raining (or not raining) in Manchester', which involves an invitation to think about or relate to it in some way (for example, fictionally, factually, and so on) without committing oneself to affirming or denying it; and of course without this imagining, or such affirmation or denial being the same thing as the presence or absence of rain in Manchester. This is an operation on the *tropic*.

S3 is very important in the concrete utopian movement of thought. The important point here, however, is that we have in S1–S3 instances of negativity or negation (or affirmation) at *three different levels*, involving negation *within reality*, negation *within factual discourse* and (at least by implication) negation *of factual discourse* within our mode of discourse when we engage in fictional or speculative, and so on, discourse. From within the epistemological process the first level will be seen to be in the intransitive dimension and the second and third in the transitive dimension. But if we switch perspectives to an ontological point of view, all three levels are seen to be constellationally contained within the intransitive dimension as parts of the world. (A *perspectival switch* moves from one transcendentally or dialectically necessary condition or aspect of a phenomenon, thing or totality to another which is also transcendentally or dialectically necessary for it.)[11]

In other words, there is a real difference between:

S1′: Being in (or travelling to) Brighton;
S2′: Making (or listening to) a statement about Brighton; and
S3′: Acting in a play (or story) about Brighton.

That is to say there is a difference between being in Brighton, being in a discourse about Brighton and being in a play or fiction about Brighton (for example, about discourse in Brighton).

The first crucial step in sequestering the possibility of referring to ontological absence or negativity, and hence real change as we understand it, was taken by Plato (and in modern times by Gottlob Frege). This consisted in tying reference to (positive) existence and presence, so that one could not refer to what was not, that is, to what was absent; one could not give an affirmative neustic or tick, $\sqrt{}$, to a negative phrastic content: $\sqrt{}(-e)$.

Against this, ontological absence is necessary in order to analyse and explain change in being, including change in our beliefs about being and change in our meta-epistemic attitudes towards being (as well as to differentiate the three).

The necessity of reference to absence

I now want to consider the extent to which reference to concepts of absence and negativity are necessary. The *meaning* or correct analysis and understanding of change always involves absence, more especially absenting; that is to say, in our ordinary understanding, change consists in, or at the very least involves the coming into being (absenting the absence) of something new or the passing out of (absenting the) being of something that was there. And this normally presupposes a continuant, an underlying substance that has or undergoes the change. Because of this, absence is at the very least necessary in order to analyse or understand the meaning of the human response to change.

Of course, in describing change we do not *have to use* the concept of absence. (Thus I did not use it in showing in Chapter 2 how, once we differentiated the transitive and intransitive dimensions, we could now coherently report, and so accommodate, scientific change.) However, upon analysis this is what it involves; that is to say, what it presupposes. In saying this, it is important to remember what I have urged in Chapter 1, namely that it is the job of philosophy (among other things) to analyse the unreflected presuppositions of our practices.

One could still argue, though, that the scientific or correct explanation of change does not involve absence, but merely the redistribution of unchanging elements or components. However, change cannot be completely explained in such a way when one is dealing with a basic or ultimate level, or when one is dealing with an emergent level, or more generally whenever one confronts a case of novelty. In the social world, because of the prevalence of emergence, change at any one level cannot be parsed in terms of the reorganisation of lower-order elements but centrally involves transformation, that is, a rupture or rift within elements or a new 'variety' at that level. Hence we have to presuppose the analysis of change as absenting, at least at that level.

However, it could still be said that such a change was caused by the impact on a thing of the reorganisation or redistribution of unchanging things in its environment, that is, by external events. But if the transformation has been caused by external pressure, there must be something about the thing in virtue of which it succumbs or responds to external pressure in this way, that is, it must be liable so to respond, so that the liability is an inner cause of the transformation, which cannot thus wholly be the result of the external reorganisation; that is, there must always be an endogenous component, as well as exogenous ones in any 'interaction' (which must thus always involve an element of 'intra-action' as well).[12]

So in the case of emergent entities, at the very least, change, involving a transformation or rupture at that level cannot be accounted for/explained totally in terms of an internal redistribution or external events, but must be explained at least in part by internal novelty or transformation, that is, as involving absenting – that is, in a non-monovalent way. This is to say that absence and absenting are irreducible in the meaning, analysis and explanation of change.

But there are two other reasons why the absenting analysis of ontological change is necessary.

What we are doing in such analysis is applying categories of change and absence to the world itself that we are perfectly prepared to apply to the transitive level, which deals with belief. But if our beliefs are themselves not to be hypostatised or extruded from the world, then we need an ontological absenting analysis of change to successfully situate change in belief. In order to avoid extruding those beliefs from the world, they must be a part of the world and so susceptible to the onto-logical analysis. Moreover, in order to make sense of the processes by which we come to change our beliefs we must understand the human operation of changing beliefs, itself, ontologically, that is, in terms of ontological absenting.

We can see one reason why extending critical realism to dialectical critical realism is necessary and implied by the concepts of basic critical realism. Extending our ontology to include negativity and absence, and *sui generis* change, is indispensable for the correct understanding of the meaning of change at any level. Furthermore, the possibility of giving a revisionary, redescriptive account of change (in terms of redistributions or external interaction) breaks down at ultimate or emergent levels and when we are considering beliefs or human actions and attitudes to beliefs. Of course, it is also the case that the concepts and categories of dialectical critical realism enormously extend the range of concepts for understanding the world.

Critical realism, in so far as it underlabours for science, must underlabour for a science that deals with changing subject matters, and this underlabouring will involve a defence and elaboration of the ideas of absence and absenting, negativity and negation in reality, and a defence of the categories and concepts we need to understand changes and their causes, including the concepts of contradiction (which includes an opposition between A and not-A) and other concepts tradi-tionally banned from use to describe the world.

The analysis of change in terms of difference

I have already noted the origins of the doctrine of ontological monovalence in a purely positive account of reality given by Parmenides. His injunction not to con-sider any negativity or change in reality is in a way the primordial pronouncement of the Western philosophical tradition. But it was Plato's subsequent analysis of change in terms of difference (an analysis that Aristotle did not question), and with it the idea that apparent change can always be redescribed in terms of different distributions of unchanging things that allowed mainstream philosophy to get away with its taboo. However, its victory proved to be a rather Pyrrhic one in that it could not coherently account for its superiority over its rivals, because a coherent account involves negation, nor could it coherently account for the processes of coming to understand its 'truth', which also involve negation. For a coherent and consistent philosophy of change, we must embrace change and absence and nega-tivity in reality, as much as in (and as including) our beliefs about reality.

To say 'Sophie dyed her hair' is different from saying 'Sophie's hair colour is different now from yesterday'. In particular it points to, and presupposes, a substan-tial process of change, which is what *explains* the difference.

Diagnostic value of absence

Focusing in particular on social analysis, absence has a remarkable diagnostic value. Looking at a social situation and asking what is *not* there, what is missing, will often give the researcher an invaluable insight into how the situation needs to change and/or how it will change.

Polysemy of absence and negation

In dialectical critical realism absence is understood to include non-existence anywhere anywhem. It is systematically bipolar, designating absenting processes, which may be of a distantiating[13] and/or transformative kind, as well as simple absence in a more or less determinate level or context-specific region of space–time. In fact it displays a four-fold polysemy, as product (that is, simple absence), process (simple absenting, for example, through divergent distantiation or substantial or non-substantial process), process-in-product (for example, as in the existential constitution of the nature of an absence by its geo-history) and as product-in-process (for example, in the iterable or non-iterable exercise of its causal powers)[14] (see Table 6.2). (These may be recursively embedded and systematically intermingled.) Absence includes, but is far from exhausted by the past and outside.

Negation and negativity

So far I have discussed absence and change but negation and negativity are important dialectical or 2E concepts that also need to be situated here. Like absence, negation has a process/product homonymy and a four-fold polysemy. This is displayed in Table 6.2. In talking of negation, it is important to differentiate *determinate* from *indeterminate* negation and absence. The Western philosophical tradition has been wont to consider only indeterminate negation, such as 'nothing'. But the main

TABLE 6.2 Polysemy and modes of absence[15]

Ontological–axiological chain	1M Non-identity	2E Negativity	3L Totality	4D Transformative agency
Concrete universal = singular	universality	a specific geo-historical trajectory	particular mediations	concrete singularity
Polysemy of absence	product	process	process-in-product	product-in-process
Causal modes of absence	transfactual causality	rhythmic causality	holistic causality	intentional causality
Concepts of negation	real negating process (substantial and non-substantial)	transformative negating process (substantial)	radical self-negating process	linear self-consciously negating process
Modes of radical negation	auto-subversion	self-transformation	self-realisation	self-overcoming

kinds of absences (and negations in this sense) with which dialectical critical realism is concerned are real determinate absences, such as we experience in hunger or the soil experiences in the absence of rain. The category of negation includes both the situation of absence and a process of absenting. It is useful to differentiate *real, transformative, radical* and *linear negation*. Real negation includes empty space (for example, the hole in the ozone layer or in a theory) as well as transformation. Transformative negation includes change induced by external as well as internal elements. Radical negation is self-transformation resulting from multiple determination within a totality. Linear negation is self-transformation in a unilinear sequence or line of transition.

6.3 Dialectic and 2E generally

I now turn to consider the other categories and concepts which dialectical critical realism introduces and/or refines at its second level, before reverting to the first level and thence proceeding to the third and fourth levels of the MELD schema.

Absence

Absence, which we have already discussed, is the central category of dialectic and of 2E, and indeed of dialectical critical realism. For whether dialectic is conceived of as argument, change or the augmentation of (or aspiration to) freedom, it depends upon the identification and elimination of mistakes, states of affairs and constraints, or more generally ills, which are argued alike to be absences.

Dialectic

Dialectic is a very old and venerable concept that I have discussed in detail elsewhere.[16] Its core meaning has to do with change, argument and/or freedom. Dialectical critical realism seeks to give a real definition of dialectic as involving the absenting of absences (including constraints and ills); and more especially as absenting absences (qua constraints) on absenting absences (qua ills [which may also be regarded as constraints]) − or, in effect, the *axiology of freedom*.[17] This definition covers ontological matters of socio-historical change, epistemological questions of remedying argument or reasoning, and ethical questions of human freedom. Argument, the socio-historical development of human being and ethics are all marked by what they lack. There is a fundamental bipolarity of absence and presence, so that negativity (or absence) is a condition of positive being;[18] and it is this essential relationship on which dialectic, which may be diffracted into a multiplicity of modes and figures, revolves.

Thus, if we identify the vocation of critical realism as underlabouring for science and practices oriented to human well-being, we may explicate this dialectically as removing (absenting) ideological rubbish (absences qua constraints) from the process of absenting absences (qua ills), such as ignorance, lack of understanding (of a particular sector or indeed the whole of reality). So dialectic in this sense really describes what critical realism is about.

We may dwell on this for a bit. At the beginning of basic critical realism – in transcendental realism – the first move was to get rid of (absent) the taboo on ontology, to undo it, by revindicating ontology. This was because the taboo (I argued) stood in the way of understanding science, which in turn blocked our efforts in the social sciences to understand the impediments to human well-being and flourishing.

The rational kernel of Hegelian dialectic

In this book I am attempting, among other things, to give an account of the uses and value of dialectical critical realism without a lot of textual reference to the writings of Hegel and Marx. However, it is important at this juncture to say something about them. It will be remembered that Marx talked about Hegel as isolating the secret of dialectic, its 'rational kernel'. Marx averred, in a letter to Engels, that if he had time, he would like to explain this secret 'in 2 or 3 printer's sheets' to the world at large.[19] Unfortunately he did not have time, and so (or so I will maintain) the rational kernel of Hegelian dialect has largely remained a secret ever since. True, in the second half of the nineteenth century a worthy text of several hundred pages appeared bearing the title *The Secret of Hegel*.[20] Regretfully, on reading this book, the secret remained as obscure as before. What then is it that excited Marx so much about Hegelian dialectic?

It is a very simple *learning process*, which indeed may be seen at work in science and in progressive social change.[21] Let me deal with science first. The process goes like this. Scientists seek to describe and explain some sector of reality. In their descriptions and explanations, they will inevitably leave something out. In many cases this will not matter; what they have left out will not be relevant to what they are seeking to explain. If, however, they have omitted a causally relevant factor, then sooner or later, as their work proceeds, the omission of this factor will generate a problem for the theory, a problem that may take the form of *contradictions* or other modes of *inconsistency* or *dualism* generally.[22] On a Kuhnian description of the scientific process, at this point we pass from normal to exceptional or revolutionary science. Failure to remedy this omission will result in the proliferation of contradictions or problems until the theory degenerates into entropic collapse. Clearly, what needs to happen when a scientific theory is in crisis is for the absence that is causing the problem, the incompleteness that is generating the inconsistencies, to be remedied. From an ontologically realist meta-perspective, this remedy will take the form of the discovery of something new (which of course was there all along) that the scientific theory had not taken into account. This discovery, once sufficient theoretical (and practical) work has been done, will eventually allow the restoration of consistency in the discipline. Generally, the role of contradiction or inconsistency in this process is to act as a *signalling device*, telling the relevant community that the universe of discourse needs to be expanded. In effect it signals to the scientific community that it has left something causally relevant out of its description of reality.

Something similar to this goes on in the social world. Thus one can take the case of the suffragettes, campaigning in the early twentieth century for the inclusion of women as electors, as part of the voting franchise. In effect, the suffragettes were saying: 'We women have been excluded from the body politic.' Thus within the first 20 or so years of the twentieth century, the electoral systems of the Western world were forced to move over to a more universal franchise.

One can also extend this second example to include a further twist of this dialectic by showing how the situation in the 1920s and 1930s had failed to remove another huge, glaring absence or omission from the body politic of the major countries of the Western world. For what had not been included were the colonies and their people. Thus one can see that a process of decolonisation would need to follow.

There is, of course, a further argument as to whether decolonisation was a substantive, or merely formal, change; and similarly one can argue about whether democracy does not need to be extended into say the economy and/or about whether one does not need to extend our existing concept or practice of democracy.

This is what I think excited Marx about Hegel's dialectic, and it surely pinpoints an essential mechanism of progress in science and social life: a *dialectic of learning processes*, whereby:

> (relevant absence generating) incompleteness → inconsistency → movement to greater totality, that is, a more inclusive or comprehensive theoretical or social situation.[23]

From the point of view of this dialectic, the crucial thing is what happens when a theory or a society faces contradictions or other kinds of problems. There are two characteristic responses to this: the dialectical or *negentropic* response, which is a movement towards greater coherence and inclusiveness; and the *entropic* or degenerative response. The prevalence of problems, whether manifest as contradictions or not, makes this a very useful schema for the analysis of social changes or non-changes (morphostases) of all types.

If this is the rational kernel of Hegelian dialectic, what is the 'mystical shell' that Marx also claimed to find? The mystical shell is precisely (or so I would urge) ontological monovalence, that is, the way in which Hegel was wont to resolve his contradictions no sooner than he announced them, in the restoration of positivity. This is what I call Hegel's *analytical reinstatement*.[24] In *Dialectic* and elsewhere I have elaborated on (i) Marx's critique of Hegel and (ii) the dialectical critical realist critique of Hegel and metacritique of Marx's critique of Hegel, a process which allows us to cast significant further light on Marxism, and so called 'actually existing socialism' in practice (see Chapter 8.3).[25]

Of course, differentiating entropic from negentropic or dialectical responses to problems and inconsistencies and so on is not to say that this is the only dimension along which to understand change. Thus we can distinguish endogenous from exogenous sources of change, revolutionary from reformist changes, and so on. Nor is it to say that there may not be a long stretch of time during which the way a situation is developing remains unclear or a long stretch of semi-equilibrium in which various alternatives to a negentropic resolution are tried out. Nor is it to make any kind of prediction. The *rational directionality of geo-history* (see section 6.7) implied by the dialectic of learning processes is at best a weak tendential one. This is especially so in a multiply fractured world of unresolved contradictions, where the dialectics of material change are diffracted in ever more complex ways.[26]

I have argued elsewhere that there is no reason to suppose that analogous processes of the dialectical kind do not apply to nature in the way in which absence, absenting and contradiction clearly do.[27]

The constellational containment of analytical within dialectical reason

Reference to Hegel's analytical reinstatement reminds me to say something about the difference between *dialectical* and *analytical* thought. Analytical thought is thought in which meanings and truth-values do not change. In science it is in fact relatively rare for meanings and truth values not to change. Generally, it is only at the end of a round of scientific enquiry – for instance, at the Leibnizian moment in the DREI(C) cycle of development I outlined in Chapter 2.4, when the research report or a paper is being prepared – that there is insistence on strictly analytical thought. It thus may be regarded as an occasionally useful moment or level of the more encompassing dialectical thought in which science, like every creative process, is more normally engaged. At certain critical moments in this process, science breaches the cardinal principle of analytical logic, that of non-contradiction, without however discarding it.[28] Thus it is best to think of a *dialectic of dialectical and analytical thought or reasoning*, in which dialectical overreaches (but does not transcend) analytical thought. More generally, dialectic can indeed be seen as the 'great loosener', freeing up our concepts from fixated or excessively fixed meanings and usages.[29]

There are a host of important categories including *process, contradiction*, and *development* that pivot on this analysis of absence, negativity and change. In particular it is important to see that the ontological employment of the category of contradiction is perfectly permissible. Thus, there is nothing wrong in saying that a sustainable world is inconsistent or in contradiction with our current levels of use of fossil fuels. Contradictions point to the need for a clear choice or resolution because, left to themselves, they will proliferate; and in themselves they put the agent in a double-bind situation, with the choice of action chronically underdetermined.[30]

Also very important in the dialectical critical realist development at 2E is the elaboration of the categories of *space, time, tense* and *process*. Space, time and causality may be especially fruitfully brought together in the idea of a *rhythmic*, or causally efficacious spatio-temporalising process (which I introduced in Chapter 4.2–4.3). It is this set of categories that underpins and informs critical realism's understanding of natural necessity in the social world, and that change is inexorable.[31] Also thematised in dialectical critical realism are the important concepts of the *presence of the past* and *future* (introduced in Chapter 4.5), and the *intrinsic exterior* or the *presence of the outside* (discussed in Chapter 8).[32] I now revert to the first level of MELD.

6.4 1M non-identity

Basic critical realism is already present at 1M and to an extent at 4D (human agency and practice). But in dialectical critical realism the ontology is deepened and the categories and concepts we may use for describing and understanding the world are considerably enhanced. 1M is the sphere under which we think ontology or being as such, and in particular being as *non-identity*. Most of the basic moves in transcendental realism involve differentiating relations of non-identity. Thus ontology is not the same as epistemology, the domain of the real is not the same as the domain of the actual, open systems are not closed, and so on. So non-identity plays a very big role at this stadion of dialectical critical realism. The two key concepts of non-identity are those of *structure* and *difference*, and we have already discussed these in Chapter 2. It was also mentioned there that ontology is not only *inexorable* but *all-encompassing*. Thus there is no way not to do ontology; and beliefs, including false and contradictory beliefs and illusions must all be allowed to be real, at least in so far as they are causally efficacious.

Dispositional and categorial realism

At 1M we have some important additions to the type of realism sustained here. Thus we have *dispositional realism*, which is realism about possibilities as well as actualities.[33] It is clear that the notion of the possible is a more encompassing one than the actual – for if an actuality is real, then so must the possibility that it actualises be real too. The analysis of dispositional realism is in fact presupposed by the analysis of causal powers and tendencies in transcendental realism. But dispositional realism is also important in ethical thought, where it plays a large role in *concrete utopianism*. Concrete utopianism involves a differentiation within the domain of possibilities of those that are real from those that are not. 'Real' here means 'realisable', and designates which possibilities may be actualised given a particular constraint. Such a constraint may be a family budget or the level of resources of a department or a school, and so on.

A second kind of realism developed here is *categorial realism*.[34] Categorial realism says that the categories and concepts developed by philosophy are themselves real. This is to say that the world is characterised not just by particular causes but by causality as such. Clearly, categorial realism is necessary if we are to present transcendental realism consistently in a transcendental realist way. Otherwise, in presenting it we would not be talking about the world, but a space somehow extruded from it, such as a space of Platonic forms. Categorial realism is important because philosophers, especially from Kant onwards, have regarded the categories as things we impose on the world, subjective impositions on being rather than inherent in being itself.

Reference and referential detachment

Following from dispositional and categorial realism, we have an analysis of *reference* as essential to semiosis or meaning-making; *referential detachment*, involving the detachment of the act of referring from what is referred to, is essential to science and everyday life. These concepts were introduced in Chapter 2.2 and 2.6. In section 2 of the present chapter we argued for an extension in the philosophical concept of the referent to include negative existence (absence and change), phrastic content generally, totalities, whole states of affairs, and so on. This is perfectly in accord with our normal usage of course.

The truth tetrapolity: a multicomponential theory of truth

Dialectical critical realism develops the analysis of *truth* that was implicit in basic critical realism.[35] According to this analysis, truth is a multi-componential concept, straddling each of four distinct meanings or components, which I refer to as *the truth tetrapolity*. This is displayed in Table 6.3, along with some key correspondences, including the *ethical tetrapolity*. The four meanings are as follows:

i.   the *fiduciary* meaning – in saying that something is true, I am saying 'you can trust me, take my word for it';
ii. the *evidential* component – this is the feature most often highlighted by philosophers. It involves saying 'there is sufficient evidence for a proposition, it is warrantedly assertible';
iii. the *expressive-referential* meaning – in saying '"the grass is green" is true', I am saying that 'the grass is green' perfectly expresses the greenness of grass. Indeed, what is a better way of reporting it? If the fiduciary aspect of truth locates it as an interpersonal or social bond and the evidential one puts it in the transitive dimension, then the expressive-referential use of truth sees it as straddling the ontological/epistemological, transitive/intransitive divide; and
iv. the *alethic* use of truth – this occurs when we say something such as 'the truth of water boiling at 100 degrees is its molecular constitution' or the 'the truth that all metals conduct electricity is their possession of a free electron'.

What this alethic use does is point to the reason or ground in the world in virtue of which, from an evidential or expressive point of view the truth *is* a truth; that is, the reason in the world, the generative structure that makes the proposition true. So the alethic concept of truth is grounded in ontological stratification; but once we have it, we may use truth in a wider ontological sense to designate quite simply anything that makes a proposition true. We thereby include in our theory of truth the referential counterpart of the expressive use of truth. This is an important addition to the critical realist armoury of concepts.[36]

Alethic truth or *necessity* is the objective pole of *three levels of natural necessity* related to human praxis: at the subjective pole lies *axiological necessity*, with the *reality principle* (which I adapt from Freud) in between. These concepts thus offer three

TABLE 6.3 Polysemy and modes of truth and untruth[37]

Ontological–axiological Chain	1M Non-identity → 7A/A identity	2E Negativity	3L Totality	4D Transformative agency
Concrete universal = singular	universality	a specific geo-historical trajectory	particular mediations	concrete singularity
Judgement form	evidential	descriptive	imperatival-fiduciary	expressively veracious
Truth tetrapolity – truth as	(4) ontological, alethic (ID)	(2) adequating (warrantedly assertible) or epistemic (TD)	(1) normative-fiduciary (IA of TD)	(3) expressive referential (TD/ID)
Modes of alethic truth	axiological necessity, reality principle alethic truth as such	praxis-dependent	totalising (oriented to maximising explanatory power)	contextualised by the dialectic of the singular science concerned
Qualities of truth	grounded	dynamic	totalising	context-sensitive
Ethical tetrapolity	(4) freedom as universal emancipation; eudaimonia or moral alethia	(2) explanatory critical theory complex (exlanatory critique + concrete utopias + theories of transition)	(1) fiduciariness	(3) totalising depth-praxis
Modes of falsity	(3) in an object or being to its essential nature (ID)	(1) about an object or being (at any one level of reality) (TD)	untrustworthiness	(2) in an object or being (at that level of reality) (TD/ID)
Form of ideology	(3) underlying generative (alethic) falsity	(1) theoretical		(2) practical
Form of alienation	(3) self-alienation	(1) conceptual		(2) practical
Holy trinity	ontological realism	epistemic relativism		judgemental rationalism
Unholy trinity	ontological monovalence	epistemic fallacy		primal squeeze on empirically controlled theory and natural necessity
Domains of Reality	Real	Empirical/Conceptual		Actual

Note. IA = the intrinsic (normative) aspect of the transitive dimension; ID = intransitive dimension. TD = transitive dimension. Correspondences with the (overlapping) domains of reality are loose.

perspectives on the same thing. The concept of alethic truth, which concerns natural necessity as such and in general, is not at all tied to specific concrete human practices, whereas axiological necessity always is, and the reality principle relates to concrete practices in general.

TINA compromise formations

Following on from the alethic sense of truth, which I call *alethic realism*, we have an important idea that we have encountered a number of times already: that of *TINA compromise formations*.[38] A TINA formation occurs when a false belief in theory is sustained by elements of a more adequate practice, in virtue of which the theory/practice ensemble manages to sustain itself. The idea at work here is that reality contains *axiological necessities*; these are imperatives that must be met for any belief (or social situation) to maintain itself.[39] Thus, as we have seen in Chapter 2.8, there is no way that a chemist or physicist, whatever their theoretical beliefs, can possibly avoid sustaining a distinction in practice between closed and open systems and therefore a distinction between the real and the actual. What happens in practice is that these distinctions are applied unselfconsciously for the most part, whilst any theoretical or philosophical apparatus that denies the distinction just runs idle, playing no role in the practice. However, in the social world TINA formations are not always so benign, for the greater role of philosophy and methodology means that false philosophical beliefs impinge on the realm of practice and so we get all kinds of mish-mash compromises with reality by virtue of which a false or otherwise inadequate theory/practice ensemble is able to stumble on. The TINA formation is accordingly a cardinal concept for the metacritique of irrealism in section 6.6 of the present chapter, which is further elaborated in Chapter 8.

The logic of emancipatory projects

Also justified by a 1M analysis is an elementary *logic of emancipatory discourse*. Typically an emancipatory project will posit a subject, such as humanity, or some section of it, that has untrammelled or effectively unlimited possibilities in virtue of the possession of a capacity or power. (This may be our capacity to work and produce goods and services for ourselves, for example.) At the same time, this capacity is constrained by the existence of a level that denies or suppresses it. (This might be the existence of class relations or gross inequalities in the distribution of resources.) So we have an effectively unlimited capacity and a superstructure that suppresses it or prevents it developing. The logic of emancipation thus consists in the jettisoning or throwing off of this superstructure. This can often be seen as an act of *disemergence*, but when it is in part or in whole within the subject it takes the form of an act of *shedding* as well as overthrow or transformation. This theme is resumed in the next chapter.

6.5 3L totality

Internal relations versus ontological extensionalism

Moving now to 3L (2E negativity was discussed in section 6.3), totality involves taking two or more things together or as a whole. Within this category the most important philosophical concept is that of *internal relations*. Two objects may be said to be internally related when a change in one affects the other.

The idea of internal relations may be illustrated by the relations between successive statements of speech acts within a discourse or action within a frame of social life generally. Thus,

D1 a statement or discourse about Brighton is, or may be, internally related to

D2 a question about Sussex or travel, but it will not typically be internally related to

D3 the absence of rain in Manchester or a game of chess in Springfield, Illinois, or

D4 the onset of the Crimean War, or

D5 the importation of bananas into Sweden.

It is sometimes possible to treat objects separately in our dealings with the natural world, but in the social world the philosophical dogma of *ontological extensionalism,*[40] that it is always possible to treat objects as distinct, self-contained individuals, atomistically, seriously breaks down. Thus the words that I utter or write now are internally related to the words in the last sentence. A question is internally related to an answer. Relations between the members of a family are clearly like this. Internal relations may be developed and systematically presented in terms of the idea of *holistic causality*. This involves a combination of internally related elements, which cohere as a whole in as much as the form of the combination causally co-determines the elements; and the elements causally co-determine (mutually mediate or condition each other) and so causally co-determine the form.

The concrete universal

Also very important here is the idea of the *concrete universal* and *concrete universality*.[41] Mainstream philosophy, at least in the analytical tradition, has normally been committed to *abstract universality*. This is the idea that for any element x its relationship with any element y may be expressed as a universal, such as 'all pens are ...'. However, there are no such abstract universals in the world. All the instances of universals we encounter in science and in everyday life are concrete universals. That is to say, they take embodied, concretised, particular forms; and as such must be analysed as *multiple quadruplicities*, that is, as involving the following four components (displayed in Table 6.3):

(a) a *universal* component, as instantiating transfactually applicable properties and laws (for example, a core universal human nature, grounded in genetic constitution);

(b) as constituted by *particular mediations* which differentiate it from others of its kind. For example, this particular woman (an instance of the universal woman) may be a nurse, trade unionist, mother of three, fan of the Rolling Stones, and so on.

Moreover each instance of such a differentiated universal will be characterised by

(c) a *specific geo-historical trajectory*. This will *further particularise* it from others who share its universal components and particular mediations (for example this particular woman may have been born in Goa thirty five years ago, and so on).

Moreover each geo-historically specific and mediated instance of a universal will also be

(d) irreducibly *unique* or a *concrete singular* (for example, this unique embodied personality, Vanirathna). This irreducible uniqueness would differentiate two instances of a universal even if they were found to satisfy all the same mediations and have the same geo-historical trajectory.

Every instance of a concrete universal must be analysed in this four-fold way; but by the same token, every particular thing or individual, will reveal these four aspects, which thus appear as the aspects of the concrete universal = singular.

Totality and constellationality

Analysing things in terms of their systematic interconnections inevitably leads to looking at things in terms of the concept of *totality*. Clearly, in science, or in a practical situation when faced with a problem, what one needs to do is to understand the world or the situation in its totality, by which one means 'in a way that includes all relevant components'.

In social life we are generally concerned with *partial totalities*, which are constituted by some external and some internal relations. In particular, one kind of partial totality is especially important, a *sub-totality*, where there is a block or hiatus between the parts of the totality. Connected to this is the concept of *alienation*. Alienation is the condition of being something other than oneself or than what is essential and intrinsic to one's nature or identity, for example, of being split off from or set over against the world from which we emerged. This important concept was introduced in Chapter 3.5 and is further discussed in Chapter 8.1.

In general, when things are internally related, I talk of *intra-connection* or *intra-action* rather than interconnection and interaction. Intra-action is as important as inaction in social life.

A very important 3L concept is that of *constellationality*. This defines a situation where one term that is normally opposed to another term overreaches and contains it. Thus, as we have seen (Chapters 2.10 and 4.3), we can talk of ontology including epistemology, that is of beliefs as real and therefore included within the subject matter of ontology, even when we continue to insist on existential intransitivity, that is, the idea that beliefs have an object independent of them. In such a situation we can say that ontology constellationally overreaches and contains epistemology. We have also seen how dialectics constellationally embraces analytics.

6.6 4D transformative praxis

Transformed transformative practice and related concepts

The dialectical critical realist dialectic is differentiated from the Hegelian dialectic in that it starts with non-identity rather than identity, involves a radically different concept of negativity and is concerned with open, not closed totalities. But, very importantly, it also has a fourth element, that of human *praxis*. This is important because it is human agency that must resolve the contradictions and dilemmas of social life, even when these are purely theoretical ones.

A fourth range of concepts is therefore developed around human agency or the idea of *transformed transformative practice*[42] and includes the notions of the irreducibility of intentionality, agency and spontaneity in social life. Thus one can neither not intend, nor not act, nor not act basically or spontaneously (without thinking about it in the moment of acting) if one is to do anything, that is, perform any action at all.[43] This is what I have called the *axiological imperative*.[44] Agency must of course be conceived of in terms of the idea of *four-planar social being*, which we have already discussed in Chapter 2 and elsewhere. Also important here is the idea of the dislocated, disjoint *duality of structure and agency* introduced in Chapter 3.

Power₂ relations and their metacritique

In dialectical critical realism the contrast between *power₂* or power-over – the kind of power exercised by masters over slaves in *master–slave-type societies* – and *power₁* or transformative capacity as such assumes increased importance. While power₂ is linked to both Hegel's master–slave dialectic and Marx's analysis of the exploitation of labour-power under capitalism, dialectical critical realism generalises it to all socially structured power relations, such as those of gender,[45] ethnicity, (dis)ability and age, through which agents or groups get their way against the overt wishes or real interests (grounded in their concrete singularities) of others.

But dialectical critical realism also relates the significance of historical power₂ relations to the forms of Western philosophy, in its metacritique₂ of that tradition. (A *metacritique₁* identifies significant absences in a theory, a *metacritique₂* in addition explains why such a theory is believed and is thus a form of explanatory critique, which I discussed in Chapter 5.)[46] Thus analytical philosophy may be seen to secrete an ontology of stasis. In this way it unselfconsciously normalises past changes and freedoms while denying present and future ones, thus helping to maintain the status quo.[47] Since an ontology of stasis is closely linked to the cardinal errors that characterise the Western philosophical tradition, such as ontological monovalence, dialectical critical realism raises fundamental questions about the relation between power$_2$ relations and knowledge.

The metacritique of irrealism

Irrealist philosophy is philosophy that is not transcendental realist, more specifically philosophy that commits the categorial errors of the epistemic fallacy (1M), onto-logical monovalence (2E), ontological extensionalism (3L) and reductionism or dual-ism (4D), thereby destratifying, denegativising, detotalising and de-agentifying being. The dialectical critical realist metacritique of irrealism[48] is structured around an analy-sis that sees irrealism as depending on a combination of (immanent) *anthroporealism* and *transcendent realism*.

The epistemic fallacy (which reduces the world to our knowledge of it) (i) con-ceals a deeply rooted *anthropocentric* bias in irrealist thought, underpinning which is what I call the *anthropic fallacy* – the analysis of being in terms of (some attribute(s)) of human being; and (ii) co-exists with the reciprocating *ontic fallacy* (which reduces our knowledge to the world, naturalising knowledge and *anthropomorphising* the world) in what I call the *anthroporealist exchanges* (see Figure 6.1).

Here the result of the categorial error of defining being in terms of attributes of human beings is manifest in the duplicity of *subject–object* (epistemic–ontic) *identity theory*: anthropocentric identity theory presupposes an anthropomorphic realist dual, the result of which may be equivocity over the independent existence of things and the dogmatic anthropomorphic reification of socially produced facts, as depicted in Figure 6.1.

At the core of anthroporealism or subject–object identity theory lies egocentric-ity and abstract universality, resulting in a repetitive uniformity and inner empti-ness, a McDonaldised world. This vista of the incessant production of sameness and nothingness, however, always both leaves traces of something determinate, a defi-nite footprint, and (or so metaReality will claim) depends upon human ingenuity and teamwork, definite degrees of inter-human solidarity and skill.

The necessary complement to anthroporealism or the reduction of being to a superficialised or depthless knowledge is an imaginary transcendent realism. This is

	TD		ID	
anthropocentricity	thought/ experience	ef ⟵ ⟶ of	material object causal efficacy	anthropomorphism

FIGURE 6.1 The anthroporealist exchanges entraining subject–object identity theory[49]

Note: TD = transitive dimension; ID = intransitive dimension; ef = epistemic fallacy; of = ontic fallacy.

required to compensate for anthroporealism's lack of a concept of ontological depth and stratification. In the absence of such a concept, an *achieved* identity theory is impossible, because regardless of the theory the world exists independently and acts transfactually. The aporias of, for example, the transdictive complex thus appear irresolvable to the identity theorist unless a transcendent realism is tacitly or implicitly invoked (for example, fideistically). At the heart of transcendent realism lies various *imaginaries*, in which reality TV, a lottery ticket, the cult of celebrity, window gazing in the shopping malls of the 'filthy rich' or the promotion of one's football team in a different culture on the other side of the world co-mingle in a fantasy world of Disneyfication, the imaginary rewards for real drudgery and/or boredom. However, just as the world of the repetition of the same in anthroporealism leaves traces and residues on material reality, so does the surrogate world of fantasy necessitate and depend on definite psychic states and real changes, however seemingly shallow (at least from the outside), in real human beings.

Together anthroporealism and transcendent realism constitute the *irrealist ensemble*. Even with a transcendent reinforcement, this internally inconsistent system, in the face of the axiological necessities it violates, requires a *defensive shield* incorporating a metaphysical λ (*ceteris paribus*) clause or safety net. The resulting TINA formation (which constitutes the *irrealist* theory problem-field solution set

$$(1) \longrightarrow \{[[(2) \quad + \quad (3)] + \quad (4)] \qquad\qquad (5)\} \longrightarrow (6)$$

identity theory $\underset{of}{\overset{ef}{\rightleftarrows}}$ ontic dual · transcendent complement

scepticism · anthroporealism · transcendent realism · defensive shield · TINA compromise formation

irrealist ensemble

(e.g. metaphysical λ clause)

FIGURE 6.2 The irrealist TINA compromise formation or problematic[50]

Note: ef = epistemic fallacy; of = ontic fallacy.

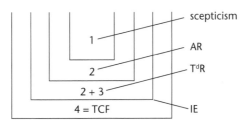

- scepticism
1 - AR
2 - T^{d}R
2 + 3
4 = TCF - IE

FIGURE 6.3 Core structure of the TINA compromise formation[51]

Note: AR = anthroporealism; T^{d}R = transcendent realism; IE = irrealist ensemble; TCF = TINA compromise formation.

or *problematic*) is depicted in Figure 6.2. Its core structure, displayed in Figure 6.3, is that of any TINA formation.

As we will see in Chapter 8.2, the epistemic fallacy is very closely bound up with ontological monovalence, the view that being is purely positive, which has its authoritative source in Plato. When Plato analysed change in terms of difference, he confined change and absence to the epistemological domain, banishing them from the world (in his terms). But the epistemic fallacy has a similar effect: since it forbids talk about the world, absence and change are repressed. Ontological monovalence is thus also at the heart of irrealism. Together with the epistemic fallacy it involves a dialectic of *fusion* and *fission* that produces irrealism's characteristic errors. Fusion collapses distinct strata of being into the level of the empirical, negativity into positivity, the parts into the whole, mind into matter; fission splits off knowledge from the world, absence from presence, the parts from the whole, and mind from matter. While apparently opposed, fusion and fission tacitly complement each other; that is, they are *dialectical antagonists* or counterparts,[52] as Aristotle and Plato arguably were,[53] united in a common mistaken problematic defined by the epistemic-ontic fallacy, ontological monovalence and what I call primal squeeze or actualism (see further Chapter 8.2). Nor are they confined to philosophy, which always resonates with its social context. Thus one form of illicit fusion in capitalist modernity is *the exchange of non-equivalents* (labour for labour-power), which is pivotal to the wage-labour/capital contract, and without which the capitalist economy could not function. This is in turn connected with the *representation of sectional interests as universal*, which is characteristic of free-market ideologies, as when sectional Anglo-American, and so on, interests are identified with those of 'the international community'. And a prevalent form of illicit fission at work in capitalism (which itself may be sourced to *generative* separation, alienation or fission) is the *non-parity of equivalents* that is evident when women and immigrants are paid less for the same work than native males, which is also connected with an ideological mechanism: *the representation of universal interests as sectional* (as when global ecological crisis is presented as a sectional, purely Green concern). Fission and fusion may thus be put critically both to vital politico-ethical and (in philosophy) to systematic-diagnostic use.[54]

The most important development within 4D is however contained in its dialectic of freedom.

6.7 The dialectic of freedom

We are at once desiring, acting creatures and judging, speaking beings, but our agency has discursive presuppositions and our judgements practical ones. Dialectical critical realism's *dialectic of freedom*[55] (or *dialectic of desire to freedom*) argues that we can derive the formal criteria for the good society, involving the free flourishing of each as a condition for the free flourishing of all, from either our agency or our discourse alone. We can do this by means of either (1) a *dialectic of agency* (or of desire and agency) or (2) a *dialectic of discourse* (or of judgement and speech action or discourse). Substantively, this involves a *totalising depth-praxis*, including research, tending in the direction of universal free flourishing and implied by the research. The combination of formal and substantive criteria, and the dialectical cross-fertilisation of each, issues in *dialectical reason*, or the *coherence of theory and practice in practice*. This is level (vii) of the levels of rationality we discussed in the last chapter, the presentation of which we postponed to this chapter: *geo-historical directional rationality*, which is powered by the pulse of freedom or the real yearning and striving of people everywhere, as the dialectic of freedom shows, to absent constraints on free flourishing.

The most compact way to present dialectical critical realism is in terms of the basic structure of the dialectic of freedom. This can be written as:

> absence – elemental desire – referential detachment – constraint – understanding of the causes of the constraint – dialectic of solidarity (immanent critique and dialectical universalisability) – totalising depth praxis – emancipatory axiology.[56]

The dialectic of agency and the dialectic of discourse each express the other pole of the coherence of theory and practice; and both effect a *double transition from form to content*: first to the action entailed by solidarity and the totalising depth-praxis, and second to the free flourishing of all as the content of the good society. As acting and speaking beings we cannot truly flourish in a social context characterised by master–slave-type social relations and alienation, and we cannot be true to ourselves unless we work towards such a society. Thus emancipation is also a coming home to ourselves, self-realisation. The logic of this cannot be brought out fully until we have a finer-grained analysis of the self, which we have in the philosophy of metaReality. Here I confine myself to the logic expounded in dialectical critical realism.

The dialectics of (1) desire and agency and (2) judgement and speech action or discourse take us to the same result. A key role is played in both dialectics by the *practico-theoretical duality* of both desire/agency and discourse.

(1) The *dialectic of desire/agency* trades on (a) the conceptual and quasi-propositional character of desire and intentional agency and (b) the fact that desire (want, need) logically entails a meta-desire for the removal of constraints on the satisfaction of desire (want, need). These take us into the provinces of discourse and sociality/solidarity, specifically the wants and actions of others. For in desiring something we are logically committed to the removal of constraints, including power$_2$ or master–slave-type relations, on the satisfaction of the desire, and thus to the removal of all dialectically similar constraints. Here it is important to recall that the concrete universal embraces all concretely singular instances of a kind, here humankind. If I exclude any human being from my concern to remove constraints, I define myself by that relation of exclusion and so limit my own freedom. Freedom is dialectically indivisible.[57]

(2) The *dialectic of speech/discourse* trades on (a) the evaluative and practical implications of factual discourse and (b) the consideration that a judgement or assertion carries the imperatival-fiduciary commitment that it is reliable and can be acted on, such that my saying 'X is true' entails 'trust me, you can act on it'. These take us back to the questions of my actions and my solidarity with the addressees of my

remarks. For to say 'trust me, you can act on it' is to say that in your circumstances we ourselves would do it, and this commits us to acting in solidarity with all such addressees.

More fully, (1) the dialectic of agency is set up by the condition that it is analytic to the concept of desire that in having a desire we have an interest in removing the constraints on it (including the constraints imposed by master–slave- or power$_2$-type relations), constraints that are ills and falsehoods to concretely singularised human nature. This stems, as already noted, from the intentionality of human praxis; that is, from the conceptual and implicitly teleological character of human agency. Thus in seeking to absent an ill we are logically committed to removing all dialectically similar ills, *ceteris paribus*. This entails absenting their causes, hence explanatory critique and totalising depth praxis. Theory/practice consistency in this process then requires that our actions and the theories informing them be both directionally progressive and universally accountable, such that they are transfactually (1M), actionably (2E), concretely (3L) and transformatively (4D) grounded. In absenting a constraint, I am thus committed to the removal of all dialectically similar constraints and thence to the removal of all remediable constraints as constraints, that is, of constraints in so far as they are dialectically similar in being constraints; and thence to a society free of such constraints and to the realisation of *assertorically imperatively sensitised concretely singularised equality* of autonomy, flourishing and freedom. (By 'assertorically imperatively sensitised' I mean oriented to *these* agents in *these* contexts in *these* processes, assertorically – not categorically – imperatival or prescriptive, sensitive to the concrete singularity of people.) This is the basic form of the dialectic of agency.

In short, the dialectic of desire or agency proceeds as follows:

> [desire to absent constraint (ill) → logical commitment to absent dialectically similar ills] → (1) absent all ills as such → (2) content of the explanatory critical theory complex [= explanatory critique + concrete utopianism + theory of transition] ↔ (3) totalising depth praxis of emancipatory axiology → (4) freedom qua universal human emancipation (moral alethia).

Turning to (2) the dialectic of judgement and discourse, we may note more generally that making a judgement implies expressive veracity, plus descriptive and evidential adequacy, as well as fiduciariness, and that each of these components is universalisable.

This stems from the condition more generally that any judgement or speech act has four internally related components or dimensions, which are implications of its being performed. In particular, it should be:

(a) *expressively veracious*, in as much as one gives one's assent to it;
(b) (assertorically) *imperatival-fiduciary*, in so far as it implies that it is reliable and can be acted on in appropriate circumstances;
(c) *descriptive*, in claiming that it indicates the way things are;

(d) *evidential*, saying that it is in principle well grounded.

Each of these four moments of the judgement form[58] is dialectically universalisable as follows:

(a) expressive veracity : 'if I had to act in these circumstances, this is what I would act on';
(b) fiduciariness: 'in exactly your circumstances, this is the best thing to do';
(c) descriptive: 'in exactly the same circumstances, the same result would ensue';
(d) evidential: 'in exactly the same circumstances, the reasons would be the same'.

Note that the imperatival and descriptive-evidential aspects together entail that practico-theoretical duality is intrinsic to the judgement-form. Assertorically imperatival sensitised solidarity entrains a dialectic of self and solidarity presupposing a commitment to remove constraints on the addressee's flourishing or, in other words, to absent her alienation from anything intrinsic to her well-being. That is to say, the goal of concretely singularised universal emancipation is implicit in every expressively veracious remark.

Universalisability is implicit in the fiduciary nature of the expressively veracious remark, and we can move progressively through the logic of simple universalisability (equality simpliciter) to that of assertorically sensitised, concretely singularised equality and thence to that of assertorically sensitised, concretely singularised autonomy. In so far as the speaking creature asserts a judgement as to what another should do or what should be the case, this implies a commitment to *solidarity*, that is, in so far as *ought* presupposes not just that the agent *can* but that the addresser *will* engage a commitment to a totalising depth praxis.

In short, the dialectic of discourse or speech action goes as follows:

> [expressive veracity → axiological commitment] → (1) fiduciariness → (2) content of the explanatory critical theory complex [= explanatory critique + concrete utopianism + theory of transition] ↔ (3) totalising depth praxis → (4) freedom qua universal human emancipation (moral alethia).

To reiterate, the dialectics of discourse and of agency have fundamentally similar overall logics, each expressing the other pole of the coherence of theory and practice in practice. Their four moments comprise what I designate the *ethical tetrapolity*[59] (see Table 6.3). Notice that in this tetrapolity the role of alethic truth in the truth tetrapolity (section 6.4, above) has its counterpart in the human moral alethia or object/ive (eudaimonia). As acting and speaking beings we cannot be true to ourselves unless we are practically oriented to such a society; nor can we flourish in a demi-real social context characterised by master–slave-type relations of domination and alienation. As we will see in Chapter 7, the deep content of these dialectics is thematised in the philosophy of metaReality in terms of the transcendentally real or alethic self; so that *emancipation is a coming home to ourselves,* or *self-realisation.*

Concepts of freedom[60]

What concept of freedom is implied in these dialectics? How do we get to the good or eudaimonistic society on these dialectics? And what is the role of solidarity? We start with a very basic concept of freedom:

1a. *Agentive freedom.* This is the capacity to do otherwise, which is analytic to the concept of intentional action.

Then we have the following dialectical progression, in which the later concepts remedy weaknesses or incompleteness in the earlier ones.

1b. *Formal legal freedom*, which neither implies nor is implied by 1a;
2a. *Negative freedom* from constraints which, since the absence of a capacity to do *x* can always be viewed as a constraint on doing *x*, is equivalent to
2b. *Positive freedom* (to do *x*, become *y*, and so on);
3. *Emancipation* from specific constraints, where emancipation is defined as the transformation from unwanted, unintended and/or oppressive structures or states of affairs to wanted, needed, and/or liberating ones; a special (and implied) case of which is then
3′. *Universal human emancipation.*

If we now introduce the concept of

4. *Autonomy* qua self-determination; we can then form the derivative concepts of
4′. *Rational autonomy* and
4″. *Universal human autonomy* in nature, which to be universalisable must be concretely singularised, that is:
4‴. *Universal concretely singularised human autonomy* in nature, specifically subject to the rights of other species and future generations.

These can now be further elaborated in the concept of freedom as

5. *Well-being* (oriented to the satisfaction of needs and the absence of remediable ills) and correspondingly
5′. *Universal concretely singularised well-being*; and thence to freedom as
6. *Flourishing*, with the emphasis turning to the presence of achievable goods and the realisation of possibilities, including possibilities for development; and
7. *Universal concretely singularised human flourishing* in nature or the eudaimonistic society, to which the logic of dialectic universalisability inexorably points, or so I argue.[61]

Note that, if the emphasis in the dialectic of desire is on freedom, that in the dialectic of judgement is on solidarity. But for each of these freedoms, a requisite form of solidarity is necessarily implicated; and the link between the freedom demanded and the solidarity to be secured is given by the logic of dialectical universalisability.

Moral realism and ethical naturalism

Dialectical critical realism is committed to a combination of moral realism and ethical naturalism, which are presupposed by the dialectic of freedom. As I deploy the term, *ethical naturalism* is the view that transitions from facts to value are not only possible in philosophy and social science but mandatory; that is, ethical naturalism is the theory and practice of explanatory critique, which was the subject of Chapter 5. *Moral realism* holds that morality is an objective (intransitive) property of the world. Ethical naturalism grounds a distinction, within moral realism, between the domains of actually existing human morality (dm_a), which is susceptible to explanatory critique, and the moral real (moral alethia or object/ive) of the human species (dm_r), which explanatory critical philosophy and science may discover. On this view, morality, like truth, has a properly ontological and alethic employment; and, like knowledge, morality has an intransitive object/ive.[62] The human moral alethia or object/ive is, I have argued, universal free flourishing in nature.[63] Moral realism is constellationally embedded within the geo-historical development of human society or four-planar social being, allowing us to define a variety of different modes in which ethical systems have stood to social actuality. Thus, where the moral real (moral alethia) is 'the real' and actually existing morality is 'the actual', we can delineate the following three patterns:

> the real *in* the actual;
> the real *beyond* and *against* the actual;
> the real *under* the actual.[64]

In Chapter 9 we make use of this schema to show the various ways in which the metaReal stands to the world of duality dominated by demi-reality.

Note that the transfactual character of moral truth means that dialectical critical realist ethics depends neither on a neo-Kantian ideal-speech situation, in the manner of Habermas, nor on a neo-contractarian original position in the style of John Rawls. However, it is well to remember that the logic of dialectical universalisability in actual history will always be a messy affair.[65] Moreover, as a transfactual, processually oriented, concretised, transformatively directional norm, this logic is subject to both multiple *ceteris paribus* clauses and a number of side constraints, including *actionability* or *feasibility*; *prefigurationality* (including means–ends consistency); *non-triumphalism* (awareness of the fallibility and limits of our knowledge); and *non-substitutionism* (the self-referentiality of all true emancipation). Non-substitutionism is entailed by the *primacy of self-referentiality* or self-transformation in social change, a principle I elaborate in the works of the spiritual turn; one changes society by first (and also) changing oneself.[66] Furthermore, although there are no a priori limits on solidarity, it must always be assertorically sensitised to the concrete singularity of the agent concerned and counterbalanced with the other priorities of a balanced life, including the necessary space for *amour de soi* (love of our [real] selves) and self-development.

However, there is the further consideration that to be practically useful the processes of solidarity and dialectical universalisation should not be *too* complicated; in particular they should allow for spontaneity and perhaps a small element of chance.

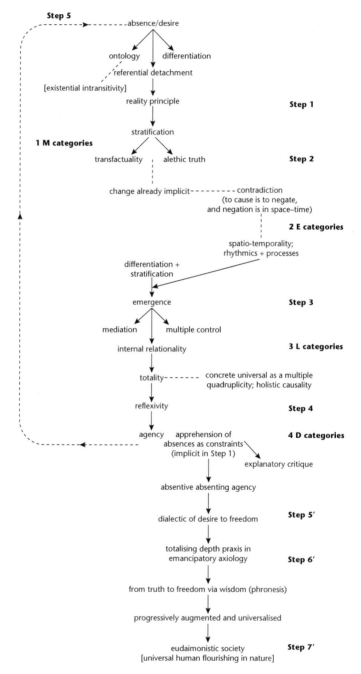

FIGURE 6.4 The dialectical presentation of dialectical critical realism[67]

It may often be best to make use of rough and ready rules of thumb or the catalaxy of existing institutions like the market (subject to overall regulation) and correct their results. In practice the realisation in actual history of the dialectic of freedom, and the interdependence of solidarity and freedom it entails will depend on the extent to which circumstances or policy permit or necessitate education or consciousness-raising oriented to all planes of social being and each of the cognitive, conative, affective, expressive and performative components of action (see Figure 3.4).

6.8 The dialectical presentation of dialectical critical realism

The main theses and categories of dialectical critical realism can be presented in just seven steps (see Figure 6.4). They start from the arguments for ontology. (1) Beginning with *absence*, taking the form of desire, we establish in one step referential detachment, the horizon of those axiological necessities that comprise the reality principle, the case for ontology and the concept of existential intransitivity, and the necessity for differentiation as a condition for scientific classification and explanation. (2) The second leap is therefore to *stratification*, entailing both transfactuality and alethic truth. Change is already implicit in the primordial act of referential detachment or even in the onset of desire. But we make this explicit from the metatheorem that to change is to cause is to negate and, if determinate, to absent; and that to contradict is to negate, and we can develop the full range of 2E categories here, from constraint through dialectical contradiction and overt conflict to non-antagonistic argumentation. We are now in the realm of space, time and tensed process; and, together with stratification and contradiction, this leads us onto (3) the plane of *emergence* and, with it, multiple control, mediation, internal relationality and thence directly into the 3L sphere of totality, which encompasses the multiple quadruplicity of the concrete universal = singular and the phenomena of holistic causality. (4) *Reflexivity* is the inwardised form of totality and manifests itself in the agency of stratified selves over distantiated space–time. (5) *Agency*, on the one hand, leads us back to our starting point of the absenting involved in anything from speech action or cooking a meal to experimental praxis. Lack, on the other hand, as suffering from constraints or ills, takes us into that absenting absentive agency intrinsic to (5′) the *dialectic of the desire to freedom* and into (6′) the *totalising depth praxis of explanatory axiology* involving counter-hegemonic struggles over oppressive power$_2$ relations to (7′) the *eudaimonistic society of universal human autonomy and flourishing*. In this process the transition from fact to value passes over into the transition from form to content, ultimately naturalistically grounded in a theory of the possibilities of a four-planar developing social being-in-nature.[68]

Notes

1 Dialectical critical realism is developed in Bhaskar, *Dialectic* and *Plato Etc.* For an excellent overview, see Alan Norrie *Dialectic and Difference* (London: Routledge 2011).

2 For explanation of the names given to these levels within dialectical critical realism and the philosophy of metaReality, see Bhaskar with Hartwig, *The Formation of Critical Realism*, 118; for a justification of these terms, which is however not central to our purposes here,

see Mervyn Hartwig, 'Introduction' to Bhaskar, *Scientific Realism and Human Emancipation*, xi–xli, xv.

3 Hartwig, 'Introduction' to Bhaskar, *Dialectic*, xiii–xxix, Table 1, xvi–xvii (modified by MH). I am indebted to Mervyn Hartwig for the excellent tables that have accompanied his expositions of my work, a selection of which I reproduce in this book.

4 Roy Bhaskar, *Philosophy and the Idea of Freedom* (Oxford: Blackwell 1991), 126.

5 See esp. Plato, *Sophist*. For discussion, see Norrie, *Dialectic and Difference*, 160–9.

6 See Bhaskar, *Dialectic*, 4–7, 38–48.

7 In *A Realist Theory of Science* I do deploy a concept of absence, treating absence as in effect real (causally efficacious) but I make no attempt to justify this in that work.

8 Bhaskar, *Dialectic*, 6–7.

9 R. M. Hare, 'Meaning and speech acts', *Philosophical Review* 79:1 (1970), 3–24, 19 ff.

10 Bhaskar, *Dialectic*, 40 f. See also my *Philosophy and the Idea of Freedom*, Chapter 7, 'Reference, fictionalism and radical negation', 112–28.

11 Bhaskar, *Dialectic*, 401; see also 115–16 and *passim*.

12 Bhaskar, *Dialectic*, 45.

13 That is, stretching out spatio-temporally (embedding), or splitting off and dislocating (disembedding).

14 Bhaskar, *Dialectic*, 39.

15 Hartwig, 'Introduction' to Bhaskar, *Dialectic: The Pulse of Freedom*, xiii–xxix, Table 2, xx (slightly modified by MH).

16 Bhaskar, *Dialectic* and *Plato Etc.*

17 Bhaskar, *Dialectic*, Chapter 2.10, 173–203, 238.

18 Outwith the universe as we know it, negativity has ontological primacy over positivity; that is, within being as a whole (which includes real absence or non-being), the negative is primary. See Bhaskar, *Dialectic*, 39 f. We now know that the universe is expanding exponentially. If the question of what it is expanding into is posed, the answer can only be real indeterminate absence. ('Outwith' is a Scottish word that nicely performs a perspectival switch on 'without' in the sense of 'outside'. As I use it, it means 'on the far side of, yet immanent within'.)

19 Marx, Letter to Engels, 14 January 1858, in Karl Marx and Friedrich Engels, *Collected Works Vol. 40, Letters 1856–1859* (New York: International Publishers, 1983), 248–50, 249.

20 James Hutchison Stirling, *The Secret of Hegel* (London: Longman, 1865).

21 See Bhaskar, *Dialectic*, Chapter 1.6–1.9.

22 Bhaskar, *Plato Etc.*, Appendix, 'Explaining philosophies', 167–89.

23 See Bhaskar, *Dialectic*, 38 and *passim*.

24 Bhaskar, *Dialectic*, 74, 311.

25 See Bhaskar, *Dialectic*, Chapter 4.7–4.8 and *Plato Etc.*, 209.

26 Bhaskar, *Dialectic*, 279–80, 300. For an interpretation of dialectical critical realism emphasising the *materialist diffraction of dialectic* as the core of the Marx–Hegel relation, see Norrie, *Dialectic and Difference*, Chapter 3.

27 See for example, Bhaskar, *Dialectic*, 26 f.

28 See for example Bhaskar, *Dialectic*, 67.

29 Bhaskar, *Dialectic*, 44, 80, 380.

30 Bhaskar, *Dialectic*, 57–9.

31 Bhaskar, *Dialectic*, Chapter 3.5–3.6 and Norrie, *Dialectic and Difference*, Chapters 3 and 4.

32 See Bhaskar, *Dialectic*, Chapter 2.8, 134–51.

33 In *A Realist Theory of Science* I speak of possibilities as real (for example, 18, 78, 177), but I do not give this position the name dispositional realism. I do this first in *From East to West: Odyssey of a Soul* (London: Routledge, 2000/2015), 53 f. Note that the page numbering in this second Routledge edition is different from the first edition.

34 I introduced the concept of categorial realism in my 'On the ontological status of ideas' (1997), 140. See also *From East to West*, 59 f. It names a position I espoused implicitly from the outset.

35 Bhaskar, *Dialectic*, 214–24.

36 *Editor's note*. Bhaskar's theory of alethic truth is significantly different from a critical realist version of alethic theory that equates alethic truth with the correspondence theory of truth (for example Porpora, *Reconstructing Sociology: A Critical Realist Approach*, 80). The correspondence theory dates back to Aristotle. Bhaskar rejects it on the grounds that there is radical non-identity between our concepts (for example, the concept of a laser beam) and what they express (for example, a laser beam), arguing that correspondence theory is a species of subject–object identity-thinking or anthroporealism (see for example Bhaskar, *A Realist Theory of Science*, 249–50 and *Dialectic*, 214–24).

37 Mervyn Hartwig, 'Introduction' to Bhaskar, *Dialectic*, xiii–xxix, Table 3, xxii (slightly modified by MH).

38 TINA stands for 'there is no alternative', and is ironically so named to indicate a false necessity that is undermined by and must be protected against its own falsity.

39 Bhaskar, *Dialectic*, esp. 118–19.

40 Bhaskar, *Dialectic*, 9–10 and *passim*.

41 See Bhaskar, *Dialectic*, 113 f.

42 Bhaskar, *Dialectic*, 9 and *passim*.

43 Basic acts are things we just do, that is, do not do by doing other things. Such acts are learnt and the capacity to perform them may be lost. See Chapter 7.4 and Bhaskar, *The Possibility of Naturalism*, 82–3.

44 Bhaskar, *The Possibility of Naturalism*, 87 f.

45 For a powerful critical realist depth-critique of gender inequality see Lena Gunnarsson, *The Contradictions of Love: Towards a Feminist-Realist Ontology of Sociosexuality* (London: Routledge, 2014).

46 Bhaskar, *Scientific Realism and Human Emancipation*, 25–6.

47 See Bhaskar, *Dialectic*, 177.

48 Bhaskar, *Dialectic*, Chapter 4 and *Plato Etc.*, Chapters 9 and 10 and Appendix. See also esp. Bhaskar, *Scientific Realism and Human Emancipation*, Chapter 3, 'The positivist illusion: sketch of a philosophical ideology at work', 224–308.

49 Bhaskar, *Plato Etc.*, 49, Figure 3.2.

50 Bhaskar, *Plato Etc.*, 50, Figure 3.3.

51 Bhaskar, *Dialectic*, 365, Figure 4.13.

52 Bhaskar, *Dialectic*, 88.

53 Bhaskar, *Plato Etc.*, 184–5.

54 Bhaskar, *Dialectic*, 168, 180–1.

55 See esp. Bhaskar, *Dialectic*, Chapter 3.10, 279–98.

56 Bhaskar, *Plato Etc.*, 166–7.

57 Bhaskar, *Plato Etc.*, 144; *Reflections on MetaReality*, 21, 219.

58 The four moments of the judgement form correspond to the four moments of my theory of truth, outlined above. See also Table 6.3.

59 Bhaskar, *Dialectic*, 262.

60 This subsection follows Bhaskar, *Dialectic*, 282–3 and *Plato Etc.*, 145.

61 See Bhaskar, *Dialectic*, Chapter 3.10, 279–98.

62 See esp. Bhaskar, *Plato Etc.*, 108–9, 151.

63 Bhaskar, *Dialectic*, 292 and *Plato Etc.*, 119n, 151, 165. *Editor's note*. cf. Smith, *To Flourish or Destruct*, esp. Chapter 6, 'Toward a theory of flourishing', 201–22. Smith's excellent book deploys a critical realist metatheory to orient its argument but does not mention Bhaskar's metatheory of free flourishing.

64 See Alan Norrie's *Dialectic and Difference*, 149–50. However Norrie refers to the moral real as the ideal rather than the real.

65 See Bhaskar, *Dialectic,* 280 and Norrie, *Dialectic and Difference*, 148.

66 Bhaskar, *From East to West*, 93; *Reflections on MetaReality*, Chapter 2, 69–117.

67 Bhaskar, *Dialectic*, 303, Figure 3.12. This figure does not directly display the categories for the critique of irrealism, but these are given in the denegation of dialectical critical realism's 1M, 2E, 3L and 4D categories.

68 Bhaskar, *Dialectic*, 301–2.

7

THE FURTHER DEVELOPMENT OF CRITICAL REALISM II

The philosophy of metaReality

7.1 Transcendental dialectical critical realism and the philosophy of metaReality: two phases of the 'spiritual turn'

There were widespread 'returns' to religion and spirituality as the second millennium CE drew to a close; my so called 'spiritual turn' was one of these. One of the cardinal reasons for these returns was undoubtedly (growing awareness of) the escalating planetary *crisis system* that the human species is now facing – and promoting. (We will discuss this in Chapter 9.2.)

One of my main motivations[1] for embarking on the spiritual turn was a concern in this context to increase the cultural resources of emancipatory movements. It was clear to me that spirituality (in the sense defined below) was a presupposition of emancipatory projects and that twentieth century emancipatory projects had by and large failed. I wanted to identify and remedy conceptual absences that played an important role in this failure, thereby also increasing the overall rationality of my system of philosophy. At a more personal level, I had a spiritual experience in 1994 that was, for me, revelatory of the deep interior of things, and took a decision to investigate this domain systematically. However, as noted in Chapter 1, there was always a certain developmental logic intrinsic to my philosophy that took it in the direction of spirituality and the theme of underlying unity and identity with a rich potential for differentiation. I sometimes refer to my spiritual turn as 'so called' because I believe that my philosophy has been strongly spiritual all along in its drive to overcome dualism, alienation and split in practice as well as in theory.

My earlier work arguably does successfully resolve all the main dualisms of Western philosophy and social theory, but with the exception of the most momentous dualism of all for human well-being – the antinomy of slavery and freedom famously noted by Rousseau: people as such are free, but everywhere in chains. If realism is true, how is it that irrealism is everywhere dominant? Irrealism is dominant because it reflects the oppressive structures of the master–slave-type society that we inhabit, so realism can be conceived to be true only if it reflects a deeper, more basic level that most of us have not fully developed or that is so occluded by heteronomous structures that we do not notice it and resign ourselves to living in a half-world or demi-reality.[2] Not only is this more basic level accessible to people everywhere, it is already pervasive in our daily lives, if largely unnoticed, I argue, informing and sustaining everything we do, the indispensable substratum of social life. This is what I call the *asymmetry of axiology and emancipation*: the world we want emancipation from dominates and occludes the spiritual infrastructure on which it depends (see further Chapter 9.2).

From East to West, published in 2000, articulating a position characterised as *transcendental dialectical critical realism*, represents the first investigative phase of the spiritual turn. It was succeeded by a second definitive phase, represented by the philosophy of metaReality, elaborated in three books published in 2002: *Reflections on MetaReality, From Science to Emancipation* and *The Philosophy of MetaReality*. Although I was concerned to articulate a spirituality that would not be hostage to institutionalised religion,[3] *From East to West* focused on religion and the thematisation of God, for two main reasons. First, because religion had a near monopoly on the topic of spirituality, and second because it was clear that much immediate progress could be made on the possibilities of inter-, intra- and extra-faith dialogue by the straightforward application of the critical realist holy trinity of ontological realism, epistemological relativism and judgemental rationality to the topic of God, thereby synthesising the dualism of sacred and profane.[4] Outside of theology departments and the like, there was a deeply entrenched taboo in the Western academy (including critical realism) on discussing the truth claims of religion[5] that I wanted to challenge in order to promote critical religious literacy, understanding and tolerance. Today there is a flourishing critical realist literature devoted to constructive critique and debate of matters religious and spiritual.[6]

The philosophy of metaReality, for its part, seeks to transcend rather than synthesise the dualisms of sacred and profane and natural and supernatural and the binary human-God. Furthermore, it differentiates sharply between spirituality and religion, holding that, although the two are connected at the limit by a notion of the absolute, the former is essentially concerned with transcendence (of dualism and oppositionality), the latter with the transcendent (what lies beyond human experience or comprehension or existence).[7] (This will be elaborated in section 7.8.) MetaReality sees spirituality as ubiquitous and as a necessary condition for everyday life; whereas *From East to West*, although it did much of the metaphysical heavy lifting necessary for the transition to the philosophy of metaReality,[8] did not satisfy the hermetic principle that I outlined in Chapter 1. Moreover, even though taking over from religion the ideas of the immanence of the divine and the actuality of enlightenment, the philosophy of metaReality substitutes for the concept God in many world religions the secular concept of the *cosmic envelope*, which links the *ground states* of all beings. Finally, in its underlabouring role metaReality issues in a sharp critique of much actually existing religiosity and its organisational forms.

Religion includes much that is false in its teaching and, as a social institution, much that is oppressive and exploitative, mired in the wider context of master–slave-type social relations.[9]

7.2 The primacy of identity and unity

The philosophy of metaReality, which I sometimes abbreviate to metaReality or PMR, involves the addition of three further levels of ontology to the four levels of dialectical critical realism:

5A: thinking being as *reflexive*, inward and spiritual;

6R: thinking being as *re-enchanted*; and

7Z/A: thinking being as involving the *primacy of identity over difference*, and of *unity over split*, and as *non-dual*. This is furthermore the level at which we pass from thinking or understanding being to *being being*. Most of this chapter will be concerned with this seventh level.

In addition, metaReality gives its own inflection to the previous levels, both generally and in terms of human ground-state qualities, as can be seen in Table 7.1. This table gives the key concepts of the philosophy of metaReality mapped onto the stadia of the developed (CR–DCR–PMR) ontological–axiological chain or the *self-structuration of being*.[10]

The seventh level, at which we are invited to think the priority of identity over difference, in a way reverses the position of 1M, the first level of development of critical realism, which thematised being as involving non-identity. Now we are prioritising identity over difference. However, the non-identity thematised at 1M involves critique of the illicit fusions of the punctualist and atomistic concepts of empiricist foundationalism. These fusions were discussed in Chapter 6. *Punctualism* and the converse fallacy of *blockism* or block universalism are irrealist theories of space–time entailed by the Humean account of causal laws, theories that deny the reality of tense and process, and hence cannot sustain an adequate concept of causality or of human transformative practice. Punctualism is entailed by the atomism of the Humean account, blockism by its actualism. Blockism postulates the simultaneous co-existence of all times and events, that is, spatio-temporal closure – the absence of an open universe. Punctualism is the converse fallacy that only the here-now exists.[11]

Underlying identities and unities are already presupposed by basic critical realism at 1M; for example, an event is a change or transformation in an enduring thing, and this underlying presupposition is further explicated in dialectical critical realism in the figures of *constellational identity*, *dispositional identity* and *rhythmic identity* at the level of ultimata for science.[12] Moreover, the concept of identity involved is a very different one from that of the empiricist tradition. The identity we are invited to think is in no way atomistic or punctual; it involves a rich, differentiating and developing identity, the sort of identity one might achieve after a deep

TABLE 7.1 Key concepts of the philosophy of metaReality mapped to the stadia of the ontological–axiological chain[13]

Stadion of the ontological–axiological chain/phase of PMR > CR	1M Non-identity/TR	2E Negativity/CN	3L Totality/EC	4D Transformative agency/DCR	5A Spirituality/TDCR	6R (Re-)enchantment/PMR	7A/Z Non-duality/PMR
Thinking being	as such and in general	as process + as for 1M	as a whole + as for 2E	as praxis + as for 3L	as spiritual + as for 4D	as enchanted + as for 5A	as non-dual + as for 6R
Form of reflexivity – immanent critique of PDM + CR	classical modernism	high modernism + 1M	modernisation theory + 1M, 2E	postmodernism + 1M, 2E, 3L	triumphalism and endism/fundamentalism + 1M, 2E, 3L, 4D	triumphalism and endism/fundamentalism + 1M, 2E, 3L, 4D, 5A	
Key PMR concepts	underlying identity–in-difference (implicitly conscious) – ground state and cosmic envelope (the absolute, non-duality, metaReality) as the truth or ground of reality; the constellational identity or unity of non-duality and duality; generalised co-presence	transcendence as ubiquitous in everyday life; transcendental identification in consciousness; transcendental emergence (creativity); accentuation of creative power of thought	unconditional love; transcendental holism or teamwork; unification, unity; reciprocity, synchronicity; synchronicity; generalisation of four-planar social being to include mental and emotional *sui generis* realities	spontaneous right-action (transcendental agency); practical mysticism; dialectically universalised synchronicity	spirituality as a necessary condition of everyday life; fulfilled intentionality; primacy of self-referentiality; universal self-realisation	enchantment – being as intrinsically meaningful, valuable and sacred; generalised hermeneutics and semiotics; enhanced human perception and hermeneutical powers, direct consciousness-to-consciousness causality	(awakening of) non-duality; being being (cosmic consciousness, at-homeness); human creative powers unbound (the unlimited self); open, unending evolution

(Continued)

TABLE 7.1 (Continued)

Stadion of the ontological-axiological chain/phase of PMR > CR	1M Non-identity/TR	2E Negativity/CN	3L Totality/EC	4D Transformative agency/DCR	5A Spirituality/TDCR	6R (Re-)enchantment/PMR	7A/Z Non-duality/PMR
Modes or forms of transcendence (non-dual components of action)	transcendental consciousness (supramental; at or of the ground state)	transcendental identification (feature of consciousness; becoming one in being)	transcendental teamwork or holism (feature of agency; becoming one in or in the context of one's agency)	transcendental agency (feature of agency; becoming one in or in the context of one's agency)	transcendental retreat into self-identity (feature of consciousness; becoming one in being)	transcendental identification and agency	transcendental consciousness
Direction of transcendence	ground of 1–4	1. outwards, onto (away from subjectivity into objectivity – loss of self)	4. with	3. on, at or in (absorption in activity)	2. inwards, into (away from objectivity into subjectivity – loss of the object)	1–4	ground of 1–4
Modes of transcendental consciousness	transcendental or supramental consciousness at or of the ground state	mindlessness (form without content: absence of content; bliss-consciousness)		mindfulness (content without form: repletion of content) → spontaneous right-action → mindlessness			

TABLE 7.1

Stadion of the ontological–axiological chain/phase of PMR > CR	1M Non-identity/TR	2E Negativity/CN	3L Totality/EC	4D Transformative agency/DCR	5A Spirituality/TDCR	6R (Re-)enchantment/PMR	7A/Z Non-duality/PMR
Principles of spirituality	self-referentiality or hermeticism (primacy of)	simultaneity	complementarity	practical mysticism	radical hermeticism (primacy of self-referentiality entails the liberation and flourishing of all beings)		
Qualities of the ground state	transcendental ground	transcendental emergence	transcendental identification or union	transcendental agency	transcendental reflection	transcendental perception	awakening of non-duality
Human ground state (*dharmic*) capacities	*will*; unbound energy or potential; freedom (the capacity to do one thing rather than another)	*creativity*; freedom as absenting constraints (negative completion)	*love*	*right-action*	*fulfilled intentionality* or self-realisation or enlightenment (positive completion)	*enchantment*	*awakening* of non-duality; universal fulfilment or peace
Conditions for self-realisation	being in your ground state or dharma (absence of atomistic ego)	clear mind, single-pointedness; mindlessness or innocence	pure heart	balanced body	absence of belief in the brute physicality of the world	enchantment	awakening

(Continued)

TABLE 7.1 (Continued)

Stadion of the ontological–axiological chain / phase of PMR > CR	1M Non-identity/TR	2E Negativity/CN	3L Totality/EC	4D Transformative agency/DCR	5A Spirituality/TDCR	6R (Re-)enchantment/PMR	7 Non-duality/PMR
Elements of the human creative process (action)	will (initial impulse or calling)	creation (emergence) thought/unthought	formation, shaping feeling or emotion	making (physical action and objectification)	fulfilled or realised intentionality (reflection of objectification to the maker)	enchanted resonance of fulfilled intentionality	awakening to the non-dual ground of fulfilled intentionality (self-and god-realisation)
Dialectic of learning	enfolded or implicit knowledge	discovery and recall or anamnesis (emergence of enfolded knowledge)	shaping (binding knowledge back into our innermost being – self-formation and elaborating it)	objectifying knowledge in practice	reflection or fulfilment		
Circles of human love	1. self	2. another human	3. all humans	4. all beings	5. the absolute		
Cosmogony (cycle of creativity of being as such, eventually perhaps repeating)	polyvalent foundational impulse (unbound energy from implicit potential enfolded in absence)	creation (transcendental emergence)	formation, shaping	making (objectification)	fulfilled intentionality of the foundational impulse (reflection of objectification back to the creator)	enchanted resonance of fulfilled intentionality	universal awakening of non-duality (self- and god-realisation); open, on-going

TABLE 7.1

Stadion of the ontological–axiological chain/phase of PMR > CR	1M Non-identity/TR	2E Negativity/CN	3L Totality/EC	4D Transformative agency/DCR	5A Spirituality/TDCR	6R (Re-)enchantment/PMR	7 Non-duality/PMR
Cosmotheogeny (cycle of cosmic creation, eventually perhaps repeating*)	self-creation of the creator *ex nihilo*‡	emergence of realm of duality, becoming and time	emergence of realm of demi-reality	individual self-realisation (commencement of return cycle‡ from alienation)	individual and universal self-realisation or eudaimonia (theosis or heaven on earth); the elimination of demi-reality	individual god-realisation (oneness with totality)	universal god-realisation; open, ongoing; the elimination of relative reality

† Corresponding to the descent of consciousness in traditional cosmotheogenesis, and to Big Bang in modern cosmological theory.

‡ Corresponding to the ascent of consciousness in traditional cosmotheogenesis.

★ Corresponding to cycles from Big Bang to Big Crunch in modern cosmological theory.

Note. 7 > 6R > 5A > 4D > 3L > 2E > 1M, so that 7A/Z constellationally contains all the rest.

learning process with a beautiful work of art or music. Nevertheless, it remains true to say that at this seventh level of ontological development we are in a sense turning our back on 'realism', at least realism as understood in terms of the independent existence of an object in a subject–object duality. For at this level the subject–object distinction breaks down; and it is in this sense that metaReality is perhaps better called a *philosophy of truth* (rather than a realism), as indicated in Table 7.2.[14]

Reflection on our ordinary concepts of identity, difference, unity and split allows us to indicate what is at stake here. If I say that two people, *X* and *Y*, are of different heights, then I am presupposing that they have something in common, which remains the same over the comparison, namely height. Indeed, it only makes sense to say of two things that they are different if they have something in common. In this way our normal use of difference presupposes an underlying identity. Similarly, if someone tells us about their experience with an alien or extra-terrestrial visitor, the fact that it is *their* experience makes it a part of our world, and their sharing it with us, even more so. It would seem that anything that human beings can come to experience or imagine must be a part of our cosmos.[15] These examples indicate intuitively how identity and unity might come to be regarded as prior to, and presupposed by difference and split, respectively.

I now want to introduce into this discussion a passage from the history of philosophy that prioritises identity and unity and suggests reasons for regarding these asymmetries – that is, the *primacy of identity and unity over difference and split* – as transcendentally inescapable. The passage in question is that concerning the 'life-and-death struggle' in Hegel's *Phenomenology of Spirit*.[16]

The life-and-death struggle

Hegel asks us to imagine a situation in which two primordial (male) human beings are fighting each other to the limit. His question is: Why, when the victor has vanquished the other, does he not kill him? Hegel's answer is that he needs him alive as a witness to testify to his valour, bravery, and so on; that he needs to spare the other in order that the other may recognise him. Thus we have a long line in post-Hegelian philosophy up to Axel Honneth that thematises the struggle for *recognition*.[17] Feuerbach, Marx and the Left Hegelians suggested another answer: the victor spares the one he vanquishes in order to make him work for him as his slave. Thus begins an alternative line of interpretation in post-Hegelian philosophy up to Sartre and the present day that thematises the *master–slave relationship*.[18] However, the master–slave relationship is normally thematised in such a way (beginning with Hegel himself when he comes on to it) that it involves a *dialectical reversal* whereby the slave, working hard and objectifying himself in the products of his work, grows stronger (augmenting his transformative capacity or his power$_1$) until he is in a position to overthrow the master and indeed the master–slave (or power$_2$) relation itself; and so unity is achieved. What Hegel's account lacks or fails to bring out, however, in contrast to his early theological writings, is that the dialectic of recognition

TABLE 7.2 Key moments and figures of the philosophy of metaReality mapped to the critical realist domains of reality[19]

Domains of Reality	Real	Actual	Empirical/Conceptual
	experiences, concepts and signs *events* **mechanisms**	*experiences, concepts and signs* **events** *[mechanisms]*	**experiences, concepts and signs** *[events]* *[mechanisms]*
REALMS OF REALITY	**ABSOLUTE REALITY** the enfolded, the implicit (the implicate order); fields of implicitly conscious possibility	**RELATIVE REALITY** the unfolded, the explicit (the explicate order)	**DEMI-REALITY** (demi-real relative reality) the falsely unfolded
SOCIAL PRINCIPLE	**love** and **peace**	struggle	**war**, control
PHILOSOPHY	**metaReality**	critical realism	**irrealism**
ONTOLOGICAL PRINCIPLE	**truth**	realism	**irrealism**
META-PHILOSOPHICAL PRINCIPLE (1)	**non-duality** (identity; identification, unity) (a property of consciousness)	**duality** (non-identity, without alienation but with the potential for it)	**dualism** (alienation)
META-PHILOSOPHICAL PRINCIPLE (2)	**truth** (most basically the revelation of identity)	**non-identity**	**mis-identification, error, falsity**
ORIENTATION TO BEING	**being being**	thinking being	**evading being**
SUBJECTIVITY–OBJECTIVITY RELATION	**unity-in-diversity**	expressive unity	**diremption** (alienation)
DIMENSIONS OF THE SELF	transcendental or alethic **self** or ground state (a field of possibility)	embodied **self**	**ego** (a real illusion)
FORMS OF ENCHANTMENT	**enchantment**	re-enchantment	**disenchantment** (emergent false level or ideology)

(Continued)

TABLE 7.2 (Continued)

Domains of Reality	Real	Actual	Empirical/Conceptual
FORMS OF FREEDOM	**peace** (dialectically = universal fulfilment)	**freedom to** (lessening of positive incompleteness or the absence of total development)	**freedom from** (elimination of negative incompleteness or heteronomous determinations)
MODES OF FREEDOM AND UNFREEDOM (non-alienation and alienation)	**autonomy** (identity – true for, to and of itself)	**unity**	**alienation**
FORM OF IDEOLOGY (demi-reality)	**underlying generative falsity** (alethic falsity)	**practical**	**theoretical**
FORM OF ALIENATION (demi-reality)	**self-alienation**	**practical**	**conceptual**
LOGIC OF MASTER–SLAVERY (demi-reality)	**exploitation**	**conditionality** of transactions	**desire** (as dominant motivation)
PATHS TO UNION WITH TOTALITY (a tri-unity)	**truth** (*jnana* yoga)	**practice** (*karma* yoga)	**love** (*bhakti* yoga)
THE HOLY TRINITY OF CRITICAL REALISM	**ontological realism**	**epistemic relativity**	**judgemental rationality**
MODES IN WHICH ABSOLUTE REALITY SUSTAINS, IS CONNECTED WITH, AND IS ACCESSED IN, THE WORLD OF DUALITY			
FORMS OF UNITY OR IDENTITY (modes in which non-duality sustains duality)	**ground** or basis (ground state cosmic envelope)	**mode of constitution** (or reproduction/ transformation) via transcendence	**fine structure** or deep interior† of all aspects of being

TABLE 7.2

Domains of Reality	Real	Actual	Empirical/Conceptual
MECHANISMS OF IDENTIFICATION (modes of connection of non-duality)	**co-presence** (a property of all beings)	**reciprocity** (a property of animate beings)	**transcendental identification** (a property of consciousness)
DYNAMIC OR EVOLUTIONARY FORM OF MECHANISMS OF IDENTIFICATION (modes of connection of non-duality)	**attraction** (integrated rhythmics)	**synthesis** (of spatio–temporally spread phenomena)	**economy** (generalised synchronicity or unfolding, inwardising englobement)
FORMS OF TRANSCENDENCE	**transcendental consciousness** at or of the groundstate	**transcendental agency** or transcendental identification in agency (solo or teamwork)	**transcendental identification** in consciousness

† Fine structure pertains to the empirical/conceptual domain because it is implicit (ground-state) consciousness and can be experienced as such. It pertains equally to the domain of the real.

Note. Correspondences are sometimes loose, particularly in the case of those between domains and realms of reality: each of the realms have real, actual and empirical/conceptual dimensions. The items in bold in the rows after the second can be arranged in a triplex structure in exactly the same way as in the second row (for further exemplification, see Bhaskar and Hartwig 2010, Table 17, p. 115). Lowermost (primary) levels can then be seen to constellationally embrace upper (secondary) levels, hence to have ontological, epistemological and logical priority over them – the priority of the enfolded over the unfolded, the possible over the actual. Where upper levels, which thus presuppose primary levels, embody categorial error and ignorance, they function to occlude lower levels. Square-bracketed levels are not given in the concept of levels without square brackets but are presupposed by them.

presupposes an at least equal and complementary dialectic of trust, nurture and care, and so of love.[20] Whatever interpretation is adopted, it is these aspects that point to underlying unity and identity.

Non-duality, duality and demi-reality

MetaReality recognises a distinction between three kinds or domains of being:

(i) non-duality;
(ii) duality; and
(iii) demi-reality.

In particular, it thematises the world of *non-duality*, which contrasts with our normal world of *duality*, where object is non-identical with and set apart from subject. This world of duality is not destroyed by the world of non-duality. Rather, it is underpinned by it. Thus when we have an example of transcendence of the world of duality, for example by the transcendental identification of two consciousnesses in consciousness (which I will discuss shortly), the two consciousnesses remain materially embodied, living in the world of duality, separate and distinct from each other, even while the consciousnesses are fused as one.

However, metaReality claims that the world of duality is dominated by the realm of *demi-reality*. The key concepts for the analysis of this realm are shown in the fourth column of the first two pages of Table 7.2. This is a world of illusion and categorial error, which is however causally efficacious and indeed dominates the world of duality in the form of the master–slave-type social relations and alienation that illusion and error both reflect and reinforce. It is a meshwork of concatenated TINA compromise formations in which categorial error is compounded on categorial error as attempts are made to patch up our theory/practice ensembles in the face of the inexorability of ontology and alethic truth.[21] Above all, in oppressing and exploiting people masters suffer from and promote the illusion that people (including themselves) are not fundamentally free, creative, loving, right-acting, spiritual and enchanted non-dual beings. Along with many of the oppressed, they all but lose sight of who they really are. There was thus a kind of geo-historical 'fall' into structural sin or evil with the rise of master–slave-type societies. Far from being primordial with the development of language and the symbolic order, and so irremediable, as a fashionable Lacano-Hegelian metanarrative has it, alienation is geo-historical and reversible.[22]

The philosophy of metaReality brings out the way in which demi-reality and the world of duality more generally is undergirded by the world of non-duality. In doing so, it regards itself as a philosophy of non-duality and characterises pre-existing critical realism, that is critical realism without the philosophy of metaReality, as a true and indeed the best available philosophy of and for the world of duality, that is, the world of non-identity, difference, structure and change. The philosophies of irrealism, on the other hand – the theoretical ideologies that pre-existing critical realism critiques – are understood as philosophies of demi-reality.

Another way of putting the distinctions between these worlds and their philosophies is to see metaReality as describing a world of *absolute reality*, pre-existing critical realism as describing the world of *relative reality* in which for most of the time we live, and irrealism as describing illusory realities or *demi-real relative reality* to which the world of duality remains in thrall. Table 7.2 maps these worlds onto the critical realist domains of reality and displays the key figures pertaining to each. We can thus rewrite our list of these worlds (above) as:

(i)   non-duality or absolute reality;
(ii) duality or relative reality; and
(iii) demi-reality or demi-real relative reality.

MetaReality claims that almost all pre-existing philosophy involves a huge scotoma or blind-spot: it has overlooked, failed to recognise the world of non-duality, a veritable immanent 'heaven on earth', on which the world of duality and the demi-real structures, attitudes and habits that dominate it totally depend. This is a huge claim, so let us see how metaReality begins to justify it.

7.3 The basic arguments for metaReality

I use the same principled method of argument to validate metaReality as for pre-existing critical realism: transcendental critique (conditional and relative transcendental arguments combined with immanent critique of rival positions). This is supplemented importantly by pragmatic arguments and retroductive and phenomenological analysis of experience and of the constitution of social life. I have elsewhere presented the main arguments in summary form in a variety of ways. Perhaps the most convenient way for the reader is to group them into (1) objective considerations, (2) subjective considerations and (3) the unity of objective and subjective considerations.[23] It should be borne in mind, however, that they are presented here in a necessarily highly condensed form; if you find them heavy going it might be advisable to skip this section on a first reading.

In (1), the method of transcendental critique is deployed to develop the philosophy of critical realism to the point where realism about transcendence leads to the self-transcendence of realism, as an absolute realm of non-duality is seen to be essential to social life as its basis or *ground*, its *mode of constitution* and its *deep interior*.[24] Thus I have already argued in section 7.1 that the truth of realism, in the context of the untruth of irrealism that is everywhere dominant, presupposes a more basic level that we have not fully noticed or developed, namely, a non-dual or metaReal level. The idea of metaReality had its inception in my reflecting on the moment of absolute transcendence or transcendental identification in scientific discovery or indeed in any process of learning or discovery – the eureka or 'aha' moment (see section 7.6).[25] The flash of insight this brings cannot be arrived at by hard work alone, although that will play an indispensable preparatory role; nor can it be derived by deduction or induction or any algorithmic formula – it comes 'out of the blue' in a moment of unthought, that is, of the suspension of thought (as some creative scientists, as well as artists, poets, and so on, attest[26]). This can be rendered fully intelligible only on the basis that it involves the union between something already enfolded within the discovering agent, brought up to consciousness by a moment of anamnesis or recall, with the alethic self-revelation of the being being known, existing outside the discovering agent; that is, that it involves the union of two beings at the level of the implicit, supramental or transcendental consciousness of their ground states. Our capacity to identify transcendentally with beings that are not explicitly conscious presupposes that they are implicitly conscious; and insofar as we can in principle identify with all beings, as is implied by the fact that we are all constituents of a single universe, bound by the same cosmic envelope, we must say that everything is both implicitly conscious and at least potentially implicitly enfolded in our own consciousnesses and those of all other beings.[27] In this way we arrive at the theory of *generalised co-presence* or interconnectedness – that at the level of fundamental possibility everything is implicitly contained within and intra-related with everything else.[28] One implication of this is that creative scientists (artists, and so on), tacitly or otherwise presuppose metaReality and are in effect *practical mystics*.[29] This is a very radical metatheory of discovery, given that science has been the paradigmatic way of knowing for Western philosophy since Descartes if not indeed Aristotle.[30]

In (2) we adopt a *pragmatic approach*, that is, one that presupposes the reality of metaReality in order to appeal to practice: in essence it argues that if you act inconsistently with your ground state, that is, transcendentally real self, you will find that you are split and unhappy (unfulfilled or unrealised) in some way. Try it, and see for yourself. Conversely, it is argued that when people act in a maximally effective way individually or collectively – as for example in Tahrir Square, Cairo, in the initial stages of the recent Egyptian revolution or in the case of the 33 Chilean miners trapped underground for more than two months in 2010 – their ground-state qualities will be to the fore: will, determination and energy, creativity and freedom, unconditional love and all its circles, right-action, a feeling of coming home to one's true self, a sense that the world is enchanted, and awakening to unity and non-duality as such (see Table 7.1). The situation in Egypt remains tragic and demi-real, but that does not gainsay the reality of the stupendous eruption of the pulse of freedom in Tahrir Square upon the fall of the Mubarak regime. On this line of argument, achieving your goals in life depends ultimately on getting in touch with your real self and clearing your embodied personality of heteronomous elements that are inconsistent with it. This is a development of my position in *Dialectic* on which emancipation and enlightenment consist ultimately in theory-practice coherence (Chapter 6.7), which is fundamentally coherent with our transcendentally real selves.[31]

The third approach (3) builds on critical realism's demonstration of the depth-stratification of being to argue the reality of a foundational level of non-duality as a *necessary condition for any being at all*. On this line we could ask, for example, where else could the eruption of pure bliss in Tahrir Square upon the fall of the Mubarak regime ultimately come from if not from the fundamental structure of possibility of the uni-verse? To say that it is a specifically *human* creative power or a human construction hardly answers the question in a thoroughgoing way. Here the argument would be that the ground-state properties of human action established by (2) are in resonance with the ground-state properties of being as such, established by (1) – as the relevant correspondences noted in Table 7.1 also suggest.

If we approach the arguments for metaReality in terms of method used to justify the idea of the three fundamental modes in which non-duality sustains relative reality – as its (i) mode of constitution, (ii) basis or ground and (iii) deep interior (see further section 7.4) – we can say that transcendental argument is the main method deployed for (ii); that (i) depends on a mix of transcendental and retroductive and phenomenological analysis of the genesis or constitution of any situation or complex in social life; and that (iii) also depends on such a mix but that phenomenological analysis of experience now comes to the fore. Here the argument is that, if one goes deeply enough into any aspect of being or consciousness, as (most classically) in mystical experience, it will reveal the qualities of bliss, emptiness, suchness, rich identity, or pure unbounded energised love, and so on, qualities that are arguably continuous with the ground-state qualities of creation, which thus infuse all the rest of being as its ontologically ultimate interior.[32] It should be noted, though, that arguments from experience alone are insufficient. Those who have had the relevant non-dual experience may find these arguments convincing but they will cut no ice with those who have had no such experience, and then there will be stalemate. MetaReality aims to be maximally inclusive, aspiring to develop an outlook that will appeal to those of no faith and all faiths.

In addition to these main lines of argument there is of course a *logic of interimplication* or *entailment* among the various propositions. Thus transcendental agency or the ultimate spontaneity of action entails *ceteris paribus* the primacy of subject- or self-referentiality, which in turn entails and is presupposed by commitment to a eudaimonistic society or universal self-realisation;[33] the collapse of subject–object duality in transcendental identification entails that reality is enchanted;[34] and so on. Furthermore, the intricate inter-articulation of the moments of the system, which is mapped in the tables in this chapter, lends plausibility to the arguments overall. This has been underlined by MinGyu Seo in relation to the logic of anti-anthropism in the development of my philosophy. Seo demonstrates that only when human beings both see themselves and act as a contingently emergent part of the cosmic totality – 'anthropocosmically' – and not as in any way split off from it, is anti-anthropism carried through to a definitive conclusion; and this is the prospect that the philosophy of metaReality holds out.[35]

A standard objection to these arguments is that human experience of the non-dual may be illusory; that is, while experience of non-duality in consciousness and agency may indeed be real and pervasive, it may not be indicative of a foundational non-dual level of being – it may be erroneous, limited, and so on, and may pertain solely to the specifically human emergent level of being. One may ask how, in that case, human agency and understanding are possible.[36] The objection tacitly endorses human-world dualism, disconnecting or splitting us off from the world from which we have emerged, presupposing that when we experience bliss (to continue our example), it is a discrete emergent phenomenon at our level of being that does not owe anything to the affordant possibilities of the world. Similarly, if it is objected that experience of absolute transcendence in the epistemological dialectic is illusory, the onus is on the sceptic who is also a scientific realist to show how in that case such moments of revelation of truth are possible. On the meta-Reality account truth is most fundamentally revelation of underlying identity.[37]

Again, it might be objected that direct mind-to-mind (better, consciousness-to-consciousness[38]) interaction with another person, namely in transcendental identity consciousness is illusory on the grounds that there is no way of knowing that identical thoughts (or the 'same' thoughts in some sense) are in two different minds.[39] But this would be to misunderstand my position. Identification does not take place at the level of actual thoughts but at the level of either our ground states or of the deep interior of our everyday dealings and perceptions.[40] If you understand what I am saying, the understanding is yours, not mine, but in the moment of understanding or listening or following there is no ego, no duality, no separation, just identification. You do not first interpret the sounds that you hear and then make out their meaning; there is no separation between the hearing and the meaning. Similarly, if you see a drawing as either a duck or a rabbit you do not first interpret it, you just see it. Of course, there will normally be a physical medium or cue – the sounds of my voice travel to you on airwaves – but your understanding me is not reducible to its physical conditions, so this is quite compatible with synchronic emergent powers materialism.[41] The immediacy of hearing, perceiving, understanding, intuiting, reading, and so on, and more generally of 'just seeing or getting' a point is irreducible in social life. The semiotic triangle collapses in these moments, and reflecting on this we see that being is intrinsically meaningful and valuable or enchanted.[42]

7.4 Principles of metaReality

As I have just argued, there are three senses in which identity or non-duality is essential to social life:

(i)   as *mode of constitution*, that is as the way social life is reproduced or transformed;
(ii) as the *basis* of social life; and
(iii) as the *deep interior* of social life, and indeed of everything that exists.

There are four main *forms of transcendence of duality*, that is, of transcendental identity or identification, or of the ingredience of non-duality in social life:

(a)   *transcendental identification* in consciousness;
(b)   *transcendental agency*;
(c)   *transcendental holism* or teamwork; and
(d)   the *transcendental self*.

(a) Transcendental identification in consciousness

Rehearsing what I argued above, when you are listening to me, or me to you, intently, the sense of a separate 'me' and 'you' disappears. Our consciousnesses become one at the level of fine structure. There is just what I am (you are) saying. Similarly, often when you are reading a book, or watching a play, the separation, distinctiveness between you and the book or the play disappears. There is a unity, which on reflection, is involved in all interaction and perception as its fine structure. You may be incredulous about this. You may want to tell me that you don't understand me, but what you are saying is that the words that you hear, the words that I utter (with which you are nevertheless one) make no sense to you. Similarly, if you cannot make out the words I am uttering, you can at least identify, are at one with the sounds that I make. This transcendental identification in consciousness is something that has been remarkably untheorised in philosophy (not to mention social theory) except with respect to the context of a small number of kinds of 'peak' experience – for example, becoming entranced with a beautiful work of art, or nature, say in an ecstatic, aesthetic 'high', or becoming engulfed in meditation on or worship of a divine figure such as Jesus or Mary. Teachers of meditation have long been aware of the paradox that if you think you are meditating, achieving the goal of transcending the world of duality, namely, transcendental identification with your real self or a state of emptiness, then you are not in non-duality! And of course it *is* difficult to achieve the kind of transcendental identifications typically attempted in prayer and meditation. But it has not been noticed that a related kind of transcendental identification is normally achieved effortlessly in everyday life and as a necessary condition for our perception and interaction alike.

(b) Transcendental agency

The second quotidian form of transcendence is transcendental or non-dual agency. This occurs at the level of what philosophers call *basic acts*.[43] Basic acts are acts that are just done, not done by doing something else. Thus for most of us, tying our shoelaces is a basic act, which we do spontaneously, that is, mindlessly (without thinking about it), though of course tying one's shoelaces is something that, as a child, one had mindfully to learn to do;[44] and of course it is a skill or accomplishment that one can, in illness or old age, lose. Whatever one does, one does ultimately spontaneously, as a basic act. Thus supposing I wish to invite a friend to dinner; I can work out the menu, go shopping and buy the food, take it into the kitchen, get all the relevant utensils out, but at some point I just have to begin cooking. Similarly, in a conversation you may think about what the correct word to use in it is (is it this? or is it that?) but when you are in a conversation at some point the thinking has to stop and you must just say something (or say nothing at all). Even with thinking itself, the thinking is the coming into your consciousness of a thought, not as such something you do by thinking about it. So transcendental agency is irreducible in our action in the world, which always presupposes a spontaneous or basic transcendental moment: in the last instance we either act spontaneously or we do not act at all. This is what I call *spontaneous right action* – action that is in and from our ground state.[45]

(c) Transcendental holism

The third kind of everyday transcendence of duality is transcendental holism, team-work or holistic synchronicity. You may experience this when preparing dinner with your partner, when you each effortlessly supplement each other's activity. Transcendental holism can be seen every day on the pavements of city streets in the way we manage to avoid bumping into each other; but it is best exemplified by reference to, for example, the sort of teamwork that is displayed in a football team in passing the ball to each other and running imaginatively in the build-up to a goal; or the acting that is done by accomplished actors in a well-rehearsed play; or the playing of a musical band or orchestra. These are all everyday examples of tran-scendental holism, when we 'click' as a team.

(d) *The* transcendental self

The fourth kind of transcendence we routinely accomplish or experience is aware-ness of the transcendental self, and in discussing this I now pass over wholly to the second sense in which identity is essential to social life, namely as a *basis* for it.

MetaReality contends that we all possess three concepts of the self:

(i)   as ego;
(ii) as embodied personality; and
(iii) as transcendentally real self or ground state.

The *ego* is the concept of self we have as separate from everyone else. This is our sense of self as an island. It is this concept of self that is the dominant one in our civilisation. It is at the heart of the philosophical discourse of modernity and of capitalist economic life, which depends on it for its ideology of possessive individu-alism and the experience of emotions such as greed and fear in one's work regime and a whole host of social practices, ranging from advertising to assessment, which are more or less necessary to it. But this sense of self, the ego, is totally illusory. No-one can possibly live separately from everyone else. Even a monk in a monas-tery is totally dependent on his fellow monks and the relations of the monastery with the outside world, at the very least for much of what is needed to meet his physical needs. But of course he is also dependent on previous generations for the teachings that he contemplates, the doctrines he recapitulates and finesses and the rituals he employs.

What then of the *embodied personality*? This Lockean sense of self is real, but it is a relative, changeable reality. As we grow up and develop, we get taller, our beliefs mature, our values change, and so on. Moreover, this sense of self is contextually variable. For many people, in some contexts, their job or partner is part of themselves, while in others it is not. For many men, their car is an essential part of their (macho) identity.

The third sense of self, the *transcendentally real self*, may be introduced by reflection on the idea of our higher or better self. This is roughly ourselves on a very good day – when we feel on top of the world and spontaneously do the right thing, act generously and kindly to all. It may begin to be justified philosophically by reflecting on what is involved in its denial. Thus when Hume tells us that he has searched everywhere for the self and been unable to find it and declares that there is no such thing as the self,[46] we may ask: 'Who is it who is saying that there is no self?' Similarly, consider the familiar postmodernist theme of the fractured self. Someone may complain that they are split, that they are hearing ten voices in their heads; but even if they are hearing ten voices, it still remains the case that there is only a single listener who is hearing the voices and that is their transcendentally real self; and if they are split, they at least know that it is *they* who are split, and this also gives an anchor or basis on which the healing of the split can begin.

This relates to the second sense in which non-duality or identity is essential to social life, as its basis or ground, but also to the third sense, as a deep interior, intrinsic to everything. This is a sense that, as we saw in section 7.3, cannot be established fully by transcendental argumentation but follows mainly from the phenomenological analysis of experience in what I call practical mysticism. Thus mystics have reported that if they go deeper and deeper into something, indeed anything, they will eventually find *sat-chit-ananda* – the bliss consciousness at the heart of being, the Buddha nature that inheres in everything, the unconditional love that permeates the world. This does have a role in metaReality. It intimates what I call the *cosmic envelope*, which connects the ground states of everything, including our real selves, in a whole or unity.

Mechanisms of identification and/or unification

There are three mechanisms of identification and/or unification in the philosophy of metaReality, the first two of which have their ultimate ontological basis in the third:[47]

(i)   transcendental identification in consciousness;
(ii) reciprocity; and
(iii) co-presence.

We have already discussed transcendental identification in consciousness. Reciprocity is when I smile at you and you smile at me. It presupposes a moment of identification that has its basis in co-presence; that is, the capacity to be one with another lies in the fact that the being or qualities of the other are implicit or enfolded within oneself. Co-presence is thus the most radical or deepest mode of identification. It is when we come to see the other as part of ourselves, an experience we have all had with a partner or child or other loved one, at least occasionally. The theory of *generalised co-presence* holds that at the level of fundamental possibility or alethic truth everything is interconnected – implicitly contained within and related to everything else. This is what makes it possible for human beings to discover the alethic truth of other beings, such as the molecular structure of a crystal or the nature of gravity and it explains why it is easy to for us to identify with our fellow human beings and why we can experience a commitment to the fulfilment and flourishing of all beings and a yearning to see being as such unfold.

I now want to develop some implications of the philosophy of metaReality. My critique of the philosophical discourse of modernity, the strands of which I first wove together in the metaReality books, will be discussed in the next chapter.

7.5 Extension of the logic of freedom

Dialectical critical realism sets out the goal of a eudaimonistic society as one in which the free flourishing of each is a condition for the free flourishing of all. We can now unpack what this involves at all four planes of social being in light of the philosophy of metaReality. We can see, in particular, that on the plane of the stratification of the embodied personality it means the *absence of ego*, that your flourishing and development becomes as important to me as my own. Most projects of trying to build a better society have been oriented to action *only on the plane of social structure*. They have ignored the question posed by Marx in the third of his *Theses on Feuerbach* as to who will educate the educators. Transformation on the plane of social structure, and in particular the abolition of master–slave-type relations is of course essential, but it needs to be complemented by equal attention to the other three planes.[48]

Marx focused overwhelmingly on the one plane of social structure, with little attention to other structures and other planes; he underestimated the role of ideas; and failed to examine the metaReal or the spiritual conditions necessary for a society in which the free development of each is the condition for the free development of all. In particular, on the plane of the stratification of the embodied personality this involves the shedding of the ego and the clearing of heteronomous elements that are inconsistent with the ground state.

The free flourishing of each as a condition for the free flourishing of all involves not only the abolition of the ego, but the *shedding of all heteronomous elements* in the embodied personality, that is, all elements that are inconsistent with one's ground state. Without this shedding, the embodied personality will be subject to endemic conflicts, with the ground state pushing one way and the heteronomous elements pushing another; so that one's intentionality will be split and undermined. It follows from this, of course, that one will not be able to achieve one's objectives in life. Hence one could say, paraphrasing the Buddha, that what you should do in your life is seek to become enlightened or *self-realised*, because this is the only thing that you can ultimately be sure to have the capacity to achieve; and attaining it is moreover a condition for your maximally efficacious agency in the world.

The mechanism of the *dialectic of self-realisation* is simple: in so far as there is an ego or heteronomous elements, the intentionality of the agent will be split, undermining the efficacy of praxis. From the standpoint of the embodied personality it is thus in its interest to become self-realised. At the same time the ground state, positive emotions such as love and (at the level of the intellect) the drive to truth all reinforce the immanent teleology to self-realisation. Thus there is a link between the immanent teleology of praxis (analysed in dialectical critical realism) and the drive to self-realisation (in metaReality), such that the eudaimonistic society can now be seen to presuppose and entail universal self-realisation. Enhanced empathy, augmented awareness of co-presence – the co-presence of ground states located on the cosmic envelope that interconnects all beings – and the tendency to *generalised synchronicity* set in motion by what I have called *the dive to the ground state* will all tend to induce an echoing, confirming, reinforcing response on the part of all dialectically similar agents or aspects of agents to action moving in an emancipating, self-realising direction.[49] This illustrates the way the logic of dialectical universalisability is played out in more concrete form in the philosophy of metaReality.

More generally and cosmologically, there is an even deeper link between the latent immanent teleology of praxis and the immanent teleology of ground states and the cosmic envelope, on which everything is enchanted and in the process of becoming one with its ground state. This link is *generalised co-presence*, the concept of which I introduced above, leading ultimately to a situation that can be characterised as one of individual and universal god-realisation.[50] This brings out the so called anthropocosmism of metaReality as a consistent anti-anthropocentricity, as noted in section 7.3. At the same time, it allows us to situate the woeful inadequacies of positivistic naturalist accounts lacking a concept of intentional agency; and of the romantic reaction to them, based on one or other form of Kantianism, with the aporia that the self remains unknowable.

7.6 Creativity, learning and education and the critique of the discursive intellect

There is a paradox involved in learning, the *paradox of the exam*. This takes the following form: when we are studying, as a student, we always attempt to revise until the very last minute; yet when we become parents or teachers, we always tell our children or students not to revise up to the last minute, to be fresh for the exam. I will come back to this paradox in a moment, but first I want to articulate a basic dialectic of learning that applies when we are coming to learn anything. The standpoint of metaReality is that the knowledge that you are trying to achieve as a student is already enfolded within you as a potential; and the task of learning (and teaching) is to unfold that potential. This is why I call this model of learning that of *unfolding the enfolded*.[51]

I can best elaborate by starting with another seeming paradox, which is that *you cannot teach anyone else anything*. That you cannot emancipate anyone else should be apparent from what I have argued in this chapter; emancipation always has to be, or involve, self-emancipation. Thus one can unlock the doors of the cells in a prison, but the prisoners have to walk out. It is on the face of it more surprising that the same principle applies to learning, but imagine trying to teach someone a logical rule, such as: 'If it is the case that either A or *not A* (but not both), then if A is the case, then it is not the case that *not A*'. Now most people will immediately get this, but if you do not, then I can perhaps write on the blackboard a metatheorem, establishing that under the circumstance envisioned, *not A* will not be the case. But what if you don't get that? It is not as if logic can, to use Wittgenstein's expression, grab you by the throat and force you to see it. You just have to see it; and if you don't see it, another approach can be applied, but at the end of the day it is you who have to get it. If and when you get it, this is the eureka moment, the self-referential 'aha' or 'I see it!'. Without the 'I see it!' the knowledge cannot be yours.

Consider your first experience of learning how to ride a bike. No doubt you fell off over and over again. Then at one point you stayed on for five or ten seconds. This was your eureka moment. You had begun to get it. But that was not of course the end of the process, because you would fall off again after ten or fifteen seconds. Moreover, you needed to learn the best technique for riding the bike in different conditions. So this was followed by a more or less lengthy period in which you learnt how to ride a bike successfully on the different kinds of terrain and in the various contexts that you were likely to encounter. Then at a certain point, you knew how to ride a bike. You could do it. And now you just do it, spontaneously, without thought. This is you as a natural being in your ground state, acting consistently with your real self. There is a similar process involved in learning French, calculus or to drive a car.

Four stages are involved. At the first stage you cannot do it, but the knowledge or capacity to do it is enfolded within you as a potential. At the second stage, you see how to do it, but haltingly. At the third stage you practice, explore, play with it, until, at the fourth stage, you can do it spontaneously. Then the knowledge is part of your being and you can perform the activity or skill relatively effortlessly – the way you speak in your mother tongue. At the second and third stages we have to carry the rules around in our heads. One might wonder, for example, which way to turn the wheel when one is reversing, or how to deal with ice or to control a skid. There is also a fifth level in which you can see your accomplishment reflected in your production or accomplishment in the world.

These five levels correspond to five *cycles of creativity*,[52] which are to be found in many ancient cosmotheogonies. These five cycles or phases are, first, the moment of *calling*. This is a moment of preparation, including a state best characterised by inner emptiness. Thus when one is beginning to learn something probably the worst one can do is fill oneself with a lot of knowledge about it. The worst thing one can do in going to one's first class or lesson is to have one's head full of a lot of information about it. On the contrary, the best way to learn is in a state of inner emptiness. The second level is called the moment of *creativity*. This is the 'I see it', the eureka moment, when light bulbs flash and you get the first glimpse of the new world opened up by this learning. The third cycle is that of *formation* or shaping, playing with it, gradually mastering the techniques and rules for this skill or activity. The fourth cycle is that of *making* or objectification. This is the moment at which the knowledge becomes part of your being, so that it can be produced spontaneously when the occasion demands. The fifth moment is the moment of *reflection*, when you can recognise your intentionality reflected in an achieved result in the world. The first four levels of course correspond in a rough way to 1M–4D in dialectical critical realism and the first five to 1M–5A in metaReality.

This schema now allows us to explain the paradox of exams. Your parents and teachers assume that you are already at the fourth stage, at which clearly you would be able to perform best when well rested. But you, as a student, recognise or fear that you are only perhaps somewhere in the second or third stage, and so desperately seek to cram your head full of information or knowledge until the last moment.

The five-stage dialectic of learning may be summed up as follows (see also Table 7.1):

1M moment of calling: the knowledge is implicit or enfolded, and preparations can begin for the learning to unfold;

2E cycle of creativity: the moment of Platonic anamnesis,[53] or the 'I see it' (primacy of self-referentiality) or the 'eureka' moment;

3L cycle of formation: the process of binding the new knowledge; so that at

4D cycle of making: it is inbuilt, part of one's being; and objectification or making can occur spontaneously, without thought;

5A cycle of reflection: the intentionality of the maker is perfectly reflected in the object or product made.

Thus the role of teaching or pedagogy is to unfold the enfolded, helping to bring out what is already there within. You cannot teach anyone else anything.

The critique of the discursive intellect and the limits of thought[54]

The intellect is just the faculty of discrimination and choice. The *discursive intellect*, which includes dialectical as well as analytical thought, is formal, calculative and discursive intellectual activity. The philosophy of metaReality does not regard thought in this sense (whether analytical or dialectical) as the crowning pinnacle of our civilisation. On the contrary, it sees it as indeed a magnificent achievement, but something with definite limits. At least equally important is the *intuitive intellect*, and both intuition and thought are possible only on the basis of *unthought* or unthinking, the suspension (conscious or otherwise) of thought.

When Descartes said 'I think therefore I am', he took the presence of thought as continuous, a constant. We can begin to reverse this process by identifying, from a critical realist standpoint, some important things that are *not* thought, that is, that are the other of thought, but which are nevertheless essential for our knowing. The five that I wish to flag here are ones we have already rehearsed in various ways.

(1) Intuition

Intuition may be involved in processes of thought but is not itself thought; it is iconic, imaginative, spontaneous and holistic intellectual activity by which we just know.

(2) Consciousness

Consciousness (capacities for awareness) constellationally embraces thought and intuition but also *supramental consciousness* or *unthought*, which is their basis or ground.

(3) Perception

Just (directly) seeing, or the non-dual becoming one with that which you would perceive or understand, which occurs without thought, is the basis of all our social life and learning.

(4) Being

The Cartesian tradition prioritises thought over being. This is an enormous mistake, for patently there is being without thought, and thought must be, if it is real or efficacious in any way, a proper sub-set, that is, a small but real part of being.

(5) Absence

Nothing creative ever comes from thought as such. The creative act or discovery, the irruption of something new, can only come from the absent beyond or between thoughts (when we stop thinking or unthink), from the epistemically unmanifested. As we have seen, an empty mind is vital for understanding anything, for if our minds are full, how could we learn anything? Clear mind or empty mind, that is, no mind, is also 'don't know mind', that is mind that is willing and open to learn, mind that has never stopped learning; and the more realised you are, the more humble you become as you understand that the whole world is your teacher and there is nothing from which you cannot learn.[55]

I now sum up this section. Alongside the discursive intellect we have the much neglected intuitive intellect; and underpinning and synthesising both is a level of supramental consciousness or unthought. Creativity always involves a moment of the suspension of thought, of unthought, and occurs most easily when the mindfulness of focused attention (ideally in a non-dual state) has passed over to the mindlessness of spontaneous 'flow', when someone is, as we say, 'in the zone'.[56] This is the level of supramental or transcendental consciousness, by which I mean the implicit consciousness of the ground state and cosmic envelope that is at once the source of the fundamental qualities of all beings and binds and coheres them as a totality.[57]

7.7 The circles of love[58]

Love is perhaps the most fundamental of all the emotions, since negative emotions such as fear or hatred are both parasitic on some rudimentary form of love and at the same time depend on love's absence or incompleteness. Love is paradigmatically unconditional. Conditional love is love mixed with some other emotion, such as jealousy or fear. Love does not calculate or barter or seek to control or shape its object. Love loves to let the other be, to flourish in their concrete singularity = universality. Love attracts love, and is self-accumulating, begetting more love. Indeed, love as automatically self-expanding is arguably the fundamental attractive force in the universe and the coherence of love, trust, sharing and solidarity is arguably the basis of human social life – what makes it possible.[59] To love and be loved is a fundamental human need as well as capacity – we cannot help but love.[60] Love is joy, sheer delight in being-becoming, bliss-consciousness.

MetaReality posits five *circles of love* corresponding to 1M-5A (see Table 7.1):

(1) love of oneself – this should be of one's ground state and of those elements within one's embodied personality consistent with it;
(2) love of another human being – if the love is from the ground state and reciprocated, then we have the situation of 'love loving love';[61]
(3) love of all human beings – through generalised co-presence, aspiring to universal self-realisation;
(4) love of all beings; and
(5) love of god, the cosmic envelope or the totality.

Re-enchantment[62]

As we have seen, the absolute non-dual or transcendental ground of reality immediately constitutes the enchanted character of relative reality via the collapse of the semiotic triangle which follows from the breakdown of subject–object duality in transcendental identity consciousness and agency. Whereas creativity corresponds to 2E absence and love to 3L totality, re-enchantment is of course the main theme of 6R. Re-enchantment means to see the world once again, through the smog of the demi-real, as it always already is – intrinsically valuable and meaningful – and to relate to it as such in our practices. This includes critiquing the opposition of sacred and profane and indeed of materialism and idealism, embracing the moral realism we discussed in Chapter 6, which sees morality as part of the world; and transforming our understanding of perception, whereby perceivers stand over against the world, to one in which perceivers are also in the world as part of what they perceive. The intrinsic value of the world is entailed by the collapse of the fact-value dichotomy.

The philosophy of metaReality allows for emergent levels of mind, emotion and supramental consciousness in such a way that the concept of four-planar social being needs to be generalised as *n-dimensionally generalised social space*. Each of the four planes can now be understood as having at least three dimensions, namely the dimensions afforded by its *evaluative* or *feeling* aspect, its *meaningful* or *mental* moment and its *transcendental* or *spiritual* dimension. This allows, for example, for mind-to-mind consciousness and other modes of non-physical connection, as we saw in section 7.3; and it involves a radicalisation of the critique of the idea of the exhaustive physicality of being – of reductive materialism.[63] If we accept the theory of Big Bang, for example, the potential for consciousness as we know it must have been present as a real possibility from the inception of space–time.

7.8 Spirituality

Although spirituality and religion converge on notions of the absolute, as already mentioned in section 7.1 the philosophy of metaReality differentiates sharply between them.[64] *Spirituality* is centrally bound up with *transcendence* in the sense of the achievement of unity and identity in a total context, as thematised above. *Religion* is essentially concerned with *the transcendent* or what lies beyond the human in the senses of a being or force transcendent to human beings and/or the cosmos, of humans becoming higher beings, and of human lives extending beyond this one in some sense. My philosophy rules none of these out – on the contrary, it endorses versions of them all,[65] but not from the perspective of any particular religion. The only view it opposes in this domain is the notion that the divine is transcendent to the cosmos.[66]

It is important to understand that metaReality is not in competition with religion. On the contrary, it seeks to underlabour for religion and help it flourish in a manner conducive to human flourishing in general. It operates at a higher level of abstraction than religion and theology. This is most apparent in my concepts of the cosmic envelope or absolute and its understanding by the *higher truth*.[67] According to the higher truth, which has adherents in all the main religions, there is only one absolute but many epistemologically relative accounts of it: God both manifests, and is accessed differently in different regions and epochs of relative reality. This is by no means to endorse judgemental relativism and the notion that all religions are equally valid (religious pluralism). The respective claims of religions can and should be rationally appraised and developed via intra-, inter- and extra-faith dialogue and assessments, and critical realist philosophy and social science can play a role here too in the critique of ethically problematic doctrines and oppressive institutional forms.[68] My own account of the abstract contours of the absolute is fallible and open to revision and not I think incompatible with the fundamental doctrines of any religion.[69] From the standpoint of epistemology, the only religious position that is opposed is absolutism (fundamentalism) or what I call the *ordinary truth*: the notion that my way is the only way and yours is definitely wrong, which I also refer to as *uniquism*.[70]

MetaReality holds that spirituality is a presupposition, not only of religious and emancipatory practices (to which I turn in a moment), but of everyday life. According to it, the whole of our social existence is underpinned by a barely noticed, but deep, spiritual or metaReal infrastructure. However, it is not that difficult to observe people acting on its basis. Thus commercial transactions, the buying and selling of commodities or stocks and shares are underpinned by trust. No transaction could be completed without this mutuality of trust. Consider what happens if I want to buy a newspaper from a newsagent and I ask her how much the paper costs. Suppose she tells me. If I don't make a gesture towards my wallet, she may become suspicious and will probably not make a move to give me the newspaper. Reciprocity of the 'do unto another as you would be done by' sort underpins all such commercial transactions. This is the reciprocity of the Golden Rule, and it is founded on the ground-state quality of trust.

Similarly, reflection on, say, the practice of war, allows us to see that many peaceful activities must be going on for the war actually to take place. There is an asymmetry here: we could of course have these peaceful activities without the war, whereas we could not have the war without them. Similarly, at the psychological level, we could say that we only choose to hate things that we could, and perhaps do, love. If a stone falls on us, we do not express hatred of, or anger at the stone. It is typically, and perhaps only, things which they also love that people hate, and the love forms a hidden basis for the hate they express. In the same sort of way, the world of instrumental so called reasoning, of means–ends rationality, is underpinned by the unconditional love we experience and give at home, and the spontaneous solidarity we show to our friends and indeed colleagues at work. Thus if someone's telephone is ringing while I pass their desk, and there is no sign of them, I will spontaneously pick it up; as we would help a colleague who had fallen and cut their knee. We would perform such acts spontaneously, without thinking. It is well known that if the workers in any organisation 'worked to rule', that is, followed the rule book, the operation would quickly grind to a halt. It is our unremarked spontaneous loving natures that keep the whole show going in all these cases. This is as true for all the relations and institutions of the world of demi-reality as it is for other more anodyne institutions and relations in the world of duality.

Reflection on the tacit metaReal level in the world of everyday life is an important resource for overcoming the crisis system we face. Thus, considering the crises at all four planes of social being, the metaReal response to the disembedding of money from the economy, and the real economy from the social structure and especially social and political control, is to seek to embed money and the economy at those levels, but also to embed the social structure in its metaReal basis. Of course we need to develop the institutions that are necessary to make this possible. The argument from transcendental identification in consciousness has already suggested that conflicts and differences are underpinned by tacit identities and I will turn to this further in the next section. I discuss healing processes on the planes of our transactions with nature and on the planes of the stratification of the embodied personality in Chapter 9.

The philosophy of metaReality sees the different religions, understood as distinct from spirituality, as involving various attempts to understand and access the absolute. In this it is susceptible of a purely secular interpretation. However, in the field of comparative religion, I have argued that the holy trinity of critical realism, namely ontological realism, epistemological relativism and judgemental rationality, can form a basis for a programme for a greater inter-faith, intra-faith and extra-faith understanding and dialogue; and that the philosophy of metaReality can underlabour more generally for theology and the philosophy of religion, especially (but not only) within the field of comparative religion.[71]

7.9 Peace and conflict resolution[72]

MetaReality contains a powerful argument for non-violence. The reason why one should not hurt another is that the other is really, given generalised co-presence, a part of oneself. Thus, *in hurting another one is hurting oneself*. In fact, co-presence, rather than the revenge of the hurt one in a subsequent life is the true basis for Gandhian *ahimsa* (or harmlessness: cause no injury, do no harm).

The philosophy of metaReality formulates two axioms or principles that may be very useful in conflict resolution. These are:[73]

> P1: the axiom or *principle of universal solidarity*, which specifies that in principle any human being can empathise with and come to understand any other human being; and
> P2: the axiom or *principle of axial rationality*, which specifies that there is a basic logic of human learning applicable to the practical order. This basic logic is used by all human communities irrespective of cultural differentiations.

P1 may be motivated by reflection on the contingency of any person's birth. If they had been born on the same day in a different country, or perhaps in the same place but at a different time, the beliefs, attitudes and habits the person came to adopt would have been very different. This shows that they could have been, that is, had the capacity to be, someone very different from the person they actually became. Moreover, even if, as a result of a rational modification of these beliefs and customs, they came to the very same beliefs and customs, and so on, that they hold now, they would have come to them by a very different route. They must therefore have had the capacity, which metaReality ascribes to their ground state, to have become very different persons from who they currently are; and they must therefore also have (or at least have had) the capacity to become one with very different persons from themselves. This capacity to become one with someone other than oneself is of course something that may become stunted in the course of a life, but metaReality posits that, however difficult and far removed from one's current concerns and dispositions, this possibility of becoming one with another is a permanent and essential possibility for any human being.

P2, the principle of axial rationality, may be motivated by the thought that people everywhere ride bicycles, drive cars, operate computers and tote machine guns. This learning proceeds by a basic dialectic of diagnosis, identification and rectification (or correction) of mistakes. As such, it presupposes a universal capacity to learn, and this presupposes also the possibility of learning the meta-process of correcting one's learning procedure, and therefore of critique. Since human beings are also linguistic, this capacity must also be expressible in language; and hence within the cultural domain proper there must also be a mechanism for the diagnosis, identification and correction of mistakes and hence for critique, including reflexive critique. Further reflection on this logic of axial rationality at work in our basic material practices of interaction with each other and the material world and, more generally, on the four planes of social being shows that there is always a possibility of critical reflection within any community (cf. Chapter 2.8).

These two principles not only underpin conflict resolution, but also collective decision-making. For they represent ways in which people can come to understand (P1) and then reason with (P2) the perspective of others. The basic process involved in P1 is of course empathy, which is ultimately transcendental identification in consciousness. An important precondition for empathy is to see the other as a human being, with hopes and dreams and fears similar to one's own. This is of course why, when a country or a community is waging war, it seeks always (especially in the popular media and at the frontline) to dehumanise the human beings of the enemy, for example, by calling them 'Jerrys' or 'uniforms' or 'pigs' or whatever. Conversely, once the process of basic human interaction, including the swapping of life stories, gets underway, then gradually the move to more difficult topics can begin. However, there may be a surprise here. For it may often transpire that what the other whom we are fighting wants is something very similar to what we want. Thus probably the overwhelming majority of soldiers fighting in the First World War wanted 'bread, peace and land'. Discussion of shared or similar objectives may point the way to the isolation of the real constraints on the attainment of these objectives. These may, for instance, lie at the level of social structure or necessitate joint work on the plane of material transactions with nature. Considering human conflict generally, what metaReality allows us to see is that the other is often merely developing a part of oneself that one has chosen not to develop or to see; so that the other is merely showing us a repressed, denied or forgotten part, aspect or possibility of oneself.

Notes

1 See Bhaskar with Hartwig, *The Formation of Critical Realism*, Chapters 7 and 8.
2 Bhaskar, *From Science to Emancipation: Alienation and the Actuality of Enlightenment* (London: Routledge, 2002/2012), 171.
3 Bhaskar with Hartwig, *The Formation of Critical Realism*, 168.
4 See Bhaskar, *From East to West*, 'Twelve steps to heaven', 65 ff. and 'Interlude: critical realism, transcendence and God' in *From Science to Emancipation*, 145–64. These passages informed the argument of Margaret S. Archer, Andrew Collier and Douglas V. Porpora in *Transcendence: Critical Realism and God* (London: Routledge 2004). See also Andrew Wright, *Critical Religious Education: Multiculturalism and the Pursuit of Truth* (Cardiff: University of Wales Press, 2007) and McGrath, *A Scientific Theology*, esp. *Vol. 2, Reality*. For discussion see *The Formation of Critical Realism*, Chapter 7 (esp. 150–1) and Chapter 8; and Roy Bhaskar with Mervyn Hartwig in 'Beyond East and West' and '(Re-)

contextualising metaReality' in *Critical Realism and Spirituality,* eds Mervyn Hartwig and Jamie Morgan (London: Routledge 2011), 187–202 and 205–17, respectively.

5 See for example Douglas V. Porpora, 'Methodological atheism, methodological agnosticism and religious experience', *Journal for the Theory of Social Behavior* 36:1 (2006): 57–75.

6 See Archer *et al.*, eds, *Transcendence*; Roy Bhaskar, Sean Estbjörn-Hargens, Nick Hedlund and Mervyn Hartwig, eds, *Metatheory for the Twenty-First Century: Critical Realism and Integral Theory in Dialogue* (London: Routledge, 2016); Andrew Collier, *On Christian Belief: A Defence of a Cognitive Conception of Religious Belief in a Christian Context* (London: Routledge, 2003); Hartwig and Morgan, eds, *Critical Realism and Spirituality* (London: Routledge, 2010); MinGyu Seo, *Reality and Self-Realisation: Bhaskar's Metaphilosophical Journey toward Non-dual Emancipation* (London: Routledge, 2014); Matthew L. N. Wilkinson, *A Fresh Look at Islam in a Multi-Faith World: A Philosophy of Success through Education* (London: Routledge, 2015); Andrew Wright, *Christianity and Critical Realism: Ambiguity, Truth and Theological Literacy* (London: Routledge, 2013).

7 Bhaskar with Hartwig, 'Beyond East and West', 189.

8 Bhaskar, *From East to West*, 'Theoretical introduction', 45–94.

9 Bhaskar with Hartwig, 'Beyond East and West', 189; Bhaskar, *The Philosophy of MetaReality*, 44, 308–9, 321, 349; *Reflections on MetaReality*, 18, 222.

10 Bhaskar, *The Philosophy of MetaReality*, 117.

11 Bhaskar, *Dialectic*, 139 f.

12 Bhaskar, *Dialectic*, 77–8, 399 and *passim*. As I note there (p. 78n.) the notion of dispositional identity was already introduced in *A Realist Theory of Science*.

13 Mervyn Hartwig, 'Introduction' to Roy Bhaskar, *The Philosophy of MetaReality*, ix–xxxix, Table 3, xxx–xxxv (slightly amended by MH).

14 See Bhaskar with Hartwig, *The Formation of Critical Realism*, 180–2. Note that, while in, say, transcendental identification in consciousness, the subject–object distinction breaks down, the consciousnesses remain that of materially embodied people and that, as materially embodied, they remain in the world of duality, even while the consciousnesses are fused as one. Editor's note. Elsewhere I have often referred to the philosophy of meta-Reality as *meta-Realism*, which seems logical both in the interest of brevity and in that it locates the philosophy in the developmental sequence of basic critical realism – dialectical critical realism – metaRealism. Bhaskar, however, did not follow suit, I expect for the reason given above: it implies that the philosophy is a realism rather than (or at least before it is) a philosophy of truth. Henceforth I will follow Bhaskar's practice.

15 Although extra-terrestrial visitors may not be real, experiences of them are, whether illusory or not; in terms of our discussion of levels of real negativity in Chapter 6, experiences of non-existent aliens are, like phlogiston or Santa Claus, real at the level of fictional discourse because they may have causal effects on people.

16 G. W. F. Hegel, *Phenomenology of Spirit*, trans. A. V. Miller (Oxford: Oxford University Press, 1807/1977), B, Self-consciousness. See also Bhaskar, *Dialectic*, Chapter 4.4–4.5.

17 See Axel Honneth, *The Struggle for Recognition: The Moral Grammar of Social Conflicts* (London: Polity Press, 1993/1995).

18 In Sartre's dialectic of the 'gaze', the master–slave theme is so pronounced that one cannot have a mutually reciprocated look. You either look, and you are the master or controller of the situation or relationship; or you are looked at and you become the subordinate victim or slave. Jean-Paul Sartre, *Being and Nothingness: An Essay on Phenomenological Ontology* (London: Routledge, 1943/2003).

19 Mervyn Hartwig, 'Introduction' to Roy Bhaskar, *The Philosophy of MetaReality*, ix–xxxix, Table 4, xxxvi–xxxix (slightly amended by MH).

20 See Bhaskar, *Dialectic*, 327.

21 For the concept of patching in this context, see Iskra Nuñez, *Critical Realist Activity Theory: An Engagement with Critical Realism and Cultural-Historical Activity Theory* (London: Routledge, 2014).

22 See for example Slavoj Žižek, *Less Than Nothing: Hegel and the Shadow of Dialectical Materialism* (London: Verso, 2012). For the concept of structural sin, see Bhaskar, *From East to West*, 64 n23, 67, 70, 76, 119, 121–2.

23 Bhaskar, *Reflections on MetaReality*, 267–9. For other ways, see Bhaskar *From Science to Emancipation*, xiv, and *The Philosophy of Meta-Reality*, xi f, 315 f.

24 This is the approach I mainly follow in *Reflections on MetaReality*; see esp. Chapter 4, 'MetaReality: In and beyond critical realism', 165–263.

25 Bhaskar, *From Science to Emancipation*, xliii–iv.

26 See for example Andrew Wiles's account in the 1997 TV documentary *The Proof* of how he arrived at the proof of Fermat's last theorem or, in literature, Marcel Proust's account of involuntary memories.

27 Bhaskar, *The Philosophy of MetaReality*, 360.

28 Analogously to the ingredience, according to some interpretations of quantum physics, of fundamental fields of non-localised *potentiae* in emergent levels of being. See for example Ruth E. Kastner, *The Transactional Interpretation of Quantum Mechanics: The Reality of Possibility* (Cambridge: Cambridge University Press, 2013) and Pete Mason, 'Does quantum theory redefine realism? The neo-Copenhagen view', *Journal of Critical Realism* 14: 2 (2015), 137–63. Nonlocality and quantum entanglement are of course regarded as beyond dispute in modern physics: at a fundamental level everything is interconnected with everything else. For the theory of generalised co-presence, see esp. Bhaskar, *The Philosophy of MetaReality*, 226 ff.

29 I introduce the concept of practical mysticism in Bhaskar, *Reflections on MetaReality*, 148 and 179.

30 Bhaskar, *From Science to Emancipation*, xliii–xliv.

31 Although the transcendentally real self is not named in *Dialectic*, it is theorised implicitly as the deep content of human speech and action, as we saw in Chapter 6.

32 Bhaskar, *The Philosophy of MetaReality*, xlii.

33 Bhaskar, *Reflections on MetaReality*, 14, 53, 148, 220; *The Philosophy of MetaReality*, 269.

34 Bhaskar, *Reflections on MetaReality*, 226.

35 Seo, 'Bhaskar's philosophy as anti-anthropism'.

36 Bhaskar with Hartwig, *The Formation of Critical Realism*, 179.

37 Bhaskar, *The Philosophy of MetaReality*, xlvii.

38 As we will see in our critique of the discursive intellect (section 7.6), this is because 'mind' freezes or fixes consciousness in an egoistic or dualistic way. See for example, Bhaskar, *The Philosophy of MetaReality*, 9.

39 *Editor's note*. Margaret Archer put this kind of objection to me in a comment on Bhaskar's manuscript. cf. Pierpaolo Donati and Margaret S. Archer, 'On plural subjectivity and the relational subject' in their *The Relational Subject* (Cambridge: Cambridge University Press, 2015), Chapter 2, 33–76. In my view Bhaskar's theory of consciousness-to-consciousness action does not contradict Donati and Archer's sociological account of the relational subject (which is consistent with the TMSA), but it is arguably a transcendental condition of the relational subject's possibility. Bhaskar's theory does not depend on 'we thinking', but it does rely on the transcendentally real self, the concept of which Donati and Archer's account lacks but could readily supply.

40 See for example Bhaskar, *The Philosophy of MetaReality*, 9.

41 Bhaskar with Hartwig, *The Formation of Critical Realism*, 183.

42 Bhaskar, *The Philosophy of MetaReality*, 317 f., 341.

43 A. C. Danto, 'Basic actions', *American Philosophical Quarterly* 2:2 (1965), 141–8.

44 *Complete* mindfulness, that is, total absorption in one's activity, is also a form of transcendental agency. See for example Bhaskar, *The Philosophy of MetaReality*, 4.

45 Bhaskar, *The Philosophy of MetaReality*, Chapter 5, 233–74.

46 Hume, *A Treatise on Human Nature, Vol. II*, Book 1, Part IV, section 6.

47 See for example Bhaskar, *The Philosophy of MetaReality*, xlviii ff.

48 Personal relations and transactions with nature were often abysmal in the so called 'actually existing socialist' countries. And of course there was no plan for, or encouragement of systematic work on the plane of the stratification of the embodied personality.

49 See Bhaskar, *Reflections on MetaReality*, 19–22. Generalised synchronicity is very different from the universal synchronicity postulated in Leibniz's reductive idealist theory of a pre-established harmony of soul-like substances or monads (see Chapter 3.4), which

(like its dialectical counterpart, reductive materialism) effectively denies the reality and knowability of geo-historical depth-stratified process, explicitly invoking a transcendent God as the cause of (actual) universal synchronicity. The tendency towards generalised synchronicity postulated by metaReality does not reduce or annul but immanently underpins and informs the geo-historical process.

50 Bhaskar, *From Science to Emancipation*, 362–3 and *The Philosophy of MetaReality*, 114.

51 See esp. Bhaskar, *From Science to Emancipation*, Chapter 11, 299–318.

52 See esp. Bhaskar, *The Philosophy of MetaReality*, 105–17.

53 This does *not* mean that that knowledge is, as for Plato, basically recollection, rather that the potential to see it, which is always already enfolded within us, is awakened. Bhaskar, *From Science to Emancipation*, 244.

54 See esp. Bhaskar, *The Philosophy of MetaReality*, Chapter 3, 121–3, 134–6, 144–52 and *passim*.

55 See Bhaskar, *The Philosophy of MetaReality*, 146–50 and *From Science to Emancipation*, 330–4.

56 See also Melanie MacDonald, 'Critical realism, metaReality and making art: traversing a theory-practice gap', *Journal of Critical Realism* 7:1 (2008): 29–56.

57 Bhaskar, *Reflections on MetaReality*, 49.

58 See esp. Bhaskar, *From Science to Emancipation*, Chapter 13, 339–63; *The Philosophy of MetaReality*, 167–232.

59 See also David Graeber, *Debt: The First 5,000 Years* (New York: Melville House, 2011).

60 Bhaskar, *The Philosophy of MetaReality*, 179 f.

61 Bhaskar, *From Science to Emancipation*, 350, 359.

62 See esp. Bhaskar, *The Philosophy of MetaReality*, Chapter 6, 275–313.

63 cf. Thomas Nagel, *Mind and Cosmos: Why the Materialist Neo-Darwinian Conception of Nature is Almost Certainly False* (Oxford: Oxford University Press, 2012).

64 Bhaskar with Hartwig, 'Beyond East and West', 187–8.

65 Bhaskar with Hartwig, 'Beyond East and West', 188.

66 The notion of the cosmic envelope, namely the notion of one universe (a uni-verse) implies that ultimately everything is immanent, bounded by the field of the cosmic envelope, the ultimatum. Bhaskar, *The Philosophy of MetaReality*, 2. Although immanent to the universe, the cosmic envelope is transcendent with respect to the ground-states of concretely singular beings.

67 Bhaskar with Hartwig, *The Formation of Critical Realism*, 7–10, 148, 151.

68 Bhaskar with Hartwig, 'Beyond East and West', 189.

69 With the exception of the doctrine of original sin, if this is understood as the permanent corruption of human nature reversible only by divine intervention, as distinct from the geo-historical 'fall' into 'structural sin', which it is up to us to reverse. I do not believe that human nature is permanently corrupted, rather it is evolving. See Bhaskar with Hartwig, 'Beyond East and West', 197.

70 See Bhaskar with Hartwig, *The Formation of Critical Realism*, 7–9, 148, 151–3 and 'Beyond East and West', 193–7.

71 Bhaskar, *The Philosophy of MetaReality*, 332–53.

72 See Bhaskar with Hartwig, *The Formation of Critical Realism*, 205–6.

73 Bhaskar with Hartwig, *The Formation of Critical Realism*, 80–1, 198; Bhaskar with Hartwig, '(Re-)contextualising metaReality', 207–8, 211, 214, 216; Bhaskar, 'Theorising ontology', 200–3.

8

CRITIQUE OF THE PHILOSOPHICAL DISCOURSE OF MODERNITY AND THE WESTERN PHILOSOPHICAL TRADITION

8.1 Critique of the philosophical discourse of modernity

The philosophical discourse of Western modernity is in many respects encapsulated by the Cartesian *cogito ergo sum*: 'I think therefore I am'. The 'think' encapsulates the false priority of epistemology over ontology (the epistemic fallacy) and of thought over body, emotion and spirit. The 'I' encapsulates the false assumption of the priority of the individual (who is propertied and tacitly gendered as male) over others and society in general, and over nature and other species.

From this basis we can derive the twin inaugurating and unifying characteristics of the problematic of the philosophical discourse of modernity: *atomistic egocentricity* and false *abstract universality*. A subject is set up in opposition to an object, and the subject relates to this object only by means of desire or fear, attachment or aversion. Other subjects too, according to this discourse, have this 'object form' and so, in place of the subject (subject–subject) relations that characterise society alone, we have object-object relations conducive to de-humanisation and reification. This couple of the atomistic ego and abstract universality has dominated the discourse of Western modernity from the outset.

Phases of the philosophical discourse of modernity

In *Reflections on MetaReality* I essayed an account of the development of the philosophical discourse of modernity.[1] I am not claiming that it is the only possible account, but it is I think a rich and suggestive one. My analysis and critique of this discourse can be set out as in Table 8.1.[2] The development of the discourse and my critique proceeds through five phases, each associated, because of the

TABLE 8.1 The philosophical discourse of modernity and the critical realist and metaReal critique[3]

The Philosophical Discourse of Modernity (PDM)		The Critical Realist and MetaReal Critique		
Moment of PDM	*Defining characteristics*	*Corresponding CR/PMR concepts and critique*	*Moment of CR/PMR*	*Main stadion and concept(s): understanding being as*
Classical modernism (CM)	(1) ego-, anthropo-centricity or -centrism, etc. (atomism) (2) abstract universality (actualism, irrealism) (both underpinned by the epistemic fallacy) the intrinsic exterior	the self as social and interrelated at a fundamental level with the cosmos; dialectical universality	TR	IM non-identity; being as structured, differentiated and changing; holy trinity: judgemental rationality, epistemic relativism, ontological realism
High modernism (HM)	(3) incomplete totality (critique of CM) (follows from (2)) (4) lack of reflexivity (critique of CM) (follows from (3))	open totality, reflexivity; critiques HM's substitutionism, elitism, reductive materialism	CN	2E process, including absence or negativity and contradiction; emergence; irreducibility of mind
Modernisation theory and practice (M)	(5) unilinearity (5′) judgementalism (5″) disenchantment	multilinearity, open systems; dialogue; (re-)enchantment	EC	3L totality; internal relationality, holistic causality, explanatory critique
Postmodernism (PM)	(6) formalism and (6′) functionalism (critique of PDM, stressing identity and difference, and rejecting universality) (7) materialism (critique of PDM)	accepts difference but reinstates unity or (dialectical) universality and critiques PM's judgemental irrationalism and lack of a concept of emancipation	DCR	4D transformative agency, reflexivity, emancipatory axiology, unity-in-diversity

TABLE 8.1

The Philosophical Discourse of Modernity (PDM) | | | *The Critical Realist and MetaReal Critique* |

Moment of PDM	*Defining characteristics*	*Corresponding CR/PMR concepts and critique*	*Moment of CR/PMR*	*Main stadion and concept(s): understanding being as*
Triumphalism	(8) ontological monovalence (a purely positive account of reality, denegating change)	ontological polyvalence, the reality of absence; accentuated critique of materialism (implicit consciousness pervades being); critique of subject–object duality; false absolute of market and other fundamentalisms	TDCR	5A spirituality the absolute (God); universal self-realisation; co-presence; transcendence
			PMR	6R enchantment, being as intrinsically meaningful, valuable and sacred 7A/Z non-duality (primacy of unity and identity over difference) or the absolute (ground state and cosmic envelope) – infinite or unending possibility; generalised co-presence; transcendence

Note: Columns should be read vertically (developmentally), such that (broadly) T/F > PM > M > HM > CM, and PMR > TDCR > DCR > EC > CN > TR.

resonance of philosophy with its social context, with a characteristic revolutionary moment in society:

(1) *classical modernism*, associated with the revolutionary moments of the English Civil War (1640–60), the American Declaration of Independence (1776) and the French Revolution (1789);
(2) *high modernism*, associated with the revolutionary moments of 1848 in Europe and 1917 in Russia;
(3) the *theory of modernisation*, associated with the moments of 1945 (the end of the Second World War and the defeat of fascism), 1947 (the Independence and Partition of India) and 1949 (the Chinese Revolution);
(4) *postmodernism*, associated with the events of 1968 and the early 1970s, together with the rise of the 'new social movements'; and
(5) *bourgeois triumphalism*, associated with the upheavals of 1989–1991 (the collapse of Soviet-style communism) and capitalist globalisation.

This last phase itself has three distinct sub-phases:

(5.1) the first sub-phase of globalisation lasts until 9/11 (2001);
(5.2) the second sub-phase of the 'war on terror' ends with the credit crunch of 2007–08; and since then we have had
(5.3) a third sub-phase of global multi-polarity (associated with the accelerated rise of the BRIC countries) and intensified and concatenated crisis.

Key characteristics of the discourse

The philosophical discourse of modernity has eight key characteristics:

(1) atomistic egocentricity
(2) abstract universality

Atomistic egocentricity is of course a defining characteristic of capitalism and much else in our contemporary 'civilisation'. It is underpinned and reinforced by a persistent model of the human being as propertied and tacitly gendered as male. Together with what I have called the classical paradigm of action (by external contact) and the celestial closure achieved by Newtonian mechanics, it forms one of the three main sources of empirical realism (see Figure 3.6).[4]

The whole point of characterising a society as modern depends on a contrast with the non-modern or pre-modern. So at first blush this contrast would seem hard to reconcile with abstract universality, which suggests that people are (as Hume remarked) 'much the same, at all times and places'.[5] However, the functioning of the modern world depended in very large part on its relations with the allegedly 'pre-modern' and 'non-modern'; this part of the world – absent in theory, but present in practice – constituted a kind of *intrinsic exterior*, an outside that was also crucially inside the modern in that the latter depended in practice on exploiting and dominating the 'non-modern'. It was natural then that high modernism, associated with figures such as Marx, Freud, Joyce and Proust, should indict classical modernism for

(3)   incomplete totality

and for a remarkable

(4) lack of reflexivity

that represented sectional interests as universal (as we saw in Chapter 6.6). However, in its proneness to *substitutionism* (which relies on some agent other than yourself to effect desirable social change) and *elitism* (deriving from the lack of an organic intelligentsia in the Gramscian sense) high modernism is itself vulnerable to some aspects of its own critique: elitism itself represents sectional interests as universal. Moreover, it is incompatible with the argument of metaReality for the principle of the primacy of *self-* or *subject-referentiality* or the *self-emancipation* of the human subject. This principle states that only we can act, no-one can do it for us, and all social change is also self-change; and while action certainly implies solidarity in removing constraints on flourishing, solidarity is not substitutionism – the educators must educate themselves, as emphasised in the concept of *transformed*, transformative praxis: if this is not effected within emancipatory movements, they will merely replace one set of master–slave relations with another. Emancipatory social change necessarily begins with self-change in this sense, we cannot rely on others (for example, the working class or elites/experts) to do it for us. As we saw in Chapter 7.5, Marx's emancipatory high modernism is additionally vulnerable to the criticism that it presupposes a spirituality that it fails to thematise explicitly or ground adequately.

The fifth feature of the discourse of modernity comes into clear view with the theory of modernisation advanced in the late 1940s,[6] characterised by

(5)   unilinearity

whereby 'developing' countries would inevitably pass through the same stages of economic and political growth as the Western world, and history as a whole is a story of unilinear progress, with Western countries in the vanguard. Critical realism critiques this as a variant of elitism and (in Popper's sense) historicism and shows that its deterministic cast is closely bound up with actualism. It is not the case that the highest form of consciousness pertains to those at the 'vanguard' of the geo-historical process; the highest form of consciousness is at the level of the ground state, which anyone can access. There are no laws of historical development inexorably determining a unique sequence; history could have been, just as it could be, very different. Intrinsic to unilinearity was a

(5′) judgementalism

whereby 'developed', 'Western' and 'modern' are not only adjudged superior to anything inconsistent with themselves (in performative contradiction with modernity's own prevalent view that rational judgements concerning matters of value are impossible) but present a model that others must follow. This was accompanied by the accentuated

(5″) disenchantment

of being that had been present in the discourse of modernity from the outset, whereby the world was increasingly drained of intrinsic meaning and value, which were sourced instead to the self-defining modern subject. During this period disenchantment found expression above all in Weberian 'rationalisation' and the Nietzschean 'death of God', entraining a line of thought that issued in the poststructuralist 'end of man' (Foucault), 'history' (Lyotard) and (through its heat-death) 'meaning' (Derrida).[7]

Postmodernism has some distinctive features of its own, which will be considered separately in the next section, but at the time it arose the

(6) formalism

and

(6′) functionalism

and

(7) reductive materialism

of modernism had also come clearly into view. By formalism I mean the glorification of formal, analytical, abstract, quantitative modes of reasoning and modes of being that characterises the discourse of modernity as a whole; and, relatedly, the prioritisation of discursive over intuitive modes of reasoning (critiqued in Chapter 7.6), which is in part reversed by postmodernism. Reductive materialism holds that the world is brutely physical, arguing that any seemingly non-physical phenomenon (for example, consciousness) fully reduces to some other identified physical entity (for example, brain-states or neural processes). Such reductionist reification has the consequence of de-agentifying human agency and downplaying the enormous creative power of thought. My critique of this position was inaugurated by the theory of synchronic emergent powers materialism and is carried through in the sublation of materialism and idealism in metaReality.

With the collapse of the erstwhile Soviet empire and the emphatic reassertion of bourgeois triumphalism, a crucial defining feature of modernism became very explicit. This is

(8) ontological monovalence

Ontological monovalence (the view that being is purely positive), together with the epistemic fallacy and actualism comprise the three members of the *unholy trinity* [8] of the Western philosophical tradition (see Figure 8.3). Monovalence is critiqued in Chapter 6. It is a categorial error that underpins further errors, which conceptually entail each other as follows: *centrism → triumphalism → endism*. These are implicit in Marx's critique of Hegel, and central to my critique of the irrealism of the Western philosophical tradition generally. Hegel exemplified all three of these errors when he said: 'World history travels from east to west; for Europe is the absolute end of history, just as Asia is the beginning'.[9] *Triumphalism* is the overweening exaggeration of human powers to know, control and so on. Politically, triumphalism found expression after 1989 in a recrudescence of neo-imperialism, reactionary nationalism and chauvinism. *Endism* is the view that history, while once real, has come to an end in the present. Thus according to twentieth century endism,[10] modernity had a beginning around about 1500, in the light of which its past appears as prehistory, and it has now arrived at an ending, an everlasting posthistory. There will of course continue to be a future, according to this view, but there will be no more qualitative social and institutional change or ideologies of change: the future will in this sense be constellationally contained within the present. Applied to our contemporary situation, endism proclaims that there are no alternatives to capitalism. Such denial of the on-going nature of geo-historicity, or *de-geo-historicisation*, is characteristic of master-classes, because the continuation of geo-history must sooner or later spell the end of their rule; and it is a potent motif of the Western philosophical tradition, which assists in rationalising that rule.[11] Endism is falsified by the irreducibly transformative nature of human praxis, which absents and creates, even as it reproduces the given.

Triumphalism was accompanied by a renascent *fundamentalism* (or *foundationalism*). Fundamentalism, whether in the form of market or religious and other fundamentalisms or a theory of epistemology, is the view that one's knowledge is incorrigible or certain because based on indubitable principles. It inevitably splits reality into two (namely that which conforms to its criterion and that which does not).[12] In late modernity fundamentalism is a cousin of postmodernism (and vice versa); like postmodernism, fundamentalism rejects universality and unity and accepts the essentiality of difference, but says 'I'm right and you're wrong' to postmodernism's 'there *is* no right and wrong'.[13] What fundamentalism ignores is that we can never start from scratch or an indubitable starting point because we are always 'thrown' into an already existing epistemological dialectic or learning process, entailing epistemological relativity and the possibility of critique. It thus arrives at the opposite conclusion to that of its dialectical antagonist or counterpart, endism or absolutism, which assumes that we are, or can be left with nothing to do. All fundamentalisms – so many symptoms of the alienation and fragmentation of being – thus turn on the provision of a false absolute or 'god' (the 'indubitable' starting point), spurred on in the last instance, as in the case of endism, by fear of change. Today, renascent religious and other fundamentalisms, summoned to account in a dialectic of violence by the false bourgeois god, the Moloch of power and money (an abstract universal), join it in suppressing creativity, love and freedom.[14]

Alternative modernities and alternatives to modernity

Critical realism and the philosophy of metaReality accept the legacy of the Axial Revolution in the middle of the first millennium BCE, which is the basis of critical science, morality and philosophy (see Chapter 3.5), but poses the questions of

(1) alternative modernities; and
(2) alternatives to modernity;

and, by rethematising the character of Indigenous society,[15] begins to explore the Kuhn-loss of the Axial world, that is, its failure to carry over into the new order the successes of the civilisations it displaced. For the rise of what we call civilisation is associated with the generation of a surplus from the countryside to the towns; the first empires; the control of irrigation schemes; the first systematic uses of money (paying the military and the like); and the establishment of a class of intellectuals and civil servants whose function is to produce ideologies justifying the status quo.

Contemporary modernity is characterised by profound alienation on all four planes of social being. As noted in Chapter 3.5, this five-fold alienation – of the creative producers from themselves, their activity, the means and materials of their production, their product and each other – may itself be traced back to the generative separation at the dawn of modernity, and indeed to the rise of earlier forms of master–slave-type societies. But the generative separation that produced an agrarian capitalism was itself overdetermined by other momentous changes at the time, in a complex which also saw the discovery of perspective and the birth of a public sphere that generated capitalism and eurocentricity,[16] alongside modernity, in the wake of the Renaissance and Reformation.

8.2 Critique of the Western philosophical tradition[17]

Signature errors of the Western tradition and their unification

We saw at the beginning of Chapter 6 that the development of critical realism expanded its ontology enormously, but in particular through the elaboration of seven successive levels of presuppositions, which are also seven levels of ontology. I now want to recapitulate these seven levels and to identify, corresponding to each, a signature philosophical error, weakness or absence characteristic of the Western philosophical tradition, together with its tendential effect in philosophy and its social meaning (in brackets). Recall that 'denegation' means 'denial in theory, affirmation in practice', entraining TINA compromise formation.

1M: the *epistemic fallacy* and actualism (destratification: there is *no depth* or transfactuality or alethic truth → denegation of ontology)

2E: *ontological monovalence* (positivisation: there is *no more history* (endism), normalisation of the status quo → denegation of negativity)

3L: *extensionalism* – no internal relations; hence, at a short remove, no real relations at all (detotalisation: there are *no splits or underlying unities-in-diversity* → denegation of totality

4D: *absence of the concept of intentional causality*, or stated more fully, of causally efficacious (intentional, materially embodied) transformative agency, together with the twin errors of reification and voluntarism *vis-à-vis* society and social structure (de-agentification: there is *no intentional causality* or embodied agency → denegation of transformative praxis)

5A: *externalism* – no interiors (de-reflexivisaton: there is *no real self* → denegation of seriousness)

6R: *disenchantment* (dis-enchantment: there is *no intrinsic meaning or value* in the world → denegation of the enchantment of the world)

7Z/A: the *inexorability of dualisms*, oppositionality and splits – which will therefore proliferate,[18] reflecting the absence of their transcendence and of a concept of non-duality (de-transcendentalisation: there is *no underlying identity and unity* → denegation of non-duality)

It is possible to unite these errors both diachronically and structurally or synchronically in terms of what I have dubbed the *unholy trinity of irrealism*, namely the epistemic fallacy, ontological monovalence and primal squeeze on the Platonic/ Aristotelian fault-line, serving to collapse ontological stratification (and alethic truth) and resulting in ontological anthropism (or anthroporealism) and actualism. One version of the diachronic unification of the *irrealist problematic* is depicted in Figure 8.1.

The reader will be familiar by now with the epistemic fallacy and monovalence. By *primal squeeze* I mean 'conducive to anthroporealism and actualism', more fully the squeeze or eliminating pressure exerted within Western philosophy by metaphysics, on the one hand, and empiricism, on the other, on empirically controlled scientific theory and its intransitive object and ontological counterpart, natural necessity. Empirically controlled theory is rendered redundant by metaphysical a priorism and rationalism, and natural necessity disappears in the empiricist problem of induction. On actualist assumptions, rationalism and empiricism (or some combination of them) seem to exhaust the alternatives. Historically this squeeze occurs on what I call the Platonic/Aristotelian fault-line generated by the epistemic fallacy and the idea it entrained that our knowledge could have indubitable foundations or an unhypothetical starting-point: lacking a non-homological account of ontological depth that could give grounds for the universal distinct from the universal concerned and other than its instances, Aristotle necessarily invoked a transcendent realism (*nous*), which his anthroporealism could not justify, in order to attribute universality to empirical regularity that was necessarily certain (see also section 8.3 and Figure 8.4). His procedure was to supplement induction with intellectual intuition or *nous* to form the indubitable starting-points or *archai* of a priori deductive reasoning in philosophy; in grasping the eternal immaterial forms of material things

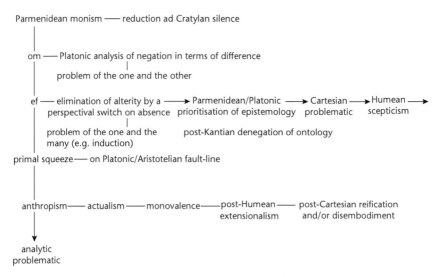

FIGURE 8.1 The irrealist problematic: a diachronic view[19]

Note: ef = epistemic fallacy; om = ontological monovalence.

by *nous*, humans participated in the self-thinking thought of God. In a posteriori science, according to Aristotle, we reason *inductively* to general laws and then we *deduce* their lower-order consequents, namely, less general laws or particular facts. This was the essence of the accepted account of science until the 1970s![20] It is the backbone of the arch of knowledge tradition, the aporias of which we identified in Chapter 2.7. Western philosophy was caught in a vice between rationalism and empiricism that eliminated multi-tiered depth and an adequate understanding of the empirically based science that can investigate it.

As we saw in Chapter 6.6, if we view the unholy trinity synchronically, irrealism comes into view specifically as a TINA compromise formation or problematic. See Figure 6.2 and surrounding text.

The unholy trinity has thus arguably determined the basic overall trajectory of Western philosophy, to which I counterpose the holy trinity of dialectical critical realism: judgemental rationalism in the intrinsic or normative dimension of the epistemological process, epistemic relativism and ontological realism. Since primal squeeze is entrained by the epistemic fallacy, mediated by actualism, the unholy trinity can be seen as the function of a couple and the question arises as to which is the more primordial or fundamental error, the epistemic fallacy or ontological monovalence. I source both ultimately to alienation and the desire to preserve the status quo (fear of change), arriving at a real definition of Western philosophy as the *Janus-faced* (enlightening/mystificatory) *aporetic and generally unconscious normalisation of the status quo ante*.[21] Considered historically, ontological monovalence determines the trajectory of the entire Western philosophical tradition from the

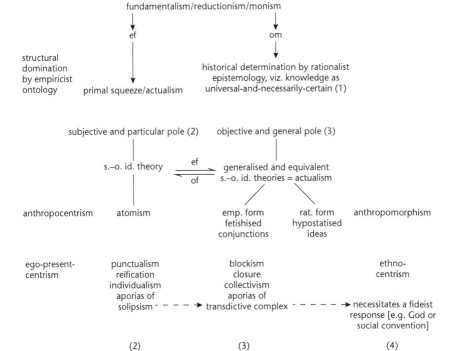

FIGURE 8.2 Historical genesis and structure of the irrealist problematic[22]

Note: ef = epistemic fallacy; emp. = empiricist; om = ontological monovalence; of = ontic fallacy; rat. = rationalist; s.–o.-id. = subject–object identity. As depicted in Figure 6.2, (1) = scepticism; (2) = identity theory; (3) = its ontic dual; (2) + (3) = anthroporealism; (4) = transcendent realism (the transcendent complement of anthroporealism).

time of Plato, who analysed change in terms of difference, but considered synchronically or from a structural point of view the epistemic fallacy and the associated ontology of empirical realism is dominant in the thought of modernity (see Figures 8.2 and 8.3). None the less, the two errors can be seen as ultimately two sides of the same coin: on the epistemic fallacy, you cannot talk about the world, so absence and change are repressed; on ontological monovalence, you can talk about the world, but in a way that rules out absence and change. However, because ontological monovalence, like the epistemic fallacy, entails the exclusion of alterity (which is by valid perspectival switch a mode of absence), ontological monovalence must be judged the more fundamental error. Moreover, In *Dialectic* and *Plato Etc.* I argue that the aporias of the irrealist problematic resonate with the social problems of generalised master–slave-type relations. On this argument, it is fear of change on the part of ruling elites, hence ontological monovalence that ultimately drives this compromise formation. It will be seen from my list of signature errors that the category of absence unifies the problems of Western philosophy, which

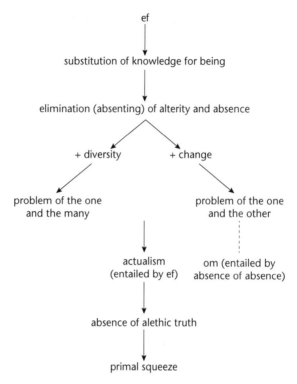

FIGURE 8.3 The unholy trinity and the problems of the one and the many and the one and the other[23]

Note: ef = epistemic fallacy; om = ontological monovalence.

occur as a result of the gulf or opposition that ensues from the absence of axiologically necessary categories.

As well as the three errors of the unholy trinity, a fourth error is almost as important, the error of *externalism* or absence of interiors.[24] However, this follows almost immediately from the trinity, mirroring its collapse of ontological depth. It depends upon the atomicity typically invoked within the Western tradition, that is, the absence of any space within entities and a corresponding fetishisation of the outer 'external' world, and is closely bound up with egocentricity and ontological extensionalism.[25] Applied to humans, it leaves no room for intentionality, or even a coherent conception of the self, and renders the whole domain of the metaReal invisible; at the extreme, it gives rise to behaviourism.

Reprise of key points of critique from earlier chapters

I now recapitulate some of the key points of the critique developed in previous chapters. In Chapter 2 we saw that mainstream philosophy cannot adequately describe either the world of everyday life or the world of the causal structures and generative mechanisms that explain it, that is the world investigated by the sciences. We also noted that ontological actualism, generated by the epistemic fallacy, inevitably develops a two-sided problem-field constituted by the insuperable problem of induction (insuperable in its own terms) and more generally the whole transdictive complex that stems from actualist presuppositions; and a deterministic deductivist account of the world, which inevitably ties knowledge, in so far as it is attainable, to closed systems. This is the arch of knowledge tradition.

There are two problems with this approach. The first is that the attempt to establish it generates insuperable (in its own terms) aporias, such as the problem of induction; and the second is that it is wrong, that is, identity theory is false: the world exists independently of our fallible and geo-historically relative attempts to know it and causal laws and the like operate transfactually, that is, independently of the conditions under which they are actualised and can be identified empirically. As we saw in Chapter 6.6, in so far as the ideal or goal of identity theory is clung to, an implicit ontological anthropomorphism is necessary for the explicit epistemic anthropocentrism, as the reification of facts and the fetishism of their conjunctions appears as the inevitable price and condition of the isomorphism of knowledge and being.[26] In the anthroporealist exchanges of identity theory (see Figure 6.1), the ontologisation of knowledge is the other side of the coin of the epistemologisation of being. But, in a world of multi-tiered ontological depth, the goal of identity can be 'achieved' only by the more or less dogmatic postulation of what is in effect a transcendent (but not a transcendental) realism, whether constituted by Aristotelian *nous*, the synthetic a priori, a democratic vote or social convention. As we have seen, anthroporealism and transcendent realism together comprise what I call the irrealist ensemble.

To the extent that the epistemic ideal or goal of identity is maintained but not read into the world, we have the variant of *unachieved* identity theory (within the rationalist strand of identity theory displayed in Figure 8.2). Here we have the zealous preservation of a sharp distinction between *epistēmē* (knowledge) and *doxa* (mere belief), as a wing of the arch of knowledge tradition from Plato to Alain Badiou[27] becomes increasingly sceptical of finding anything in the ordinary material world that satisfies the elevated criteria of knowledge – criteria that are false, but flow inevitably from the epistemic fallacy (anthropism) and actualist-deductivist presuppositions.

In Chapter 3 we noted the errors of conflationism, the identification of social structure and agency or the epiphenomenalisation of either one or the other, generating an incoherent (or impossible) account of the relationship between them. But equally important is the endemic dualism of the philosophy of the human sciences, and in particular the absence of any connection between thought and action, making intentional agency itself impossible (in its own terms). We also identified in Chapter 3 the dominance of the personal by the social for much of human history; but we were able to give a sharper definition of this in Chapter 7 by isolating the dominance of the demi-real in the world of duality, and the seeming emasculation of the spiritual infrastructure of society (the world of non-duality or the meta-Real). However, we saw that the demi-real, like the other, less noxious structures and forms in the world of duality, is actually totally dependent on the world of non-duality, that is, on the spiritual or metaReal infrastructure that it denegates.

Turning to Chapter 4, we noted how the epistemic fallacy makes change impossible (that is, if the world were as presupposed by the fallacy, it would not be a world of change) and how the actualism and deductivism that it entrains makes understanding and the rational deliberation of policy in open systems likewise impossible. For understanding and rational deliberation depend on the capacity to make the distinctions between the domains of the real and the actual, and between open and closed systems, distinctions that are unavailable to mainstream or irrealist philosophy. We also saw how important the concept of ontological emergence is in allowing us to sustain the various kinds of laminated systems we identified in Chapter 4.

In Chapter 5 we saw how the dichotomy between fact and value makes the rational informing of values impossible, generating an anti-naturalism. This is buttressed by the view that values are subjective impositions on the world, that is, by disenchantment at the level of 6R, including moral irrealism. It quickly follows from this that our discourse and powers of persuasion and argument cannot have an effect on policy (the rational choosing of values); nor can our policy rationally change the world, because of the de-agentification induced by mind–body dualism (identified in Chapter 3). So the whole epistemic sphere, including philosophy as well as science, becomes entirely epiphenomenal. Instead of being constellationally embedded within ontology, epistemology and the epistemic sphere generally become totally dislocated from the world, which has been actualistically misdescribed. The hypostatisation and detotalisation of philosophy quickly follows from this. It becomes a discourse running idle, with no real effect in the world other than obfuscation and reinforcement of the status quo.

Thus it was Plato's achievement, as a good servant of the master-class, to take change off the ontological agenda; so that by the time that a public sphere came to be celebrated in modernity, philosophers and intellectuals generally experienced a Hegelian Unhappy Consciousness (split or divided consciousness), knowing that, on the one hand, change (indeed dramatic change) is happening in the world, but being unable, on the other hand, to credit any way in which philosophy (or indeed scientific knowledge or rationally argued discourse) could possibly affect it, that is, make a positive difference. So we have a picture of intellectuals talking about a world in which they were impotent to intervene to make it a better world, as indeed was any rational discourse.

In a way, once an actualist ontology had been established, this was an inevitable outcome in a master–slave-type social context. Thus in Chapter 2.6 we saw how ontological actualism and the induction–deduction problem-field characteristic of the arch of knowledge tradition makes the application of knowledge, and hence policy, and hence rationally-informed change impossible. So the philosophers have painted a picture of the world in which human beings cannot make a difference. This poignantly expresses the dehumanisation of human beings and the de-agentification of agency. We are somehow pre-determined to behave in accordance with the 'course of nature', including of course our compliance with the powers-that-be (whose proxy the 'course of nature' so often in the social world appears to be). But actually, as the argument of Chapters 3, 6 and 7 makes clear, the course of nature depends at least in part on us, while the powers-that-be depend totally upon our continuing tolerance of them.

8.3 So how did it get to be this way?

A closer look at the development of the irrealist problematic

In what follows I look more closely at the historical story of the development of the errors identified in section 8.2 into the full blown ideological monster that is mainstream philosophy. If we start with the dispute between the Parmenidean and Heraclitean camps in ancient Greece, the first thing to note is that there are at least two interpretations of Heraclitus. The first is as a theorist of flux and the second is as a theorist of explicable change, that is, as a proto-theorist of structured being and becoming.[28]

Of course, the first interpretation also has its absurd Cratylan variant which would make the rational reporting of change impossible. (Cratylus was a Sophist and contemporary of Socrates who trumped the Heraclitean dictum that you cannot step into the same river twice – because it is continually changing – by saying that you cannot step into it even once.[29]) But even if we take Heraclitean philosophy as a theory of flux, albeit in its non-absurd form, it was a sufficient threat to the goals of Parmenidean monism for Plato to consider that analysing change away by means of difference was essential to safeguard reason, which had to be certain and unchanging. The effect of the Platonic operation is of course to hypostatise philosophy and indeed knowledge, to extrude or detotalise it from the world. For, patently, philosophy would be pointless unless epistemic negation, absence and change were to be allowed. This is the first effect of the Platonic operation: to confine change to our knowledge. But simultaneously with Plato's analysis of change in terms of difference, the dominance of the problem of the one and the many (with its emphasis on the irreducibility of difference) over the problem of the one and the other (with its emphasis on the irreducibility of change) was established (see Figure 8.3, and also 8.1). And with it the dominance of the analytical over the dialectical tradition (stressing the essential connection of opposites and the inexorability of change), and over Eastern (Taoist), mystical and other traditions, involving (as we saw in Chapter 7) critiques not just of analytical thought but of thought per se (that is, the discursive intellect), had also been effected.

Moreover, within this problem-field of the one and the many, it is the many that is bound to secure victory over the one, which fixes the subsequent trajectory of Western philosophy as involving a variety of theories of difference. By the time of Aristotle, it is clear that an achieved actualist identity theory can be established only at the biological level of the individual and the species and that this necessitates recourse to a neo-Platonic moment of *nous*, necessary to confer deductive certainty on an otherwise unending series of inductive hypotheses. This is what I call the Platonic/Aristotelian fault-line. The overall cast of irrealist philosophical thought has now been firmly established. Thus, it is clear that Aristotelean *nous* cannot do the job that ontological stratification can secure (see Figure 8.4).[30] Rather, it marks the point at which Western philosophy becomes prone to insoluble taxonomic and explanatory aporias. There are problems of universals and induction, to which Aristotelian *nous*, Christian faith, Cartesian certainty, Humean custom, Kantian synthetic a priori, Fichtean intellectual intuition, Hegelian autogenetics or Strawsonian dissolution cannot provide an answer.[31] It is clear that once real determinate absence with its link to change has been sequestered, and subject–object identity theory and actualism are ensconced on the throne, the anthroporealism of philosophy must inevitably lead to the generation of a new transcendent in the absence of any concept of ontological stratification, that is, of a concept of the transfactuality of relatively enduring causal structures and generative mechanisms in open systems.

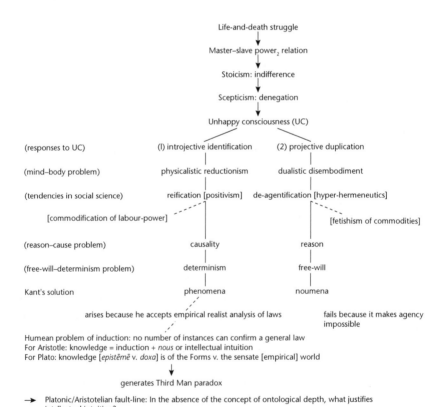

FIGURE 8.4 The Unhappy Consciousness of modern Western philosophy stuck on the Platonic/Aristotelian fault-line[32]

Figure 8.4 shows the way in which the unholy trinity of errors was played out in the philosophical discourse of classical modernism.

The Western tradition takes a subjective turn in modern times with the establishment of the Cartesian problem-field. Unserious Cartesian doubt leads inevitably to Humean scepticism; and on to what I have elsewhere described as the Humean turntable of Western philosophy.[33] It is of course Humean scepticism that Kant is expressly concerned to counter. But the Kantian moment in philosophy sees the involution of our rational intuitions and the development of an anti-Copernican standpoint, as suggested in Chapter 2.10. Apart from the performative contradiction involved in the unknowability of Kant's own premises of the transcendental subject, and therefore of the agent who must effect the Kantian synthesis required to produce knowledge,[34] the knowledge that is produced is of a world that is still described by Humean causal laws. This poses a huge problem for agency, including any moral agency; so that Kant had to resort to the idea of an unjustified primordial choice by every agent, a choice outside time and in the noumenal realm, a choice that must consist in that of a world synchronised with the whole history of the phenomenal world that actually prevails. Patently, this involves the collapse of any morality, including any notion of causal responsibility by particular agents for one rather than another sequence of events. The most portentous result of the Kantian enterprise for post-Kantian philosophy is, however, dichotomy and dualism, in which subjects are split off from the world that they would describe and explain, a dichotomy only weakly repaired in the synergies of the third *Critique*.

This dualism goes on to take various forms, including phenomenology and the hermeneutics of Heidegger, in which an authentic human world is segregated from the world of nature. There are also the Gadamerian or Winchian forms of hermeneutics, which I critiqued in *The Possibility of Naturalism*. In one guise or another, the dichotomised neo-Kantian world is taken over in critical theory, especially in its Habermasian form. We also find it in the analytical tradition, most evidently in the two-worlds or two-languages theory of Friedrich Waismann, following the later Wittgenstein, and in the anomalous monism of Donald Davidson and contemporary analytical philosophy.

Nietzschean perspectivism brings out the subjective implications of this dualism very clearly in the doctrine that there are no facts, only interpretations; so that the judgemental relativism in which the irrealist tradition culminates is very clear. This judgemental relativism becomes even more pronounced in postmodernism and poststructuralism generally. By now the epistemic fallacy has taken a linguistic form, of course, but the implications, in terms of ontological irrealism and judgemental irrationalism are the same – never more so than in the tradition of so called continental philosophy in the works of Gilles Deleuze and Jacques Derrida. In the latest manifestation of this wing, Slavoj Žižek invokes a rediscovered Hegel, but produces an impotent, purely retroactive Hegelianism; while Alain Badiou's philosophy involves a form of Platonism in which mathematical ontology takes the form of *epistēmē*, and in which nothing in the material world can be described as knowable except for the sheer event, which is a celebration of the purely singular, the abstracted event. The event is abstracted from the open-systemic context of its formation, its interpretation and its effect.

The progressive face of Western philosophy

We have been investigating the negative side of Western philosophy's Janus face. We can give a more positive interpretation to the development of modern philosophy by seeing it in terms of a succession of metacritiques$_1$, involving the identification of key absences. Thus, Kant may be seen as engaged in the metacritique$_1$ of the Cartesian ego from which modern philosophy starts, arguing that an objective manifold is a condition of possibility of the transcendental unity of apperception that allows us to synthesise the empirical manifold presented by a world unknowable in-itself. Hegel in his metacritique$_1$ of Kant sees the transcendental unity of self-consciousness as a social, not purely individual achievement, ultimately grounded in a public world of moral order, enshrined in the constitutional structures of his rational state. Marx in his metacritique$_1$ of Hegel identifies in turn the real basis of the Hegelian state in civil society (later, modes of production) founded on the alienation and exploitation of labour-power, and radically generalises Hegel's dialectic of mutual reconciliation into a dialectic of de-alienation, arguing that capitalism is a geo-historical product, destined to make way for a society in which the 'free development of each is a condition for the free development of all'.[35]

Dialectical critical realism argues that this goal can only be achieved by a further radicalisation of Marx's dialectic of de-alienation into a dialectic of liberation from the totality of master–slave-type relationships; and that this moral goal of universal human emancipation is a presupposition of the most elemental desire, the first initiating act of referential detachment, induced by negativity in the guise of absence. The philosophy of metaReality further radicalises this argument, insisting that this goal cannot be achieved except on all four planes of social being, including in particular the plane of the stratification of the embodied personality, where it involves the shedding of the ego and of all elements of the embodied personality that are inconsistent with the ground state (for example, jealousy, greed, and so on). From this perspective, we are able to begin to envisage totalising depth praxis that would produce a plausible, concretely utopian model of flourishing within the eudaimonistic society, necessary for the actionability of the project of universal human emancipation.

In this context it is worth rehearsing the transitions from Kant to Hegel to Marx and thence the abortive attempt to introduce actually existing socialism in the Soviet Bloc (which I revisit here as an example of the vain attempt to realise a better human society on the basis of action at only one plane of social being, the plane of social structure.)[36] I have argued that the three keys to Hegel's philosophy are:

(a) *realised idealism*, resulting, in opposition to transcendental realism (or what may be called 'epistemological materialism'), in the epistemic fallacy and ontological actualism;

(b) *constellational monism*, based on the privileging of thought in the speculative illusion (the illusion that the world can be reduced to an autonomised philosophy), to which we may oppose the synchronic emergent powers materialism (or 'ontological materialism') of critical naturalism; and

(c) *endism*, or ontological monovalence, which of course undermines the force of the transformational model of social activity (or what may be called 'practical materialism').

Subjectively, these were motivated by Hegel's

(a★)   desire to realise the traditional goals of philosophy within an immanent metaphysics of experience, that is, an achieved identity theory;

(b★)   commitment to a philosophy of unity-in-diversity; and

(c★)   attempt to avoid Unhappy Consciousness without succumbing to the fate of the Beautiful Soul. (The Beautiful Soul is Hegel's archetypal figure for alienation, the Unhappy Consciousness for a self that is divided between identifying with the powers that be (introjection) and escaping into a fantasy world (projection). The Beautiful Soul attempts to resolve its problems by withdrawing from the world, the Unhappy Consciousness by a process of introjection/projection. The Unhappy Consciousness is aware of its self-division but unable to overcome it.)

While Marx is critical of Hegel's realised idealism, his constellational monism (in the form of logical mysticism) and his endism, it is arguable that he himself is vulnerable to critique on just these scores. Thus I have argued that there are clear actualist, unidimensional and endist strands within Marx and subsequent Marxism. We can appreciate the significance of these strands, transmitted from Hegel, if we revisit the question of the fate of actually existing socialism.

We are prone to forget today that in the 1960s it was widely assumed that the Soviet Union was bound to overtake the West, and indeed in the near future. On the one hand there were the material, and especially technological achievements of the Soviet Bloc, ranging from the crucial role that the USSR played in the defeat of Nazism, through to such achievements as the first person in space, the first satellite, and so on. On the other hand there were the patent, visible effects in the West of Soviet military, political and ideological competition, and in particular of the balance of power between the Soviet-style socialist bloc and the Western-style capitalist democracies which made possible, between 1917 and 1989, Keynesianism, the welfare state, the growth of trade unions, the existence for long periods of time of social democratic (including labour) governments, feminism and the rise of the new social movements, an augmentation of civil rights and decolonisation. By 1989–1991 the Soviet-style regimes had completely collapsed. What explains this?

One factor in their early success was their capacity to import Western technology and modernise their economies at a very fast rate, under the aegis of central planning. They had practically achieved the limits of such import substitution by the mid-1960s. After that, the absence of a source of creative, innovative dynamism within the economy itself, such as was provided in the West by monetary incentives and the profit motive generally, contributed greatly to their economic stagnation. For what they had tried to do was to realise socialism on the basis of a strategy orientated to one plane of social being, namely the social structure, and moreover to one particular social structure, economic relations of production, in one particular country, the USSR. They had indeed successfully taken control of the relations of production. However, they had not passed control of the labour process, as Marx had enjoined, to the immediate producers in the labour process but instead retained control in the hands of party managers. So capitalism was replaced, not by socialism but by a commandist party state.

Marx's own critique of Hegel's constellational monism and speculative illusion led him, moreover, into a serious miscalculation of the role of thought and ideas – astonishingly, given the part that 'class consciousness' and social scientific theory were earmarked by his own work to play in changing the world. At the same time he had followed Hegel's sociological reductionism of ethics, leading to a disregard for morality and constitutional procedures. Thus, there was no culture in the Soviet Union of discussing the ethical implications and presuppositions of the project for a new and fundamentally better society. Instead, the pretence that the regime was in some way introducing a different kind of society gave way, first, to the weak rhetoric of 'socialist humanism' and then to an even weaker rhetoric to the effect that what was being developed in these societies was something that could be seen as a way of producing more and better material goods, such as washing machines, motorcars and holidays on the Black Sea! It was, alas, only too obvious that 'actually existing socialism' was failing in these regards by the late 1980s.

The Janus-face of postmodernism

Let me engage a retrospect on this trajectory by reverting to the theme of the discourse of modernity. Earlier, I isolated eight cardinal features of this discourse:

(1) atomistic egocentricity
(2) abstract universality
(3) incomplete totality
(4) lack of reflexivity
(5) unilinearity and judgementalism
(6) formalism
(7) materialism
(8) ontological monovalence.

Let us now note the features of one particular, radical form or phase of the discourse, namely the discourse of postmodernism. Its principle features are:[37]

(1★) relativity
(2★) linguisticism (often the linguistic fallacy in one of its two forms)

(3★)   ontological irrealism
(4★)   judgemental irrationalism
(5★)   a heightened (but unsustainable) sense of reflexivity
(6★)   proximity to the politics of identity and difference
(7★)   lack of universality
(8★)   lack of totality
(9★)   lack of the concept of emancipation
(10★)   traces of suppressed discourses (for example, the emotions).

Epistemic relativism now comes very much to the fore, but the relativity of belief is not constellationally englobed by an existentially intransitive ontologically real world that the beliefs are about. Consequently, we have judgemental irrationalism, normally in a linguistic key. The emphasis on the transitive dimension to the exclusion of the intransitive does serve to induce a heightened sense of reflexivity whose transience, however, prevents any reflexive mode or practice from fulfilling its main task of enabling subjects purposefully to design courses of action that they believe will realise their concerns, precisely because they lack any durability.[38] Ultimately, it follows that this reflexivity cannot coherently influence the world in which we must act.

At the same time there is a welcome critique of abstract universality, in terms of an accentuation of individual and collective difference. But what necessarily departs is any sense of universality, of human being, of the things we share in common and more generally of the universality implicit in any adequate cognitive claim. There is no sense of the universal as either transfactual or concrete, no sense of it as transcending experience or actuality and no sense of it as balanced by particular mediations, specific trajectories and irreducible uniqueness in the concrete universal. The concepts of totality and emancipation thus also fall by the wayside. More generally, difference is emphasised at the cost of an understanding of structure and change, since postmodernism's ontology draws via Nietzsche on the doctrine of Heraclitean flux. The problem of the one and the many is emphasised at the cost of the one and the other. In that sense, postmodernism is in the main an anti-Platonic move on a Platonic terrain.[39]

The regressive face of the philosophy of modernity

Common to the discourses of modernity, including those of postmodernism, is a view of the ontology of our world as consisting only of *bodies and language*. This is the position, ultimately, of Wittgenstein, Heidegger, Rorty and the group of philosophers and thinkers whom Badiou calls 'democratic materialists'.[40] Members of this group often add to bodies and language: *chance*.[41] This is a nod in the direction of Darwinism. Badiou, of course, will himself add to this expanded list *the event* as a source of truth and subjectivity. The abstracted event appears out of the blue, as something magical without presuppositions or (apparent) causes or material continuity, as something with which we can choose to identify or not. In an echo of

Pascal and Kierkegaard, we must wager: *either/or*. Either way, however, it can make no difference on Badiouan assumptions. This is because the world in which we act is regarded as already effectively actualistically determined, whether it is knowable and known, as in an achieved identity theory, or not. So subjective alignment with the event can make no difference to what happens. In collapsing ontological emergence and the possibility of transformative change, ontological actualism collapses our hopes and aspirations to make a better world in virtue of our rational agency, informed by enhanced explanatory knowledge of the mechanisms and structures of the world. The legacy of actualism, that is, of the induction-deduction or arch-of-knowledge problem-field remains the same. The message is clear:

> *Human beings cannot rationally change the world.*

That they can is the theme of our concluding chapter, as of the whole book.

Notes

1 Bhaskar, *Reflections on MetaReality*, 25–68, 165–74. See also Bhaskar, *From Science to Emancipation*, 125–68 and *passim*; *The Philosophy of MetaReality*, *passim*.
2 See also Mervyn Hartwig, 'Bhaskar's critique of the philosophical discourse of modernity', *Journal of Critical Realism* 10:4 (2011): 485–510.
3 Hartwig, 'Introduction' to Bhaskar, *The Philosophy of MetaReality*, Table 2, xxvii–xxix (slightly modified by MH).
4 Bhaskar, *A Realist Theory of Science*, 198.
5 David Hume, *An Enquiry Concerning Human Understanding*, ed. Peter Millican (Oxford: Oxford University Press, 1747/2007), Section VIII, 60 [80].
6 Its classic statement came a decade later: W. W. Rostow, *The Stages of Economic Growth: A Non-Communist Manifesto* (Cambridge: Cambridge University Press, 1960).
7 Bhaskar, *Reflections on MetaReality*, 169–70.
8 'Holy' puns on 'holes' or absences.
9 G. W. F. Hegel, *Lectures on the Philosophy of World History. Introduction: Reason in History*, trans. H. B. Nisbet (Cambridge: Cambridge University Press, 1837/1975), 197.
10 See especially Francis Fukuyama, *The End of History and the Last Man* (London: Penguin, 1992) and Niklas Luhmann, 'The future cannot begin: temporal structures in modern society', *Social Research* 43:1 (1976), 130–52.
11 Bhaskar, *Dialectic*, 64.
12 Bhaskar, *Dialectic*, 300.
13 Bhaskar, *Reflections on MetaReality*, 41, 97.
14 Bhaskar, *Reflections on MetaReality*, 242; *The Philosophy of MetaReality*, 347.
15 See esp. Chris Sarra, *Strong and Smart: Towards a Pedagogy for Emancipation. Education for First Peoples* (London: Routledge, 2008) and Gracelyn Smallwood, *Indigenist Critical Realism: Human Rights and First Australians' Well-being* (London: Routledge, 2015).
16 See Nick Hostettler, *Eurocentrism: A Marxian Critical Realist Critique* (London: Routledge, 2013).
17 For the dialectical critical realist critique, see esp. Bhaskar, *Dialectic*, Chapter 4, 308–85 and *Plato Etc.* Chapters 9, 10 and Appendix, 175–245; for the metaReal critique, see my metaReality books *passim*.
18 See Bhaskar, *Plato Etc.*, Appendix, 'Explaining philosophies', 219–45.
19 Bhaskar, *Plato Etc.*, 173, Figure 8.4 (slightly modified by MH). The unholy trinity is viewed here from the perspective of the primacy of ontological monovalence.

20 Bhaskar, *Plato Etc.*, 9.
21 Bhaskar, *Plato Etc.*, 216. I argue that its mystificatory function predominates, especially in contemporary philosophy.
22 Bhaskar, *Plato Etc.*, 235, Figure A.13.
23 Bhaskar, *Dialectic*, Figure 4.7, 356. The unholy trinity is here presented from the perspective of the primacy of the epistemic fallacy. In Figure 8.1 it appears under the sign of the primacy of ontological monovalence.
24 See Bhaskar, 'Critical realism in resonance with Nordic ecophilosophy', 18.
25 See for example, Bhaskar, *Dialectic*, 9.
26 See Bhaskar, *Scientific Realism and Human Emancipation*, Chapter 3.
27 Alain Badiou, *Being and Event*, trans. Oliver Feltham (London: Continuum, 1988/2010) and *Logics of Worlds: Being and Event, 2*, trans. Alberto Toscano (London: Continuum, 2006/2009).
28 Bhaskar, *Plato Etc.*, 176–7; Norrie, *Dialectic and Difference*, Chapter 7.
29 See Bhaskar, Plato Etc., 53n. According to Aristotle, Cratylus eventually avoided speech altogether, merely pointing. How he thought that avoided the dilemma we do not know. For, by his silence, he was saying something; just as in pointing he was indicating a relative persistent.
30 See also Norrie, *Dialectic and Difference*, 169–76.
31 See Bhaskar, *Dialectic*, 309–10.
32 Bhaskar, *Plato Etc.*, 6, Figure 1.1.
33 See Bhaskar, *Plato Etc.*, 193 ff.
34 cf. Bhaskar, *From Science to Emancipation*, 11; 'Theorising ontology', 195.
35 Bhaskar, *Plato Etc.*, 209–10.
36 The following recapitulates the argument in Bhaskar, *Dialectic*, esp. 333–6 and Chapter 4.6–4.8, 336–53 and *Plato Etc.*, esp. Chapters 6.1–6.2, 115–23, and 10.1, 202–9.
37 Bhaskar, *Reflections on MetaReality*, 33 ff.
38 Margaret S. Archer, *The Reflexive Imperative in Late Modernity* (Cambridge: Cambridge University Press, 2012), Chapter 7.
39 See Norrie, *Dialectic and Difference*, Chapter 7.
40 Badiou, *Logics of Worlds*, 1 ff.
41 For example, Richard Rorty. See Bhaskar, *Philosophy and the Idea of Freedom*, 'Section One: Anti-Rorty', 1–136.

9

CRITICAL REALISM AND THE ONTOLOGY OF THE GOOD SOCIETY

9.1 The dialectical development of critical realism and the collapse of the arch of knowledge tradition

Critical realist philosophy has typically developed through a double metacritique$_1$, in which some significant absence is noted in mainstream philosophy, or more especially in the philosophical discourse of modernity, an absence which *also* reflects an incompleteness in the development of critical realism up to that time, so that new developments function to metacritique its earlier phases. Thus, the big absence identified at the beginning of critical realism (1M) was the absence of ontology, and then the absence of ontological stratification (or a stratified ontology). With the development of dialectical critical realism (2E) the massive absence of absence itself was identified as a crucial scotoma or blind spot. The successive levels of the MELDARZ/A schema brought out the absences of internal relationality (3L), intentional causality and transformative praxis (4D), spirituality and inwardness generally (5A), enchantment (6R) and non-duality (7Z/A). Critical realism has thus itself developed dialectically, by the identification and rectification of absences in philosophical orthodoxy and in its own previous phases. Later in this chapter I will briefly recapitulate some of the highlights of its development in general, but first I want to look specifically at how critical realism can contribute to our understanding of the ontology of a good or eudaimonistic society, oriented to the flourishing of each as a condition of the flourishing of all.

In previous chapters we have seen how the arch in the arch of knowledge tradition, with its impossible combinations of induction and deduction, empiricism and rationalism, has collapsed; and how the duplicitous combination of anthropocentrism and anthropomorphism, and of the epistemic and ontic fallacies, in which certain knowledge is achieved at the price of reified facts and fetishised conjunctions necessary for an actualist achieved identity theory, can be sustained only by the invocation of a complementing transcendent or other-worldly realism as tacitly underpinning or explicitly contrasting with this world. However, the primal squeeze on the Platonic–Aristotelian fault-line resulting in ontological de-stratification and actualism continues to exact a heavy price. For in an actualist world our trans-formative agency becomes unsustainable, and so does any possible efficacy in the world of new and more adequate ideas, whether philosophical or scientific, techni-cal or lay. This is an enormous price to pay. Intentional causality and transformed transformative praxis or rational agency become possible again when actualism is replaced with, on the one hand, dispositional realism, so that possibilities are real and may be actualised in alternative and better ways; and, on the other, ontological stratification (and alethic truth), so that the reality of transfactually efficacious structures and mechanisms is differentiated from that of the events and regularities that they contingently generate. This allows for the possibility of explanatory knowledge rationally informing individual and collective praxis, so that the world can potentially, under appropriate conditions, be transformed for the better (albeit that there will still be counterfinality and unintended consequences as well).

However, actualism cannot even establish satisfactorily its nugatory result (the demise of agency), in virtue of, at the pole of general knowledge, the aporias of the transdictive complex and, at the pole of particular knowledge (or any knowl-edge at all) (see Figure 8.2) the longstanding so called 'scandal of philosophy'. This was articulated by Heidegger, who remarked that the scandal was not that proof of the reality of the ('external') world had yet to be given, but that '*such proofs are expected and attempted again and again*'.[1] However, we do of course know that our world came into existence long before human being and that it, and the cosmos, which is after all being, will survive our species, human being. Moreover, we know – it is a condition of the possibility of science – that the laws of nature to which we are subject, exist and operate quite independently of our activities. The absurdity of denying or doubting at least some of this has recently been articulated in the movement known as speculative realism. Thus Quentin Meillassoux has pointed to the absurdity of thinking that the truth embodied in an *arche*-fossil of its pre-historic existence could somehow be ruled out by the fact that there were no human beings around at the time to witness and measure it.[2] At the same time as Meillassoux affirms the pre-existence of being to human being, his speculative real-ist colleague Ray Brassier affirms the contingency and finitude of human being, homing in on the fact that human beings, like all sentient life, are bound in the end for extinction.[3] For critical realism, which distinguishes clearly between ontology and epistemology – the intransitive dimension of the objects studied by science and the transitive social process of studying them – and which understands the latter as constellationally embedded within the former (while situating, furthermore, the epistemic fallacy as a major fault-line in Western philosophy), such results are of course no surprise.

At the same time as speculative realists have been mounting their challenge to the mainstream's theories of existence and truth, new realists in analytical philosophy of science and metaphysics have been challenging the mainstream's theory of causality, which revolves of course around the Humean theory of causal laws. However, speculative realists have not been much interested in causal realism, while causal realists have drawn back from tackling questions of existence and truth per se. Moreover, just as the insight of speculative realists referred to above can be nicely situated by reference to the critical realist distinction between the intransitive and transitive dimensions, so the insight of the analytical realists can be situated in terms of the critical realist distinction between the domains of the real and the actual – between the possession and transfactually efficacious exercise of powers and tendencies, on the one hand, and their actualisation or manifestation as particular event sequences and regularities, on the other. Although it is true to say that basic critical realism arrived at these pertinent distinctions thirty or more years earlier,[4] and that the insights of these two newer forms of realism remain seriously incomplete and compromised unless taken together, their piecemeal emergence now is certainly to be welcomed and is a sign, perhaps, of a major wave about to break.

How are we to explain the resurgence of realism, leaving aside critical realism, in philosophy? Perhaps partly in terms of the enormity of the problems humanity faces, and the alarm felt by conscientious people in disciplines seemingly incapable not only of addressing but even of registering them. Here critical realism is on very strong ground, because not only does the theory of intentional causality show how thought can be efficacious in the world, but the theory of explanatory critique shows how we can and must pass from fact to value. The radicalisation of the theory of explanatory critique in dialectical critical realism into the dialectic of desire to freedom via the dialectics of agency and discourse represents the ethical high point of dialectical critical realism, and presents a serious challenge to more conventional accounts of the good life. The rational geo-historical directionality established by dialectical critical realism is however a very long-run one, while our crisis is immediate and very much in the short run. It is here that the philosophy of metaReality comes into its own. This is because, while it shares the vision of a eudaimonistic society, which it further develops and radicalises, its claim is that the key elements of such a society are already immanently present in the here-and-now of everyday life. Although it does not say that *all* that has to happen is for them to be recognised (for there is a great deal of work that needs to be done in shedding everything that is inconsistent with those elements), it does both allow a resetting of the terms of the debate and shows some of the ways in which dialectical universalisability and the dialectic of freedom can work themselves out; for example, through the transcendental identification in consciousness that comes from enhanced empathy or through the expanding unities of developing awareness made possible by co-presence. To reiterate, co-presence is the interrelatedness of everything at the absolute level of being – a level that sustains and is ingredient in everything we do without exhaustively constituting or saturating it, and which we awaken to when we come to understand that at the deepest level of being all is in all: that the starry heavens are within us, and we are within them.[5]

Thus what I call the dive to the ground state will awaken or evoke an echo, through the mechanism of co-presence, even though we are not currently aware of it, with every other who is 'in this respect, situation or relation like me',[6] that is, with every dialectically similarly situated other. You can see this very clearly at work, for example, in the consciousness of peoples throughout the Pacific whose island homelands are being threatened by rising sea levels; these peoples have a deep understanding of my philosophy without having to go to the trouble of reading it. In relation to the global crisis system, human beings are indeed 'all in it together', and only the solidarity that comes from getting into our ground states will bring solutions. Such a dive will have a maximally universal effect – acting both outwardly and inwardly – towards a situation of *generalised synchronicity*. This is what I call *the universal silent revolution*.[7]

Moreover, metaReality can speak to the excellent capacity of human beings everywhere to respond to acute crises. The present crisis, though still remaining invisible to many as a crisis, is certainly acute. In the ensemble of conditions necessary for humanity to find a resolution here, critical realism can certainly play an important *double* role in education and consciousness-raising. First, and corresponding to its role as a transcendental underlabourer (metaphysics$_\alpha$[8]), through clearly articulating the ontology of the problems and elucidating conceptual means for finding solutions to them, for example, clearly distinguishing the activity of searching for the mechanisms at work in some pathological tract of actuality from looking for empirical regularities. Second, and corresponding to its role as conceptual analyst (metaphysics$_\beta$), it can play an important mediating role between abstract philosophy and emancipatory practice in articulating sketches of ways forward on the four planes of social being, sketches that need to be developed into concrete utopian prospectuses. To indicate some of the possibilities here, let us look in turn at the contributions of dialectical critical realism and the philosophy of metaReality to a philosophical ontology of human flourishing and the good society.

9.2 Critical realism and the ontology of the good society

Elements of the good society

Some of the elements necessary for the construction of the ontology of a good society have been assembled in previous chapters. Thus we differentiated in Chapter 3 persons from society, and agents from persons; and the concept of the self, analysed in Chapter 7, from our idea of the person, in the sense of the embodied personality of the human being. Our sense of self, which is normally continuous from early infancy, precedes the development of a personal identity, which in turn precedes the development of a social identity, corresponding to which one may differentiate the person as social *actor* from the person as *agent*.[9] Moreover, in Chapter 7 we differentiated three concepts of the self: the self as ground state, the self as embodied personality (or a person in the world of duality) and the self as ego, which was argued to be illusory.

In Chapter 6, we saw how the dialectics of desire or action and of discourse or judgement both converge on the idea of the eudaimonistic society as a society in which the condition for the free development or flourishing of all is the free development of each. This is the ethical high point of dialectical critical realism, which was radicalised in the philosophy of metaReality (Chapter 7) by taking into account the further development of the embodied personality, including the jettisoning of the ego and of heteronomous elements inconsistent with its ground state, necessary for the realisation of such a eudaimonistic society. We also rehearsed the development of the concept of freedom, from simple agentive freedom, to positive and negative freedom, through emancipation and autonomy, to well-being, flourishing and universal human flourishing. Each rung on the development of freedom entails a co-equal development of solidarity, the link between desire and solidarity being provided by our dependence on others and the interdependence of each upon all. The mechanism effecting these transitions was the logic of dialectical universalisability, where the attempt, say, to satisfy a desire, or to remove a constraint implies a commitment to solidarity with the satisfaction of all dialectically similar desires and the removal of all dialectically similar constraints. In the philosophy of metaReality, the logic of universalisability is given a further twist by the idea of co-presence, and the goal of a eudaimonistic society oriented to universal human flourishing can be seen to involve the idea of universal self-realisation. Dialectical universalisability may be supported and empowered by practices enabling enhanced empathy and expanded co-presence, but it still has much to do if it is to knit the sense of solidarity explicit in the judgement form and, I have argued, implicit in all human action as well as discourse.

Crisis system

It is clear that in the contemporary world we are faced with a situation of global crisis, or indeed concatenated global crises; so much so that one could talk of this poly-crisis as a *crisis system*.[10] One can identify the contours of this crisis at each of the four planes of social being. Most striking is perhaps the *crisis of the four e's*. Thus on the plane of material transactions with nature, it is most obvious in the form of *ecological* crisis; on the plane of social interactions between people, it most obviously takes the form of an *ethical* or moral crisis, stemming from the growing inequalities and imbalances in already skewed distributions of resources, both allocative and authoritative, and more generally of life chances and opportunities. On the plane of social structure the most obvious crisis is an *economic* one; while on the plane of the stratification of the embodied personality we have various acute *existential* crises.

On the plane of social interactions, the crisis over authoritative resources takes the form of a crisis of legitimacy, which may extend to the whole political sphere and is accentuated by the contemporary attenuation of democracy. This crisis is further exacerbated by growing inequality in the distribution of allocative resources and wealth and more generally of life chances and well-being (including health and opportunities or capabilities). In addition to these normative crises on the plane of social interaction, we have the existential crises induced by violence and war, terror and the threat of terror. On the plane of social structure, the most obvious crisis is an economic one, with money becoming effectively disembedded from the real economy and the economy becoming disembedded from the social structure (social regulations and control generally) and the social structure in turn becoming disembedded from its spiritual or metaReal infrastructure. On the plane of the stratification of the embodied personality, we have various existential crises, from crises induced by ontological insecurity to crises induced by the postmodern fracturing of the sense of self, to crises of narcissism and various forms of physical addiction (alcohol, drug abuse, and so on) and psychotic and/or neurotic states.

Impediments to the realisation of the good society

Moreover, we are faced by a number of impediments or counteracting forces blocking the dialectic of freedom in contemporary social realty:

(1) the domination of the personal by the social, of enablements by constraints and of power$_1$ by power$_2$;
(2) the current imbalance between freedom and solidarity and the concomitant weakening of – and deficit in – solidarity and the sense of solidarity;
(3) the atrophying of the public sphere;[11] and
(4) the increasing lag of the moral evolution of the species behind its technological evolution.

The drive to freedom, with its weak but definite geo-historical directionality, is clearly identifiable throughout the world today, for example, as a drive to self-determination at work with the start of the Arab Spring in 2010 and elsewhere; that the actual world is very tragic and demi-real does not gainsay the reality of the pulse of freedom beating inexorably beneath it or irrupting into the domain of the actual in the early days of, for example, the Egyptian revolution of 2011. However, there is equally no doubt that this drive to freedom faces imposing counter-forces such as those indicated in (1)–(4) above. An additional problem is that the various crises feed into each other: the ecocrisis exacerbates the economic crisis, which produces ethnic and political tensions, which threaten the international political structure or system; so that we have in effect the concatenation of the crises in such a way that they mutually reinforce one another.

As part of the ethical tetrapolity (see Chapter 6.7) dialectical critical realism spells out the requirements for any progressive change as (i) explanatory critique; (ii) concrete utopianism; (iii) theories of transition (which together constitute the *explanatory critical theory complex*) as part of (iv) totalising depth praxis.[12]

Resources of metaReality

As a precursor to a fuller, more concrete exercise in *concrete utopianism*, we may begin to sketch out some of the resources that the philosophy of metaReality can bring to counter these counter-forces to the drive to enhanced freedom.

At this point it will be convenient to provide a brief summary of metaReality. MetaReality is not a transcendent or other-worldly philosophy[13] and the spirituality it identifies is immanent and actual (not just possible). However, the conceptions of identity and unity it works with are very different from those prevalent in mainstream philosophy. The identity involved is rich, differentiating and holistically developing from an original identity-in-difference.

As we have seen, there are three senses in which social life presupposes the priority of identity. These involve, respectively, identity as non-duality, as basis or ground and as deep interior. In turn, there are four forms of identity: transcendental identification in consciousness, transcendental agency, transcendental holism or teamwork and the transcendental self. The self for its part must be analysed in a tripartite way as consisting in an absolute ground state, a relative and shifting embodied personality and an always illusory ego. This sets for human beings the twin goals of achieving (or restoring), first, consistency between the embodied personality and the ground state and, second, elimination of the illusory ego.

When the embodied personality of the self is inconsistent with its ground state, the intentionality of the agent will be split. Self-realisation depends on the unification or restoration of consistency between embodied personality and ground state. Self-realised human beings may be said to be negatively complete, but positive completeness depends additionally on the abolition of all oppressive or master–slave-type relations and the elimination of all heteronomous states on all four planes of social being, together with the clearing up of their material residues. Together, the criteria for negative and positive completeness deepen the criteria for the satisfaction of a eudaimonistic society by elucidating further necessary conditions for human well-being and flourishing. This, in turn, allows us to identify the ways in which the project of universal self-realisation both extends and is required by the axiology of freedom in dialectical critical realism, that is, the process of absenting constraints on absenting ills.

The foregoing is then developed in an argument in which the domain of the spiritual or metaReal is seen to be ubiquitously presupposed in the practices of everyday life. These are conducted for the most part in terms of the categories of the world of duality and under the influence of that exploitative, oppressive and categorially false part of it that I call demi-reality. This presupposition in practice of the spiritual may be illustrated by the way in which trust underpins commercial transactions; or the way in which war presupposes some peaceful activities, a degree of peace – but not vice versa; and the way in which we use our creative ingenuity to remain stuck or addicted or our loving concern to fuel a host of negative emotions, from jealously to hatred. All these forms exemplify an *asymmetry of axiology* (or of *axiology and emancipation*):[14] what we want emancipation from dominates and occludes the deeper reality on which it depends, hence we can have the normally under-recognised good or 'heavenly' state without the eye-catching and dominant bad or 'hellish' state – but not the other way round.

This has profound implications for our understanding, critique and replacement of the demi-real world of alienation, oppression and growing inequity and injustice.

For there is *no society without human agency, and no human agency without non-duality and the ground state.*

If the metaReal is an unacknowledged but real sub-structure of social life, for the most part conducted and conveyed at the level, and in the idiom of the world of duality, but under the sway of the demi-real, then we can say all of three things. We have the *metaReal* (a) *in* (b) *under* and (c) *against the actual.*[15] The metaReal is certainly in and a part of the actual, though a largely unrecognised one; it is certainly dominated by the world of duality and demi-reality within that world; but, especially if developed in the concrete utopian imagination, it depicts and holds out a vision, albeit one only instantiated in microcosm, of a better way of doing things and an alternative order of human being and social life. In this respect the metaReal is 'opposed' to the actual, as its immanent critic or a standing indictment of it.

There is another consequence of great moment for our concatenated crisis today. MetaReality affirms that the only way of avoiding a split in intentionality and the failure and unhappiness that ultimately ensues is to eliminate the inconsistencies between the ground state, which one cannot lose, and the rest of one's personality. This will involve the *shedding* both of the ego, the illusory sense of a separate 'I', and of the heteronomous characteristics in the embodied personality, that is, those features of it that are inconsistent with its ground state. This will inexorably involve a *simpler but inwardly richer and deeper existence.*

This in turn will inevitably involve[16]

(1) overall de-growth; and
(2) enhanced use of the underdeveloped powers of humanity, together with such aids to them as IT technology.

Thus I think it has been shown beyond doubt that it is not possible to combine ecological viability and further net growth. This is of course consistent with growth in some sectors and some countries and with a radical redistribution of resources and wealth. But overall it must be net de-growth. Of course, whether or not it is possible to have capitalism and de-growth is a moot point.[17]

An end to growth is not however the same as an end to development, in two senses. First, on the terrain of economics, in the context of a world of growing inequalities, there needs to be a radical redistribution in favour of the poor, sick and disabled, the young and the old, the oppressed and the needy. Together with this redistribution, we must encourage a flowering of new transitional and ecologically friendly technologies, discovered or invented and produced and functioning without any overall increase in use of energy. This must be accompanied by a profound reorganisation of our life-long learning, so that we learn to enjoy and share not just information, but knowledge, ideas and wisdom, and to become adept in the skills of the imagination and the use of empathy. Thus, in learning to become one with the other whom we are not (or think we are not), we learn that we need no longer bear the pain of the repression or exclusion of a part of ourselves. Second, development will take place at the level of the greater fulfilment of our individual and collective human nature consistently with our responsibilities to other species and unborn generations, that is, toward the goal of universal human flourishing or the free flourishing of each as a condition of the free flourishing of all.

Enhanced use of our underdeveloped powers can be illustrated by considering the phenomenon of hypermobility, incessant travel in fuel-guzzling cars and planes. Is there any real need for most, perhaps 95 per cent, of the passenger flights from, say, Northern Europe or the USA to the continent of Australia? If one wants to visit Australia, perhaps to take in the Sydney Opera House or the Gold Coast or Uluru, why not watch a film or video of them or go on the Internet or make a telephone call to a friend there or read a book or talk to and empathise with someone who has been there. Of course, one will have to do some inner work, delve into our inward space a bit, use our imagination. But how much more rewarding this is and better for ourselves and the planet (including of course Australia) than a 20 hour flight! Again, who really needs to go to the Grand Canyon? At least just to *see* it when we can experience it on film? Who needs frequent face-to-face business meetings when we can web- or teleconference? Our aided imagination and consciousness generally can take the place of an enormous amount of current travel.

A final question remains: How can metaReality help in our concatenated crisis system? This is equivalent to the question: Are there any intrinsic limits to alienation in four-planar social being? MetaReality identifies a limit to the alienation and crisis we experience at each of the planes. On the plane of social interactions between people, this comes from the irreducibility of transcendental identification in consciousness in interaction, manifest in the consideration that when we do not agree, we must to some extent still understand each other (even to mark our disagreement). Similarly, the person who is split ten different ways or hears ten different voices, at least *hears* the different voices – there may be ten different voices, but there is only one listener, there is one person who is split, a real self on which to bootstrap. This then is the limit on the plane of the stratification of the embodied personality. The limit on the plane of material transactions with nature comes from the fact that human beings are natural beings. Nature is not apart from us, we are a part of it. The destruction of nature is not only murder, but suicide, and must be treated as such. The limit on the plane of social structure is more complex, and best discussed by reference to an example such as the 2007–08 credit crunch. The solution here is the re-embedding of money in the real economy, and the re-embedding of the real economy in the social and political infrastructure on which it depends, together with the re-embedding of the social infrastructure in its metaReal spiritual sub-structure. In the case of the social structure and our transactions with nature, more than individual intentionality and agency is required. We need collective decision-making and action, of course, and here metaReality invokes the axioms of universal solidarity and axial rationality, which serve to bridge alleged incommensurabilities and opposed interests.

As for the neo-liberal counter-forces to the dialectical critical realist drive to freedom, the domination of the personal by the social begins to look less decisive when we appreciate the structural asymmetry of axiology posited, and the possibility of geo-historical reversal afforded by metaReality. This involves the dependence of the social structure and power$_2$ on the spiritual infrastructure of society, and the sense in which we need inter-human trust to sustain any commercial transaction or master–slave-type relationship; the sense in which the overt world of work and instrumental rationality presupposes a 'domestic' regime revolving (at least partially) around unconditional love and involving non-contractual relationships.

Or consider the apparent collapse of solidarity. Such solidarity may have been suppressed, but has it been lost? I would argue, not. In crisis situations, human beings will very often dive to their ground states and the power it affords. From the behaviour of the Chilean miners trapped underground to the impeccable behaviour of those who felt the full force of the Japanese tsunami, we can witness this time and time again. Of course, what we need to do is to take every opportunity to expand our capacities for empathy and our sense of co-presence. These will augment our capacity to use and follow the logic of dialectical universalisability wherever it takes us (so that, for example, the death of someone in Boston can be compared to that of a person in Afghanistan).

As for the imbalance in our moral evolution, this can be offset partly by exploiting some of our technological evolution, for example, through the establishment of networks of virtual solidarity in the digital age, solidarity that has already on many occasions not remained in the office or living room, but taken to the streets.

Finally, the concatenated character of the crises can also be stood on its head – as, for instance, arguments for de-growth and radical redistribution inform our new strategy for the economy or for organising work and the structure of daily life.

9.3 Advantages of critical realism

Critical realism possesses several related kinds of advantage over its irrealist rivals. First is its maximal inclusiveness – ontologically, epistemologically, methodologically.[18] Second, we have seen that non-critical realist/irrealist positions are subject to destructive, including Achilles' Heel critique, which isolates a weakness or blindness in a position at what is considered by its proponents to be its strongest point. Irrealist positions include, among theories of science, empiricism, neo-Kantianism and supra-idealism of a social constructivist or poststructuralist sort; and, among theories of social science, positivism, neo-Kantianism, hermeneutics, critical theory, social constructivism and poststructuralism.

However, these other positions in practice must (of axiological necessity) presuppose at least some elements of critical realism. As such they constitute TINA compromise formations. Now, because of the heightened methodological reflexivity today, at least in the social sciences, in practice this means that critical realism must be adopted *ex ante*, explicitly and methodologically self-consciously.

Nevertheless, critical realism can certainly embrace adherents of other positions,[19] at any rate in so far as they do not seek to impose their negative methodological injunctions on critical realists or others.[20] In practice, my wager is that many will come to embrace critical realism, if only as a result of an appreciation of its greater inclusiveness.

Weaknesses in critical realism

Possible weaknesses in critical realism include its relative underdevelopment of epistemology in comparison with ontology; its relative neglect of some parts of four-planar social being, for example, of developmental psychology and of the role of worldviews and analogous *Gestalts* in the formation of belief and action. The kind of taxonomies put forward by, say, Ken Wilber's school of Integral theory may be helpful here.[21]

Detailed engagement with the various sciences and with practices of emancipation is also as yet lacking. There is a dearth of relatively detailed 'middle-level' work in relation to most of the natural sciences and many of the social sciences. Here, useful lessons may be learnt from the complex thought of Edgar Morin,[22] as well as the studies of earlier generations of philosophers of science such as Bachelard or even Feyerabend. When it comes to detailed engagement in or with practices of emancipation, critical realism is not much better off. Much mediating work (and concrete utopianism) remains to be done if critical realism is to become a successful underlabourer for human emancipation, as it aspires to be.

Notes

1 Martin Heidegger, *Being and Time*, trans. John Macquarrie and Edward Robinson (Oxford: Blackwell, 1927/1962), 249 (205), original emphasis.
2 Quentin Meillassoux, *After Finitude: An Essay on the Necessity of Contingency*, trans. Ray Brassier (London: Continuum, 2008).
3 Ray Brassier, *Nihil Unbound: Enlightenment and Extinction* (London: Palgrave 2010).
4 See Groff, 'Introduction to the special issue on causal powers' and Assiter, 'Speculative and critical realism'.
5 Bhaskar, *The Philosophy of MetaReality*, 71, 351.
6 Bhaskar, *Reflections on MetaReality*, 19.
7 Bhaskar, *Reflections on MetaReality*, 22.
8 See Bhaskar, *Scientific Realism and Human Emancipation*, Chapter 1.3. Metaphysics$_\alpha$ is the formal transcendental investigation of the presuppositions of human practices (thematised in Chapters 1.1 and 2.8, above), whereas metaphysics$_\beta$ subjects the general conceptual frameworks deployed in scientific research and practical programmes to critical scrutiny (exemplified in Chapter 4, above).
9 See Archer, *Being Human*, Chapters 3, 7, 8 and 9.
10 See Næss *et al.*, eds, *Crisis System*.
11 This is not just in the form of a welfare state and publically controlled production, but in the sense of places to meet and collectively discuss matters of social policy and communal life.
12 Bhaskar, *Dialectic*, 258–70, 286.
13 The various forms of transcendence I have identified are of transcendence-within-immanence, not immanence-within-transcendence, *pace* Jolyon Agar's interesting *Post-Secularism, Realism and Utopia: Transcendence and Immanence from Hegel to Bloch* (London: Routledge, 2014).
14 Bhaskar, *Reflections on MetaReality*, 115–16, 192, 228, 240; *The Philosophy of MetaReality*, 152 f.

15 To once again borrow Alan Norrie's nice formulation in his *Dialectic and Difference*, 149–50.

16 The remainder of this section draws heavily on Bhaskar, 'Critical realism in resonance with Nordic ecophilosophy'.

17 See Næss *et al.*, eds, *Crisis System*. More generally, this raises the questions of (a) alternatives to capitalism (cf. Hans Despain, '"It's the system, stupid": structural crises and the need for alternatives to capitalism', *Monthly Review* 65:6 (2013), 39–44); and (b) alternatives within capitalism, for example, worker-owned or co-operative enterprises (based on principles of economic democracy), or more highly regulated mixed economies (coupled with enhanced political democracy), with a public sector oriented to use-, rather than exchange-value or at the very least to the creation, rather than extraction, of value (see for example, Will Hutton, 'So the West is a write-off? Beware those economic forecasts', *The Observer* (London), 29 December 2013.)

18 See Bhaskar and Danermark, 'Metatheory, interdisciplinarity and disability research', Part IV.

19 See Bhaskar with Hartwig, *The Formation of Critical Realism*, Chapter 4, 'The critical realist embrace: critical naturalism'.

20 Bhaskar with Hartwig, *The Formation of Critical Realism*, 77–8.

21 See Bhaskar *et al.*, eds, *Metatheory for the Twenty-First Century: Critical Realism and Integral Theory in Dialogue*.

22 See for example, Edgar Morin, *Seven Complex Lessons in Education for the Future*, trans. Nidre Poller (Paris: UNESCO, 1999) and Paul Marshall, 'Towards a complex integral realism', in *Metatheory for the Twenty-First Century*, eds Bhaskar *et al.*, 140–82.

BIBLIOGRAPHY

Ackroyd, Stephen and Karlsson, Jan Ch. 2014. 'Critical realism, research techniques, and research designs', in *Studying Organisations Using Critical Realism: A Practical Guide*, eds Paul K. Edwards, Joe O'Mahoney and Steve Vincent (Oxford: Oxford University Press), Chapter 2, 21–45.

Agar, Jolyon. 2014. *Post-Secularism, Realism and Utopia: Transcendence and Immanence from Hegel to Bloch*. London: Routledge.

Archer, Margaret S. 1988. *Culture and Agency: The Place of Culture in Social Theory*. Cambridge: Cambridge University Press.

Archer, Margaret S. 1995. 'Realism and morphogenesis' in her *Realist Social Theory*, Chapter 5, reprinted in *Critical Realism: Essential Readings*, eds M. S. Archer *et al.* (London: Routledge, 1998), Chapter 14, 356–82.

Archer, Margaret S. 1995. *Realist Social Theory: The Morphogenetic Approach*. Cambridge: Cambridge University Press.

Archer, Margaret S. 2000. *Being Human: The Problem of Agency*. Cambridge: Cambridge University Press.

Archer, Margaret S. 2003. *Structure, Agency and the Internal Conversation*. Cambridge: Cambridge University Press.

Archer, Margaret S. 2012. *The Reflexive Imperative in Late Modernity*. Cambridge: Cambridge University Press.

Archer, Margaret S., ed. 2013. *Social Morphogenesis*. Dordrecht: Springer.

Archer, Margaret S. 2015. 'How agency is transformed in the course of social transformation: Don't forget the double morphogenesis', in *Generative Mechanisms Transforming the Social Order*, ed. M. S. Archer (Dordrecht: Springer, 2015), 135–58.

Archer, Margaret S. 2015. 'Introduction: other conceptions of generative mechanisms and ours', in *Generative Mechanisms Transforming the Social Order*, ed. M. S. Archer (Dordrecht: Springer), 1–26.

Archer, Margaret S., Collier, Andrew and Porpora, Douglas V. 2004. *Transcendence: Critical Realism and God*. London: Routledge.

Archer, Margaret S., Bhaskar, Roy, Collier, Andrew, Lawson, Tony and Norrie, Alan, eds. 1998. *Critical Realism: Essential Readings*. London: Routledge.

Assiter, Alison. 2013. 'Speculative and critical realism', *Journal of Critical Realism* 12:3, 283–300.

Badiou, Alain. 1988/2010. *Being and Event*, trans. Oliver Feltham. London: Continuum.

Badiou, Alain. 2006/2009. *Logics of Worlds: Being and Event, 2*, trans. Alberto Toscano. London: Continuum.

Bellah, Robert N. 2011. *Religion in Human Evolution: From the Paleolithic to the Axial Age*. Cambridge, MA: Belknap Press.

Berger, Peter L. and Luckmann, Thomas. 1966/1991. *The Social Construction of Reality: A Treatise in the Sociology of Knowledge*. Harmondsworth: Penguin.

Bhaskar, Roy. 1975. 'Feyerabend and Bachelard: two philosophies of science'. *New Left Review* 94, 31–55; reprinted in his *Reclaiming Reality: A Critical Introduction to Contemporary Philosophy* (London: Routledge, 1989/2011), Chapter 3, 26–48.

Bhaskar, Roy. 1975/2008. *A Realist Theory of Science*. London: Routledge.

Bhaskar, Roy. 1979/2015. *The Possibility of Naturalism: A Philosophical Critique of the Contemporary Human Sciences*. London: Routledge.

Bhaskar, Roy. 1986/2009. *Scientific Realism and Human Emancipation*. London: Routledge.

Bhaskar, Roy. 1989/2011. *Reclaiming Reality: A Critical Introduction to Contemporary Philosophy*. London: Routledge.

Bhaskar, Roy. 1991. *Philosophy and the Idea of Freedom*. Oxford: Blackwell.

Bhaskar, Roy. 1993/2008. *Dialectic: The Pulse of Freedom*. London: Routledge.

Bhaskar, Roy. 1994/2010. *Plato Etc.: The Problems of Philosophy and their Resolution*. London: Routledge.

Bhaskar, Roy. 1997. 'On the ontological status of ideas', *Journal for the Theory of Social Behaviour* 27:2/3, 139–47.

Bhaskar, Roy. 2000/2015. *From East to West: Odyssey of a Soul*. London: Routledge.

Bhaskar, Roy. 2002/2012. *From Science to Emancipation: Alienation and the Actuality of Enlightenment*. London: Routledge.

Bhaskar, Roy. 2002/2012. *The Philosophy of MetaReality: Creativity, Love and Freedom*. London: Routledge.

Bhaskar, Roy. 2002/2012. *Reflections on MetaReality: Transcendence, Emancipation and Everyday Life*. London: Routledge.

Bhaskar, Roy. 2007. 'Theorising ontology', in *Contributions to Social Ontology*, eds Clive Lawson, John Latsis and Nuno Martins (London: Routledge), 192–204.

Bhaskar, Roy. 2010. 'Contexts of interdisciplinarity: interdisciplinarity and climate change', in *Interdisciplinarity and Climate Change*, eds Roy Bhaskar, Cheryl Frank, Karl Georg Høyer, Petter Næss and Jenneth Parker (London: Routledge), 1–34.

Bhaskar, Roy. 2012. 'Critical realism in resonance with Nordic ecophilosophy', in *Ecophilosophy in a World of Crisis: Critical Realism and the Nordic Contributions*, eds Roy Bhaskar, Karl Georg Høyer and Petter Næss (London: Routledge), 9–24.

Bhaskar, Roy and Danermark, Berth. 2006. 'Metatheory, interdisciplinarity and disability research: a critical realist perspective', *Scandinavian Journal of Disability Research* 8:4, 278–97.

Bhaskar, Roy, Danermark, Berth and Price, Leigh, eds. In press. *Interdisciplinarity and Well-being*. London: Routledge.

Bhaskar, Roy, Estbjörn-Hargens, Sean, Hedlund, Nick, and Hartwig, Mervyn, eds. 2016. *Metatheory for the Twenty-First Century: Critical Realism and Integral Theory in Dialogue*. London: Routledge.

Bhaskar, Roy with Hartwig, Mervyn. 2010. *The Formation of Critical Realism: A Personal Perspective*. London: Routledge.

Bhaskar, Roy with Hartwig, Mervyn. 2011. 'Beyond East and West', in *Critical Realism and Spirituality,* eds Mervyn Hartwig and Jamie Morgan (London: Routledge), 187–202.

Bhaskar, Roy with Hartwig, Mervyn. 2011. '(Re-)contextualising metaReality', in *Critical Realism and Spirituality,* eds Mervyn Hartwig and Jamie Morgan (London: Routledge), 205–17.

Brassier, Ray. 2010. *Nihil Unbound: Enlightenment and Extinction*. London: Palgrave.

Brown, Gordon. 2009. 'The ontological turn in education', *Journal of Critical Realism* 8:1, 5–34.

Campbell, N. R. 1919. *Foundations of Science: The Philosophy of Theory and Experiment*. New York: Dover.

Collier, Andrew. 1989. *Scientific Realism and Socialist Thought*. Hemel Hempstead: Harvester Wheatsheaf.

Collier, Andrew. 1994. *Critical Realism: An Introduction to Roy Bhaskar's Philosophy*. London: Verso.

Collier, Andrew. 1999. *Being and Worth*. London: Routledge.

Collier, Andrew. 2003. *On Christian Belief: A Defence of a Cognitive Conception of Religious Belief in a Christian Context*. London: Routledge.

Danermark, Berth, Ekström, Mats, Jakobsen, Liselotte and Karlsson, Jan Ch. 2002. *Explaining Society: Critical Realism in the Social Sciences*. London: Routledge.

Danto, A. C. 1965. 'Basic actions', *American Philosophical Quarterly* 2:2, 141–8.

Despain, Hans. 2011. 'Karl Polanyi's metacritique of the liberal creed: reading Polanyi's social theory in terms of dialectical critical realism', *Journal of Critical Realism* 10:3, 277–302.

Despain, Hans. 2013. '"It's the system, stupid": structural crises and the need for alternatives to capitalism', *Monthly Review* 65:6, 39–44.

Donati, Pierpaolo and Archer, Margaret S. 2015. 'On plural subjectivity and the relational subject', in *The Relational Subject*, eds Pierpaolo Donati and Margaret S. Archer (Cambridge: Cambridge University Press), Chapter 2, 33–76.

Evenden, Martin. 2012. 'Critical realism in the personal domain: Spinoza and the explanatory critique of the emotions', *Journal of Critical Realism* 11:2, 163–87.

Fairclough, Norman. 1995/2010. *Critical Discourse Analysis: The Critical Study of Language*. Harlow: Pearson.

Fairclough, Norman. 2003. *Analysing Discourse: Textual Analysis for Social Research*. London: Routledge.

Fairclough, Norman. 2007. 'Critical discourse analysis', in *Dictionary of Critical Realism*, ed. M. Hartwig (London: Routledge), 89–91.

Fukuyama, Francis. 1992. *The End of History and the Last Man*. London: Penguin.

Giddens, Anthony. 1979. *Central Problems of Social Theory*. London: Macmillan.

Giddens, Anthony. 1984. *The Constitution of Society: Outline of a Theory of Structuration*. Cambridge: Polity.

Goodman, Nelson. 1955. *Fact, Fiction, and Forecast*. Harvard: Harvard University Press.

Graeber, David. 2011. *Debt: The First 5,000 Years*. New York: Melville House.

Groff, Ruth. 2009. 'Introduction to the special issue on causal powers', *Journal of Critical Realism* 8:3, 267–76.

Gunnarsson, Lena. 2014. *The Contradictions of Love: Towards a Feminist-Realist Ontology of Sociosexuality*. London: Routledge.

Habermas, Jürgen, 1976/1979. *Communication and the Evolution of Society*. Boston: Beacon Press.

Hare, R. M. 1970. 'Meaning and speech acts', *Philosophical Review* 79:1, 3–24.

Harré, Rom. 1972. *The Principles of Scientific Thinking*. London: Macmillan.

Hartwig, Mervyn. 2007. 'Critical realism', in *Dictionary of Critical Realism*, ed. M. Hartwig (London: Routledge), 97–8.

Hartwig, Mervyn. 2007. 'MELD', in *Dictionary of Critical Realism*, ed. M. Hartwig (London: Routledge), 97–8.

Hartwig, Mervyn. 2009. 'Introduction' to *Scientific Realism and Human Emancipation*, by Roy Bhaskar, xi -xli, xv.

Hartwig, Mervyn. 2009. 'Introduction' to *Dialectic: The Pulse of Freedom*, by Roy Bhaskar, xiii–xxix.

Hartwig, Mervyn. 2011. 'Bhaskar's critique of the philosophical discourse of modernity', *Journal of Critical Realism* 10:4, 485–510.

Hartwig, Mervyn. 2012. 'Introduction' to Roy Bhaskar, *The Philosophy of MetaReality*, ix–xxxix.

Hartwig, Mervyn and Morgan, Jamie, eds. 2012. *Critical Realism and Spirituality*. London: Routledge.

Hegel, G. W. F. 1837/1975. *Lectures on the Philosophy of World History. Introduction: Reason in History*, trans. H. B. Nisbet. Cambridge: Cambridge University Press.

Hegel, G. W. F. 1807/1977. *Phenomenology of Spirit*, trans. A. V. Miller. Oxford: Oxford University Press.

Heidegger, Martin. 1927/1962. *Being and Time*, trans. John Macquarrie and Edward Robinson. Oxford: Blackwell.

Hempel, Carl G. 1965. *Aspects of Scientific Explanation and Other Philosophical Essays*. The Free Press: New York.

Honneth, Axel. 1993/1995. *The Struggle for Recognition: The Moral Grammar of Social Conflicts*. London: Polity Press.

Hostettler, Nick. 2013. *Eurocentrism: A Marxian Critical Realist Critique*. London: Routledge.

Hume, David. 1740/1934. *A Treatise of Human Nature, Vol. II*. London: J. M. Dent.

Hume, David. 1747/2007. *An Enquiry Concerning Human Understanding*, ed. Peter Millican. Oxford: Oxford University Press.

Hume, David. 1779/2008. *Dialogues Concerning Natural Religion*. Oxford: Oxford University Press.

Hutton, Will. 2013. 'In language and action, there's a new brutalism in Westminster', *The Observer* (London), 29 June.

Hutton, Will. 2013. 'So the West is a write-off? Beware those economic forecasts', *The Observer* (London), 29 December.

Kastner, Ruth E. 2013. *The Transactional Interpretation of Quantum Mechanics: The Reality of Possibility*. Cambridge: Cambridge University Press.

Kuhn, Thomas. 1962/1970. *The Structure of Scientific Revolutions*. Chicago: University of Chicago Press.

Locke, John. 1690/1975. *An Essay Concerning Human Understanding*. Oxford: Oxford University Press.

Luhmann, Niklas. 1976. 'The future cannot begin: temporal structures in modern society', *Social Research* 43:1, 130–52.

MacDonald, Melanie. 2008. 'Critical realism, metaReality and making art: traversing a theory-practice gap', *Journal of Critical Realism* 7:1, 29–56.

Marshall, Paul. 2016. 'Towards a complex integral realism', in *Metatheory for the Twenty-First Century: Critical Realism and Integral Theory in Dialogue*, eds Roy Bhaskar, Sean Esbjörn-Hargens, Nicholas Hedlund and Mervyn Hartwig (London: Routledge), 140–82.

Marx, Karl. 1973. *Grundrisse*. Harmondsworth: Penguin.

Marx, Karl. 1958. Letter to Friedrich Engels, 14 January, in Karl Marx and Friedrich Engels, *Collected Works Vol. 40, Letters 1856–1859* (New York: International Publishers), 248–50.

Mason, Pete. 2015. 'Does quantum theory redefine realism? The neo-Copenhagen view', *Journal of Critical Realism* 14:2, 137–63.

McGrath, Alistair. 2001. *A Scientific Theology: Volume 1 Nature*. London and New York: T&T Clark.

McGrath, Alistair. 2002. *A Scientific Theology: Volume 2, Reality*. London and New York: T&T Clark.

McGrath, Alistair. 2003. *A Scientific Theology: Volume 3, Theory*. London and New York: T&T Clark.

McWherter, Dustin. 2013. *The Problem of Critical Ontology: Bhaskar Contra Kant*. London: Palgrave Macmillan.

McWherter, Dustin. 2015. 'Roy Bhaskar and post-Kantian philosophy', in Ruth Porter Groff, Lena Gunnarsson, Dustin McWherter, Paul Marshall, Lee Martin, Leigh Price, Matthew L. N. Wilkinson and Nick Wilson, 'In memoriam Roy Bhaskar', *Journal of Critical Realism* 14:2, 119–36, 124–7.

Meillassoux, Quentin. 2008. *After Finitude: An Essay on the Necessity of Contingency*, trans. Ray Brassier. London: Continuum.

Morin, Edgar. 1999. *Seven Complex Lessons in Education for the Future*, trans. Nidre Poller. Paris: UNESCO.

Moth, Rich. Unpublished discussion paper. 'How do practitioners in community health teams conceptualise mental distress? – the pentimento model as a laminated system'.

Naess, Petter. 2004. 'Predictions, regressions and critical realism', *Journal of Critical Realism* 3:1, 133–64.

Næss, Petter and Price, Leigh, eds. In press. *Crisis System: A Critical Realist and Environmental Critique of Economics and the Economy*. London: Routledge.

Nagel, Ernest. 1961. *The Structure of Science: Problems in the Logic of Scientific Explanation*. London: Harcourt, Brace and World.

Nagel, Thomas. 2012. *Mind and Cosmos: Why the Materialist Neo-Darwinian Conception of Nature is Almost Certainly False*. Oxford: Oxford University Press.

Nellhaus, Tobin. 1998. 'Signs, social ontology, and critical realism', *Journal for the Theory of Social Behaviour* 28:1, 1–24.

Norrie, Alan. 2010. *Dialectic and Difference*. London: Routledge.

Nuñez, Iskra. 2014. *Critical Realist Activity Theory: An Engagement with Critical Realism and Cultural-Historical Activity Theory*. London: Routledge.

Nussbaum, Martha. 2011. *Creating Capabilities*. Harvard: Harvard University Press.

Oldroyd, David. 1986. *The Arch of Knowledge: An Introductory Study of the History of the Philosophy and Methodology of Science*. London: Methuen.

Outhwaite, William. 1987. *New Philosophies of Social Science: Realism, Hermeneutics and Critical Theory*. London: Palgrave Macmillan.

Pigden, Charles R., ed. 2010. *Hume on Is and Ought*. Basingstoke: Macmillan.

Porpora, Douglas V. 2006. 'Methodological atheism, methodological agnosticism and religious experience', *Journal for the Theory of Social Behavior* 36:1, 57–75.

Porpora, Douglas V. 2016. *Reconstructing Sociology: A Critical Realist Approach*. Cambridge: Cambridge University Press.

Price, Leigh. 2014. 'Critical realism versus mainstream interdisciplinarity', *Journal of Critical Realism* 13:1, 52–76.

Psillos, Stathis. 2007. 'Inference', in *Dictionary of Critical Realism*, ed. M. Hartwig, 256–7. London: Routledge.

Reeves, Craig. In press. *The Idea of Critique*. London: Routledge.

Rogers, Tim. 2004. 'The doing of a depth-investigation: implications for the emancipatory aims of critical naturalism'. *Journal of Critical Realism* 3:2, 238–69.

Rostow, W. W. 1960. *The Stages of Economic Growth: A Non-Communist Manifesto*. Cambridge: Cambridge University Press.

Sarra, Chris. 2008. *Strong and Smart: Towards a Pedagogy for Emancipation. Education for First Peoples*. London: Routledge.

Sartre, Jean-Paul. 1943/2003. *Being and Nothingness: An Essay on Phenomenological Ontology*. London: Routledge.

Scriven, Michael. 1959. 'Truisms as the grounds for historical explanation', in *Theories of History: Readings from Classical and Contemporary Sources*, ed. Patrick Gardiner (New York: Free Press), 443–75.

Scriven, Michael. 1962. 'Explanations, predictions and laws', *Minnesota Studies in the Philosophy of Science* 2, 170–230.

Seo, MinGyu. 2008. 'Bhaskar's philosophy as anti-anthropism: a comparative study of Eastern and Western thought', *Journal of Critical Realism* 7:1, 5–28.

Seo, MinGyu. 2014. *Reality and Self-Realisation: Bhaskar's Metaphilosophical Journey toward Non-dual Emancipation*. London: Routledge.

Shipway, Brad. 2011. *A Critical Realist Perspective of Education*. Routledge: London.

Smallwood, Gracelyn. 2015. *Indigenist Critical Realism: Human Rights and First Australians' Well-being*. London: Routledge.

Smith, Christian. 2010. *What Is a Person? Rethinking Humanity, Social Life, and the Moral Good from the Person Up*. Chicago: University of Chicago Press.

Smith, Christian. 2015. *To Flourish or Destruct: A Personalist Theory of Human Goods, Motivations, Failure, and Evil*. Chicago: University of Chicago Press.

Steinmetz, George. 1998. 'Critical realism and historical sociology', *Comparative Studies in Society and History* 40:1, 170–86.

Stirling, James Hutchison. 1865. *The Secret of Hegel*. London: Longman.

Stoljar, Daniel. 'Physicalism', in *The Stanford Encyclopedia of Philosophy* (Spring 2015 Edition), ed. Edward N. Zalta, retrieved on 24 February 2016 from http://plato.stanford.edu/archives/spr2015/entries/physicalism/.

Whewell, William. 1989. *Of Induction, With Especial Reference to Mr. J. Stuart Mill's System of Logic*. London: John W. Parker.

Wikipedia contributors. 2015. 'Climatic Research Unit email controversy', 30 September. *Wikipedia, The Free Encyclopedia*, retrieved on 25 February 2016 from https://en.wikipedia.org/w/index.php?title=Climatic_Research_Unit_email_controversy&oldid=683477293.

Wilkinson, Matthew L. N. 2015. *A Fresh Look at Islam in a Multi-Faith World: A Philosophy of Success through Education*. London: Routledge.

Wilkinson, Matthew L. N. 2015. 'Towards an ontology of educational success: Muslim young people in humanities education', in his *A Fresh Look at Islam in a Multi-Faith World: A Philosophy of Success through Education* (London: Routledge), Chapter 6, 117–50.

Winch, Peter. 1958. *The Idea of a Social Science and its Relation to Philosophy*. London: Routledge and Kegan Paul.

Wittgenstein, Ludwig. 1921/1922. *Tractatus Logico-Philosophicus*, trans. Frank Ramsey and C. K. Ogden. London: Kegan Paul.

Wright, Andrew. 2007. *Critical Religious Education, Multiculturalism and the Pursuit of Truth*. Cardiff: University of Wales Press.

Wright, Andrew. 2013. *Christianity and Critical Realism: Ambiguity, Truth and Theological Literacy*. London: Routledge.

Žižek, Slavoj. 2012. *Less Than Nothing: Hegel and the Shadow of Dialectical Materialism*. London: Verso.

INDEX